RESTA… …AFÉS

2008 · 2009

PUDLO
ALSACE

by Gilles Pudlowski

HOTELS · GOURMET SHOPS

About the Author

GILLES PUDLOWSKI is a journalist and restaurant critic for the French weekly maga-zine, *Le Point*; a contributor to *Saveurs* and *Bon Voyage* magazines; cultural commenta-tor and critic; a historian of French culinary traditions; and the author of two cookbooks, *The France the Beautiful Cookbook* and *Great Women Chefs of Europe*, as well as many other books and guides. He is the author of *Pudlo Paris* and *Pudlo France*, published by The Little Bookroom.

About the Translators

SIMON BEAVER (chief text translator) grew up in the South of England, but moved to Paris nearly 30 years ago. For two and a half decades now, he has been adapting books, TV and movie scripts, songs and biographies into English, writing subtitles and record-ing voice overs. Whenever he can, he spends time at his second home on the Normandy coast, in England or in Andalusia.

ALICE BRINTON is a former news journalist who now specializes in French wine and gastronomy.

LIAM GAVIN is an independent translator who works on both technical and literary projects.

CATHERINE SPENCER is a freelance editor, translator, and writer who has lived in France and now lives in Morocco. She specializes in non-fiction and literary translation.

LUCY VANEL (chief food translator) is a food journalist, photographer, and writer who has lived and worked in Lyon, France since 2000. She serves as a Manager of the eGullet Society for Culinary Arts and Letters, and is co-host of the France forum there. She re-cords her experiences though the seasons in a blog about living, writing and cooking in Lyon, France, Lucy's Kitchen Notebook. http://kitchen-notebook.blogspot.com

PHYLLIS FLICK (food translator) is an American living in Paris who has written about Paris and French life for various publications including the *TimeOut Eating and Drink-ing Guide to Paris*. She is also co-host of the eGullet Society for Culinary Arts and Letters France forum.

TAMAR ELSTER (additional food translations) is an editor at The Little Bookroom.

RESTAURANTS · CAFÉS

2008 · 2009

PUDLO
ALSACE

by Gilles Pudlowski

HOTELS · GOURMET SHOPS

TRANSLATED BY SIMON BEAVER

with Alice Brinton, Liam Gavin and Catherine Spencer
Food Translations by Lucy Vanel with Phyllis Flick

The Little Bookroom • New York

© 2008 The Little Bookroom
Portions originally published as *Pudlo France 2008-2009*
© 2008 Michel Lafon
Originally published in French by Michel Lafon as
Guide Le Pudlo France by Gilles Pudlowski

With the assistance of Alain Angenost, Marc Baise, Olivier Binst,
Francis Brayer, Dominique Bruiere, Didier Chambeau, Jean-Pierre
Espiard, Phyllis Flick, Maryse Grimont, Sylvain Knecht, Denys Michel,
Jean-Francois Neyroud, Marc Horwitz, Jérome Berger, Sophie Elusse,
Véronique Gauthier, Michele Maublanc, Francois Morel, Elisabeth
Morin, Albert Nahmias, Didier Nicolas, Sylvie Nouaille, Sylvie Pistono,
Muriel Pragier-Pudlowski, Michael Pudlowski, Sylvie Rouge-Pullon,
Elisabeth Rocher, Maurice Rougemont, Jean-Daniel Sudres

English translation: Simon Beaver with Alice Brinton,
Liam Gavin and Catherine Spencer
Food Translation: Lucy Vanel with Phyllis Flick
Additional Food Translation: Tamar Elster

Book design: Louise Fili Ltd

A catalog record for this book is available from the Library of Congress

Published by The Little Bookroom
435 Hudson St., 3rd floor
New York NY 10014
editorial@littlebookroom.com
www.littlebookroom.com

1 3 5 7 9 0 8 6 4 2

Distributed by Random House, Random House International,
and in the UK and Ireland by Signature Book Services

PUDLO ALSACE 2008·2009
TABLE OF CONTENTS

INTRODUCTION: EAST TO EDEN

This paradise in eastern France now stands at the gates of Paris, thanks to the brand new TGV Est high-speed rail link. Today, Strasbourg is a mere two hours and 20 minutes from Paris; Saverne and the Northern Vosges two hours; and the wine route, Colmar and the Ballons natural park slightly more, but only just. Now you can reach France's most exotic region in the blink of an eye, and avoid getting lost on the way.

The people of Alsace speak French with a drawling accent, reminding us that Germany is next door, Switzerland not far off, and Luxembourg and Belgium just a few miles of turnpike away. The region is famous for its half-timbered houses, flowered villages, warm welcome, immaculate cleanliness and smile at every door, as well as a cuisine raised to the level of high art.

Queen of taverns (called "*winstubs*" in Alsace), land of inns and flambéed tarts, realm of brewers, winegrowers and distillers, *charcutiers* and confectioners, Alsace has, more than any other region, maintained the high standards of its traditional cuisine. Nouvelle cuisine is looked on with suspicion and the menus written in the local dialect often require a glossary. In short, eminently gourmet Alsace has staunchly and successfully defended its identity against every whim of fashion.

Having explored its treasures for a quarter century already, the writer of these lines—a love-struck devotee of this fine province—has found himself endlessly obliged to enlighten his fellows from the "heartlands" of France: far from Siberian, the Alsatian winter is a positive enchantment; fall there is as blessed a season as it is in New England (and the Vosges are the French Vermont); the sprawling towns are charmed villages and the homes—from the humblest to the most sumptuous—firstly taverns.

A paradise for delighted gourmets? Naturally, that is very much the nature of Alsace. It is not simply a stronghold of tradition, shrewdly conserving its choucroute, cervelas, schiffala, bürespäck, streusel and kougelhopf; it has also adjusted to the times, concocting a very Alsatian cuisine, modernizing its matelote, fine-tuning the cooking times and temperatures of its foie gras and game, and preparing frogs and snails in a thousand different ways, all without ever blunting the connoisseur's appetite.

Famous restaurants and star chefs—named Haeberlin, Jung, Husser, Westermann, Mischler, Albrecht, Paul or Paulus, Stamm or Schillinger—compose symphonies of keen modernism and joyous tradition. The menus in the *winstubs*, or wine bars, are odes to local custom and the wines (which bear the names of their grape variety—nine or ten of them, depending on whether we include the rare Klevener de Heiligenstein) exude a magnificent diversity of bouquets.

Flavorsome and convivial, Alsace has a smile for all, cultivating the warm welcome like a fine art. By all means, pay a flying visit on the high-speed train, but be ready to return. Alsace is a kaleidoscope of regions: Outre Forêt, beyond Haguenau; the floral village route towards Wissembourg; the Ried plain by the Rhine, an Eden for hunters and anglers; and the Munster valley, land of farmhouse inns; or Sundgau, the southern county that flirts with the Jura and boasts fried carp at every turn.

In its endless variety, Alsace is worth a thousand detours, a hundred trips and dozens of delicious stopovers. The purpose of this guide is to make it all clear, helping you tell apart the Bürestübel (in Pfulgriesheim) and the Bürehiesel (in Strasbourg); the *winstubs* of the Haut-Rhin and Mulhouse district, celebrating fleischnaka (or escargots de viande) and the Bas-Rhin *winstubs*, dedicated to presskopf and sausage of every form and kind. Naturally, Alsace also boasts an abundance of fine Chinese, Italian and "fusion" establishments.

From Vieux-Ferrette to Sélestat, and Molsheim to Rouffach, take time to discover this region. Alsace is in faster, easier reach than before, but proud as ever of its image and traditions. Whether you come for a weekend, a short stay, a return trip or an extended vacation, you may well find it is your own personal paradise too.

GILLES PUDLOWSKI

HOW TO USE THIS GUIDE

Listings—The hotels, restaurants, shops and rendezvous in the guide are listed by town/city. These towns and cities are in alphabetical order ignoring articles—le, la, les, etc. (so Le Havre is listed under the letter H). Under the heading of each town or city you will find hotels and restaurants listed in our order of preference—hotels according to their appeal and facilities, followed by restaurants according to the quality of their food. A hotel with a restaurant that we particularly like (that is not listed separately) is classified as a restaurant. At the back of the guide there is an alphabetical index of all venues.

Ratings and symbols—The names of hotels and restaurants are followed by symbols showing our ratings.

● Restaurant
■ Hotel
▼ Gourmet shop
◆ Rendezvous

Hotel / Restaurant:
⌂ / **SIM** Simple
⌂ / **COM** Comfortable
⌂ / **V.COM** Very comfortable
⌂ / **LUX** Luxurious
⌂ / **V.LUX** Very luxurious

Green indicates a particularly charming establishment.

○ Very good table
◎ Excellent table
◎◎ Grand table

⬧ Good value for money
❀ Very peaceful hotel
🛖 Historical significance
🏠 Promotion *(higher rating than previously)*
✪ New to the guide

AWARD WINNER

Baker of the Year—Patrick Dinel, *Au Pain de mon Grand-Père*, Strasbourg

Patrick Dinel, a native of Nancy, intellectual and keen convert to the cause of authentic baking, is very much at home with his dough. Assisted by his son Bruno, he tends to the leaven in his kneading trough and plies his trade in full view of the customers in his rustic store with its wood-burning oven. What he produces has a delightfully old-fashioned flavor. Charentes-Poitou butter, Breton shortbread, whole grain breads, ciabatta, olive fougasse, spelt wheat Coronne, Pogne de Romans, rye Chaperon, soy flour Bûcheron, the delightfully rustic round loaf of stone-ground wheat flour and the Kamut newly revive the baker's spirit of Alsace. Aficionados of local produce need not worry, though: he also purveys a superb kouglof, streussel, Chinois, pretzel and onion tart all well worth the detour. A word of advice: at peak times, you can expect to join a long line of customers!

THE BEST
TABLES IN ALSACE

THE BEST VALUES FOR MONEY (🕭)
THE MOST PEACEFUL HOTELS (❀)

PEACEFUL HOTELS

HOW TO USE THE MAP OF ALSACE

The regional map of Alsace shows towns and cities where there are very good, excellent and grand tables (○, ○○, ○○○), our good value for money selections (⊙), grand hotels (🏨, 🏨) and particularly charming hotels, whatever their level of category (🏠) and outstandingly peaceful hotels (❀). Towns or cities with a hotel or restaurant of another kind featured in the guide are in bold type with a green location dot, but no symbol.

The small inset map of France shows where Alsace lies in relation to the rest of France.

Bon voyage!

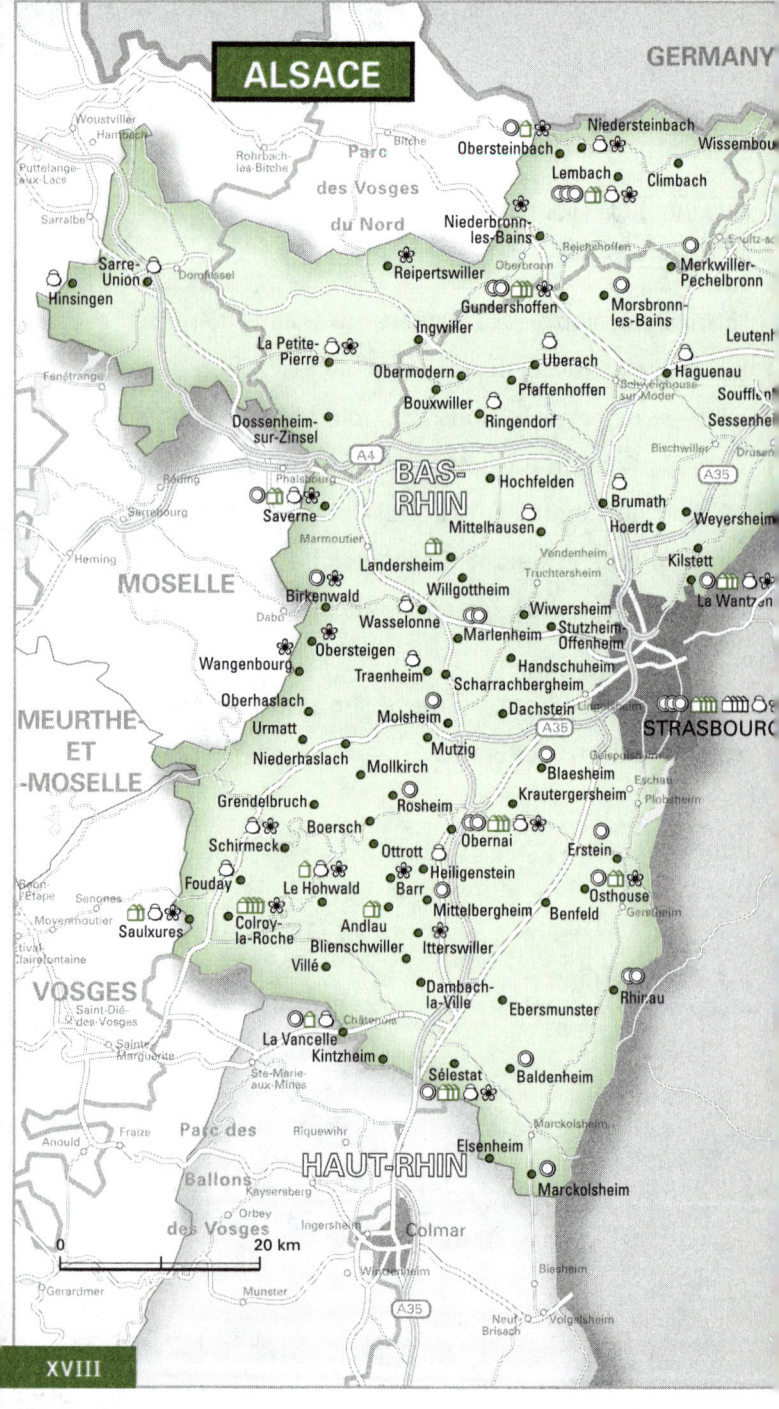

ALSACE

FRANCE

BAS-
RHIN

0   10 km   20 km

terbourg

Seltz

Sainte-
Marguerite

Ste-Marie-
aux-Mines

Châtenois

Liepvre

Saint-
Hippolyte

Thannenkirch

Ribeauvillé

Bergheim

Marckolsheim

Fraize

Arnould

Kaysersberg

Riquewihr

Zellenberg

Beblenheim

Illhaeusern

Lapoutroie

Kientzheim

Ostheim

Les Trois-Epis

Ammerschwihr

Artzenheim

GERMANY

Labaroche

Colmar

Orbey

Katzenthal

Gerardmer

Niedermorschwihr

Turckheim

VOSGES

Wintzenheim

Ingersheim

Biesheim

Wettolsheim

Volgelsheim

La Bresse

Munster

Husseren-
les-Châteaux

Eguisheim

Neuf-Brisach

Hohrodberg

Muhlbach-
sur-Munster

Gueberschwihr

HAUT-
RHIN

Cornimont

ures-sur-
lotte

Soultzmatt

Westhalten

Rouffach

Kruth

Guebwiller

Pfalz
Ht-Rhin

Fessenheim

St-Amarin

Murbach

Jungholtz

Le Grand
Ballon

Ungersheim

Parc des Ballons

Ensisheim

des Vosges

Wittelsheim

Sewen

Thann

Cernay

Kingersheim

Masevaux

Pfastatt

Rixheim

Giromagny

Guewenheim

Mulhouse

Valdoie

Diefmatten

Landser

A35

Kembs-
Loechlé

Belfort

Sierentz

Danjoutin

Bartenheim

Bâle

Dannemarie

Altkirch

Saint-Louis

Huningue

TERRITOIRE
DE
BELFORT

Hirsingue

Grandvillars

Della

Feldbach

Folgensbourg

Buschwiller

Sochaux

Hagenthal-le-Bas

Audincourt

Ferrette

Hagenthal-le-Haut

ndeure

Oberlarg

Ferrette

Kiffis

SWITZERLAND

XIX

ALTKIRCH

68130 Haut-Rhin. Paris 458 –
Colmar 61 – Bâle 35 – Thann 27.
ot-altkirch.com.

The Museum of Popular Tradition here reminds us that this sleepy little sub-prefecture perched on high ground was the capital of the Sundgau region. It watches over the surrounding lakes, orchards and "Route de la Carpe Frite" (Fried Carp Route) and cherishes the memory of Jean-Jacques Henner, son of Bernwiller and glorious painter of this peaceful countryside.

 HOTELS-RESTAURANTS

In Bettendorf (68560). 9 km via D432 and D9b.

■ **Au Cheval Blanc** ⌂
4, rue de Hirsingue.
Tel.-Fax 03 89 40 50 58.
Closed Wed. din., Thu., 2 weeks Dec., 2 weeks Apr.
7 rooms: 26–42€.
Prix fixe: 9€, 13€, 18€, 24€.
A la carte: 30€.

Philippe Petit-Richard watches over this rustic inn, delighting his following with classical but tasty concoctions. The chef's terrine, hot Munster cheese with cumin cream sauce, salmon served on a bed of sauerkraut, veal kidneys and the sliced block of cinnamon ice cream are precisely prepared and sensibly priced. A charming welcome and neat rooms.

In Carspach (68130).

■ **Auberge Sundgovienne** ⌂
Baerenhute, rte de Belfort 3 km w via D419.
Tel. 03 89 40 97 18. Fax 03 89 40 67 73.
www.auberge-sundgovienne.fr
Hotel closed Christmas–end Jan.
Rest. closed Sun. dinner, Mon., Tue. lunch, Christmas–end Jan., 1 week beg. July.
28 rooms: 42–80€.
1 suite: 87–105€.
Prix fixe: 12€, 21€, 27€, 38€, 48€, 11€ (child).
A la carte: 45–55€.

This contemporary motel is looking healthy indeed. Véronique Hermann provides a cordial welcome, the rooms are neat as a pin and Jean-Bernard concocts dishes with a contemporary flavor. An absolutely delicious escargot cake, seared pike-perch filet, oven-crisped pork trotter with foie gras and the pear crêpe are splendid. Well-chosen wines by the glass.

In Hirtzbach (68118). 4 km s, then D432 and D7.

● **Hostellerie de l'Illberg**
17, rue de Lattre-de-Tassigny.
Tel. 03 89 40 93 22. Fax 03 89 08 85 19.
hostelillberg@tiscali.fr
www.hostelillberg.fr
Closed Sun. dinner, Mon.
Prix fixe: 23€ (weekday lunch), 33€, 43€, 59,50€, 90€.
A la carte: 60€.

Jean-Luc Wahl has enlarged his establishment, adding a pleasant little bistro (Le Bistro d'Arthur), and continues to offer his own individual reinterpretation of Alsace tradition. Duck foie gras, escargots in tempura mille-feuille and the grilled sirloin steak with a bone marrow tartine favorably impress. The tarte Tatin is excellent and Delphine Midou's service elegant and friendly.

▼ SHOPS

CHOCOLATES & PASTRIES

▼ **La Gourmandise**
36, rue Charles-de-Gaulle.
Tel. 03 89 40 98 86.
The sweet-toothed come to enjoy melon-strawberry mousse, Swiss chocolates and ice creams in a range of flavors.

▼ **La Griotte**
13, rue Charles-de-Gaulle.
Tel. 03 89 40 92 54.
King of desserts, Hubert Ueberschlag delights us with his chocolate-mint "Antarctica", or the "croc blanc", with white chocolate mousse and berry coulis.

RENDEZVOUS

TEA SALON

◆ **René Muller**
8, rue J.-J.-Henner.
Tel. 03 89 40 08 64.
In the paneled lounge we treat ourselves to gâteaux landais or linzer torte and little butter pastries with cinnamon, raisins, almonds or chocolate.

AMMERSCHWIHR

68770 Haut-Rhin. Paris 438 –
Colmar 8 – Sélestat 26 – Saint-Dié 48.
ma.ammer@calixo.net.
The Tour des Sorcières (Witches' Tower), the fortified gate opening onto the vineyards and the sundial are the landmarks in this village at the gates of Colmar, whose pride and joy is its Kaefferkopf wine.

 HOTELS-RESTAURANTS

■ **A l'Arbre Vert**   🛏️⌂
7, rue des Cigognes.
Tel. 03 89 47 12 23. Fax 03 89 78 27 21.
arbre.vert@wanadoo.fr
info@arbre-vert.net
www.arbre-vert.net
Closed mid-Nov.–mid-Feb.
Rest. closed lunch, Tue.
16 rooms: 39–62€. 3 suites: 48–72€.
Prix fixe: 21€, 35€, 47€.

It would be hard to come up with anything more Alsatian than this large house, once the property of a village luminary and now a welcoming hostelry in the hands of Joël Tournier offering comfortable rooms, a range of facilities and a restaurant that remains staunchly loyal to local tradition. Foie gras served hot and cold, pikeperch with beer-seasoned cream sauce, pan-seared veal steak and the warm soufflé with seasonal fruits go well together, at reasonable prices, with a string of Alsace wines.

■ **Aux Trois Merles**   ⌂
5, rue de la 5e-DB.
Tel. 03 89 78 24 35. Fax 03 89 78 13 06.
auxtroismerles@wanadoo.fr
www.auxtroismerles.com
Closed Sun. dinner, Mon., mid-Jan.–mid-Feb.
12 rooms: 28–54€.
Prix fixe: 14,50€, 42€. A la carte: 50€.

Didier Louveau has adopted Alsace, but his Norman roots have left him with an abiding taste for seafood. The scallop and jumbo shrimp salad, cod tagine with lemon and sundried tomatoes and the roasted monkfish with a fine ratatouille display true skill. A fine pressed chestnut terrine for dessert and tremendously friendly service. Simple rooms for overnight stays.

● **Les Armes de France**   ◎LUX
1, Grand-Rue.
Tel. 03 89 47 10 12. Fax 03 89 47 38 12.
aux-armes-de-france@wanadoo.fr
www.aux.armes.de.france.com
Closed Wed., Thu.
Prix fixe: 25€ (weekday lunch), 30€, 32€ (Sat., Sun. lunch), 42€. A la carte: 55€.

It is always delightful to visit Philippe Gaertner, a convert to the cause of simplicity. Having inherited his precision and sureness of hand from his father Pierre, a student of Point, he uses these talents to leisurely reinterpret fine regional produce. On the plate, this results in escargot and parmesan mille-feuille, sturgeon filet served on a bed of julienned fennel and the duck foie gras medallion with dried fruit chutney. Desserts, which include rice pudding served with vanilla-seasoned rhubarb compote, are a return to childhood. Supervised by the friendly Simone, the service is absolutely flawless. The wine list is rich in regional vintages and the check is very reasonable given the joys to be found here.

SHOPS

BREAD & BAKED GOODS

▼ Beyl

16, Grand-Rue.
Tel. 03 89 78 23 72.
www.beyl.fr

This village baker has built up a solid reputation based on country loaves; bread with rye, bacon or poppyseeds; and bouchon (cake with almonds and raisins soaked in Marc de Gewurz).

ANDLAU

67140 Bas-Rhin. Paris 500 – Sélestat 17 – Molsheim 25 – Strasbourg 39.
otandlau@netcourrier.com.

This is one of the melting pots of the Alsace wine-growing region, with its theatrical scenery, abbey dedicated to St. Richard, Bear fountain, amphitheater of vines and great Kastelberg, Moenchberg and Clos du Val d'Eléon vintages.

 HOTELS-RESTAURANTS

■ Zinckhôtel

13, rue de la Marne.
Tel. 03 88 08 27 30. Fax 03 88 08 42 50.
zinck.hotel@wanadoo.fr
www.zinckhotel.com
18 rooms: 59–95€.

Each room in this former mill is different. Guests can choose between Thousand and One Nights, Zen or fifties décor. Daniel Zinck has also fitted out large reception rooms.

● Au Boeuf Rouge   COM

6, rue du Dr-Stoltz.
Tel. 03 88 08 96 26. Fax 03 88 08 99 29.
auboeufrouge@wanadoo.fr
Closed Wed. dinner (off season), Thu. (off season), 10 days Feb., 3 weeks June–July.
Prix fixe: 15€, 24€, 30€. A la carte: 48–53€.

This 17th-century post house is coming back to life in the hands of Pierre Kieffer. Formerly with Jung in Strasbourg, he excels at preparing his region's produce

with subtlety and lightness of touch. A foie gras medallion, Anna Kieffer pike fish quenelles, pike-perch served on baked vegetables and potatoes and the apple and cherry dessert pay serene tribute to timeless Alsace. On the *winstub* side, the spread includes tartes flambées (regional flat savory tarts), a local head cheese and aspic terrine and choucroute. A professional welcome and prompt service.

● L'Auberge de   ⑪SIM
l'Ancienne Scierie

73, rue du Maréchal-Joffre.
Tel. 03 88 08 23 65. Fax 03 88 08 84 51.
Closed Tue. dinner (exc. Bank holidays), Wed. (exc. Bank holidays).
Prix fixe: 9,50€ (lunch), 27€. A la carte: 35€.

Monique Kientz, a woman of character, runs this great paneled tavern on the edge of the forest towards the Hohwald region. There, we savor traditional specialties and pleasant dishes of the day, not to mention food roasted in the huge fireplace. Tourte vigneronne (a covered pie with minced veal and pork in cream), beer-braised ham shank, mixed brochette, the veal escalope with Munster cheese, rum savarin and the tartes flambées served in the evenings are a delight for all.

● Le Relais de la Poste   SIM

1, rue des Forgerons.
Tel. 03 88 08 95 91. Fax 03 88 08 57 16.
Closed Mon. (off season), Tue. (off season), Jan., Feb.
Prix fixe: 16€, 7€ (child). A la carte: 35–40€.

A strict Alsatian décor with contemporary artwork in this establishment run by Pierre Zinck, which combines quality, simplicity and generosity. A creamy cep soup, crayfish and goat cheese salad, stuffed pork trotters and a fig Tatin are meticulously served and gently priced. Andlau and Mittelbergheim wines are on the agenda.

Au Val d'Eléon

19, rue du Dr-Stoltz.
Tel. 03 88 08 93 23. Fax 03 88 08 53 74.
contact@valdeleon.com
www.valdeleon.com
Closed Sun. dinner, Mon.
Prix fixe: 11€, 12,50€.
A la carte: 30€.

Dominique Philippe has turned this corner *winstub* into a pleasant spot. Goose foie gras with potatoes, pike-perch with noodles and the frozen Marc de Gewurz kouglhopf are splendid.

BALDENHEIM

67600 Bas-Rhin. Paris 440 – Colmar 28 – Strasbourg 52 – Sélestat 9.
Close by the border, this Ried district village built on alluvial Rhineland soil is in Alsace hunting country. The game here—waterfowl, mallard, woodcock and teal—takes flight with a flurry of wings.

●	RESTAURANTS

● La Couronne

45, rue de Sélestat.
Tel. 03 88 85 32 22. Fax 03 88 85 36 27.
la-couronne-baldenheim@wanadoo.fr
Closed Sun. dinner, Mon., Thu. dinner,
2 weeks beg. Jan., 1 week at end July,
1 week beg. Aug.
Prix fixe: 32€, 47€, 59€, 68€.
A la carte: 70€.

In the heart of the village, Angèle Trébis' inn is a magnet for gourmets of every kind who all appreciate her son-in-law Daniel Rubiné's traditional tricks. In the hushed dining room with its fine woodwork and meticulously laid tables, they make short work of the frog legs, monkfish medallions Rossini, the venison medallions with fresh chanterelles and the seasonal fruit vacherin. All these regional dishes of good stamp are washed down with Alsatian wines. The service is very enthusiastic and the check still honest.

BARR

67140 Bas-Rhin. Paris 434 – Colmar 39 – Strasbourg 35.
mairie.barr.ot@wanadoo.fr.
This winegrowing town with its period houses, vineyards, theatrical main square and exhumed canals has many charms.

 HOTELS-RESTAURANTS

■ Château Landsberg

133, vallée de Saint-Ulrich.
Tel. 03 88 08 52 22. Fax 03 88 08 40 50.
www.chateau-landsberg.com
Closed beg. Jan.–end Mar.
Rest. closed Mon.–Thu.
3 rooms: 65–125€.
7 suites: 99–140€.
Prix fixe: 30€.
A la carte: 35€.

Fatima Wehrling and Corinne Sekula's old fortified farm offers many pleasures. Along with its light, peaceful rooms, it boasts a Jacuzzi and heated swimming pool. In the restaurant, the duck foie gras terrine, saffron-seasoned salmon, pork cheeks in Pinot Noir sauce and a raspberry shortbread cookie are accompanied by lively local wines.

■ Au Château d'Andlau

113, vallée de Saint-Ulrich.
Tel. 03 88 08 96 78. Fax 03 88 08 00 93.
www.hotelduchateau-andlau.fr
Rest. closed Sun. dinner, Mon., 2 weeks Nov., 2 weeks Jan.
22 rooms: 44–65€.
Prix fixe: 25€, 35€.
A la carte: 35–40€.

This hotel standing between river and forest provides a range of rustic rooms and a pleasant restaurant. Honed by Christian Boulard, the Alsatian-style crayfish bavarois, lemon-mint-seasoned skate wing, Indian-style monkfish filet, Middle Eastern-style lamb in a crêpe bundle and the spiced chicory candy are up to scratch. A superb wine list.

■ Le Brochet

9, pl de l'Hôtel-de-Ville.
Tel. 03 88 08 92 42. Fax 03 88 08 48 15.
hotel@brochet.com
www.brochet.com
Closed New Year's.
23 rooms: 50–69€.
Prix fixe: 15€, 18€, 21€, 7,50€ (child).
A la carte: 30€.

This half-timbered 16th-century residence is now a traditional hotel with friendly rooms in yellow shades with a tasteful regional restaurant. The onion tart, the three-fish choucroute, the honey-glazed duck breast and a frozen kouglof are pleasant.

■ Le Manoir

11, rue Saint-Marc.
Tel. 03 88 08 03 40. Fax 03 88 08 53 71.
info@hotel-manoir.com
www.hotel-manoir.com
Closed Jan.–end Feb.
18 rooms: 59–89€.
Half board: 80–131€.

Right in the heart of town, this hotel is a strategic staging post for families exploring Alsace. The traditional rooms are pleasant and the discount prices from the fourth night on are welcome.

● Le Potin `SIM`

11, rue du Général-Vandenberg.
Tel. 03 88 08 88 84.
Closed Mon., Tue.
A la carte: 28–35€.

This "Parisian" bistro in the heart of a winegrowing town—Hervé Duhamel's rural replica of the Café Flore—is very pleasant. At any hour, customers can read the day's papers, enjoy a coffee or beer on tap and snack on a country platter or an onion tart. The pike-perch filet simmered in wine, the pork cuts and charcuterie on a bed of sauerkraut prepared with goose fat and the lemon or chocolate tart frankly deserve an ovation. An interesting choice of wines and a terrace in summer.

● Winstub du Manoir   SIM

6, rue Saint-Marc.
Tel. 03 88 08 07 36.
Closed Sat. lunch, Mon., Jan.
Prix fixe: 25€. A la carte: 30€.

Laurent Finck, who worked at the Zimmer-Sengel in Strasbourg, has just taken over this tavern in the town center with its rough plaster and beams, where he presents a varied menu that willingly wanders away from the beaten path. Local head cheese and aspic terrine, the grilled pikeperch with coriander-seasoned cream, the oven-crisped Munster and marinated herring served with fried potatoes and a warm cherry tart make an excellent impression.

● S'Barrer Stubel   SIM

4, pl de l'Hôtel de Ville.
Tel. 03 88 08 57 44.
Closed Mon., Jan.
Prix fixe: 18€. A la carte: 25–35€.

In the first floor dining room with its low ceiling and woodwork, or on the less convivial second floor, Jacky Schmitter (who owns the Brochet just opposite) serves foie gras seasoned with Gewurztraminer, pikeperch served in the local-style on a bed of sauerkraut, ham braised in Pinot Noir and house spätzle, followed by a frozen kouglof seasoned with Marc de Gewurz.

In Gertwiller (67140). 1 km e via N422.

● Auberge du Maennelstein   SIM

154 A, rte de Strasbourg.
Tel. 03 88 08 09 80. Fax 03 88 08 10 37.
Closed Mon. dinner, Tue. dinner, Wed. dinner, 27 Dec.–8 Jan.
Prix fixe: 13€, 19€, 8€ (child).
A la carte: 35€.

This large, modern, crossroads hostelry is also a *winstub*. Eric and Marie-Claude Schoen's shrewd preparations champion the local cuisine. A quail and Port sauce *verrine*, Munster cheese in puff pastry, a four-fish choucroute, stuffed quail with flavorful meat sauce and variations on the chocolate theme for dessert are up to scratch.

▼   SHOPS

BISCUITS

In Gertwiller. 1 km e via N422.

▼ Fortwenger

144, rte de Strasbourg.
Tel. 03 88 08 96 06.
In his little factory out back, Gérard Risch lets us in on the secrets behind his celebrated gingerbread, cinnamon feuilleté, langues (small tongue-shaped cookies), florentins and macarons.

▼ Lips

110, pl de la Mairie.
Tel. 03 88 08 93 52.
www.paindepices-lips.com
Jean-Michel Habsiger deftly concocts his memorable Alsatian gingerbread, along with decorated heart-shaped cookies, waffles and macarons.

CHARCUTERIE

▼ Pierre Baltzinger

6, rue des Boulangers.
Tel. 03 88 08 90 37.
Pig breeder and artisan Thierry Schweitzer has taken over the Baltzinger store and remains faithful to tradition. His knacks (knackwurst, a small Alsatian sausage), cervelas, hams and accompaniments for choucroute or kassler are of consistently high quality.

REGIONAL PRODUCTS

▼ Le Pot à Crinoline

30, rue des Cigognes.
Tel. 03 88 08 07 74.
Pottery, engraved bottles, tablecloths, Soufflenheim pots, Betschdorf stoneware, fine wines and eaux de vie are carefully selected by Reine Bachert.

◆   RENDEZVOUS

TEA SALON

◆ Jacky Oster

31, rue du Collège.
Tel. 03 88 08 92 49.
Pound cakes (pistachio, orange) and elaborate desserts (raspberry, choco-

late-banana, kirsch, caramelized black coffee, vanilla-peach-cinnamon, Mont Blanc) are all splendid. To be savored with selected teas.

BEBLENHEIM

68980 Haut-Rhin. Paris 438 – Colmar 11 – Ribeauvillé 5 – Sélestat 19.
This small village on the Alsace wine route boasts listed vintages, such as Mandelberg and Sonnenglanz, redolent of sun and almond trees.

●	RESTAURANTS

● L'Auberge du Bouc Bleu

2, rue du 5-Décembre.
Tel. 03 89 47 88 21. Fax 03 89 86 01 04.
Closed Wed., Thu., 2 weeks Feb. vac.
Prix fixe: 25€, 32€, 10€ (child).
A la carte: 70€.

Daniel Friess plays to an unusual score in this charming inn on the wine route. A native of the Bas-Rhin village of Blaesheim converted to the joys of Gascony, he combines produce from the two regions rather successfully. Duck foie gras terrine or seared escalope, duck breast and cep salad, monkfish blanquette with seasonal vegetables, beef shoulder roast served with slow-simmered shallot and the fine vanilla bean, Armagnac and brown sugar crème brûlée are frankly gratifying. Keep an eye on the à la carte prices, which tend to add up rapidly!

BENFELD

67230 Bas-Rhin. Strasbourg 29 – Colmar 40 – Obernai 14 – Sélestat 19.
grandried.ot.benfeld@wanadoo.fr.
A town on the highway by the Ried river, with a historic past and an antique dealers' village.

●	RESTAURANTS

● Le Petit Rempart

1, rue du Petit-Rempart.
Tel. 03 88 74 42 26. Fax 03 88 74 18 58.
www.petit-rempart.fr

Closed Mon. dinner, Tue. dinner, Thu. dinner, 2 weeks Feb., 3 weeks Aug.
Prix fixe: 9,30€, 24€, 29€, 7,90€ (child).
A la carte: 45€.

Jean-Marie and Francis Grass run their little family establishment meticulously. In the dining room, with its woodwork and coffered ceiling, Jean-Marie prepares traditional regional dishes that Francis serves with gusto: duck foie gras seasoned with Gewurztraminer, pike-perch with Pinot Gris sauce, beef filet medallion Rossini with duck foie gras and a mint charlotte with chocolate coffee sauce, all very well crafted.

BERGHEIM

68750 Haut-Rhin. Paris 450 – Sélestat 8 – Colmar 14 – Strasbourg 50.
Ancient alleyways, high gates and fine fortifications. The world seems to be unaware of this winegrowing village despite its wealth of attractions.

	HOTELS-RESTAURANTS

■ Chez Norbert

9, Grand-Rue.
Tel. 03 89 73 31 15. Fax 03 89 73 60 65.
labacchante@wanadoo.fr
www.cheznorbert.com
Closed 10 days beg. Nov., 3 weeks Mar., 1 week beg. July, Rest. closed Wed. lunch, Thu., Fri. lunch.
10 rooms: 60–90€. 2 suites: 115€.
Prix fixe: 22€, 48€, 9€ (child).
A la carte: 35€.

At this rustic winegrowing farm, the functional rooms are furnished in contemporary style. In the restaurant, La Bacchante, chef Adrien Kliem serves duck foie gras, a snail and walnut cassolette, grilled salmon served over sauerkraut, tender roasted oxtail and a Kirsch-seasoned frozen kouglof, and Sabine Schalck recommends the proper wine.

● La Wistub du Sommelier   SIM

51, Grand'Rue.
Tel. 03 89 73 69 99. Fax 03 89 73 36 58.
www.wistub-du-sommelier.com
Closed Tue. dinner, Wed., 2 weeks Jan.,
2 weeks July.
Prix fixe: 16€, 19,90€. A la carte: 35–40€.

Patrick Schneider's *winstub* is an institution on the wine route. Wooden tables, banquettes and ceramic stove set the tone in this eatery that still has its antique stamp. Here, we savor beautifully crafted local dishes. Head cheese in aspic terrine with vinaigrette, goose foie gras, a pike and crayfish quenelle, veal kidney with creamy mustard sauce and a poached Williams pear with semolina flan.

● L'Auberge des Lavandières   SIM

48, Grand'Rue.
Tel. 03 89 73 69 96. Fax 03 89 73 37 02.
contact@leslavandieres.fr
Closed Mon., Tue.
Prix fixe: 19€, 27,50€.
A la carte: 38€.

Frédéric Ancelot from Bayon, who learned his trade at the Bistroquet in Belleville, has taken an innocuous inn and turned it into a very good, low-priced restaurant. Together with his wife Nathalie, a native of Guebwiller who formerly worked in the dining room at the Fer Rouge, he presents the freshest produce of the moment. Foie gras slow-cooked in the ultra-gentle heat of a steam oven accompanied by a dried fruit chutney, jumbo shrimp with sesame in salad, pike-perch filet served on pissaladière, cod filet with zucchini mousse in a lasagne mille-feuille, tartes flambées (thin crusted local tarts garnished with cream, onions and bacon) served at lunch and dinner and a house frozen kouglof make a marvelous impression. All the village's winegrowers feature on a list that is fraught with temptation.

67440 Bas-Rhin. Paris 460 – Strasbourg 33 – Molsheim 22 – Saverne 11.
A village at the foot of the Vosges, a step away from Dabo rock in the heart of Alsace's "Little Switzerland".

■ ⬤ HOTELS-RESTAURANTS

● Au Chasseur

7, rue de l'Eglise.
Tel. 03 88 70 61 32. Fax 03 88 70 66 02.
hotel.au-chasseur@wanadoo.fr
www.chasseurbirkenwald.com
Closed Jan. Rest. closed Mon., Tue. lunch, Thu. lunch.
21 rooms: 60–83€. 3 suites: 120€.
Prix fixe: 15€ (lunch), 39€, 52€, 65€, 10€ (child).
A la carte: 55€.

Times are still changing at the Gasses' establishment. Refurbished with wood paneling, the dining room in this Relais du Silence hostelry is charming indeed, like the hunting-themed bistro the Jägerstübe, friendlier than the seventies facade. The luxurious rooms, swimming pool and fitness center make this hotel a good-natured stopover. The cuisine—always prepared with refinement by Roger, the father—has become light, fresh and a touch Southern in the hands of Yann, the son, formerly at the Ducasse restaurant in Monaco. There is no pretension on the plates here, just dishes that sparkle with freshness and truth. The game terrine, a poultry and aspic terrine, scallop carpaccio, grilled turbot served with creamy chanterelle risotto, veal kidney with hand-rolled egg noodles and mustard sauce and a tender veal cutlet with vegetables served from a cocotte at the table are splendid, exemplary variations on theme of pure, fresh produce. The desserts follow the same rules: a frozen vacherin, local steamed bread with preserved fruit (dampfnüdle) and a hot fruit soufflé are tailored classics.

BLAESHEIM

67113 Bas-Rhin. Paris 491 – Molsheim 15 – Strasbourg 19 – Sélestat 34.
A step away from Strasbourg-Entzheim airport, an urbane village in the heart of the sauerkraut fields.

 HOTELS-RESTAURANTS

■ Le Boeuf

32, rue du Maréchal-Foch.
Tel. 03 88 68 68 99. Fax 03 88 68 60 07.
auboeuf.resa@wanadoo.fr
www.hotel-au-boeuf.com
Closed 2 weeks beg. Jan., 2 weeks end July–mid-Aug. Rest. closed Fri., Sat. lunch.
22 rooms: 56–130€.
Prix fixe: 15€, 25€, 8,50€ (child).
A la carte: 45€.

This village inn is a handy halt on the airport road. Sandra and Eric Walter provide comfortable, contemporary guest rooms and dishes like the dining rooms, in a very Alsatian style. They include presskopf, head cheese and aspic terrines, fish choucroute, three-game and potato baekeofe and a cold quince dessert or the kirsch parfait, all reliably prepared.

● Schadt

8, pl de l'Eglise.
Tel. 03 88 68 86 00. Fax 03 88 68 89 83.
schadt@wanadoo.fr
Closed Sun. dinner, Mon., end July–beg. Aug.
Prix fixe: 30€, 45€, 60€.
A la carte: 60€.

We love the rough good humor of this inn opposite the church. In the dining room with its frescos by Tomi Ungerer, Raymond Waydelich and Christian Geiger, we make short work of the roguish dishes concocted by the mercurial Philippe Schadt. Duck foie gras in brioche, pike-perch filet with morel mushrooms, the divine fried catch of the day, the beef Rossini and a seasonal fruit vacherin are washed down with first-rate Alsatian wines.

▼ SHOPS

BREAD & BAKED GOODS

▼ **Daniel Schadt**

2, rue des Prés.
Tel.-Fax 03 88 68 82 61.
Daniel Schadt, brother of Philippe mentioned above, prepares splendid breads (country style, sourdough, with beer, with walnuts), a famous bannette moisson and an exquisitely light kouglof.

BUTCHER & CHARCUTERIE

▼ **Daniel Baur**

55, rue du Maréchal-Foch.
Tel. 03 88 68 82 13.
Daniel Baur supplies knacks, hure de porc (potted pig's head in aspic), stuffed piglet, ham, smoked meats, sausages and choucroute garnie of excellent quality.

BLIENSCHWILLER

67650 Bas-Rhin. Paris 505 – Strasbourg 43 – Sélestat 11 – Dambach 3.
An unobtrusive halt on the wine route, this authentic village has charm to spare with its pleasant cellars, great wine (Winzenberg) and the Vosges mountains nearby.

 HOTELS-RESTAURANTS

■ Hôtel Winzenberg

58, rte des Vins.
Tel. 03 88 92 62 77. Fax 03 88 92 45 22.

Winegrowing family the Dresches have had the bright idea of providing rustic, typically Alsatian guest rooms in their home. The breakfasts here are enough to coax the latest of risers from their bed and the check is well behaved.

● Le Pressoir de Bacchus SIM

50, rte des Vins.
Tel. 03 88 92 43 01.
lepressoirdebacchus@wanadoo.fr
Closed Tue., Wed. lunch, Christmas, Feb. vac., 2 weeks beg. July.
Prix fixe: 24€, 9€ (child). A la carte: 43€.

Good humor is the rule in this authentic *winstub*. The local wines selected by Gilles Grucker are hard to resist. We first met his wife Sylvie at her parents' Clos des Délices back in Ottrott. Now she delights us with her hunter's salad with wild pigeon filet and raspberry-infused vinegar, her carp ravioli with minced young onions and a light smoky cream sauce and the pheasant filet with a side of creamy polenta flavored with chanterelles and a fine lingonberry sauce. The crème brûlée duo is not bad and the prices remember their manners.

BOERSCH

67530 Bas-Rhin. Paris 488 – Strasbourg 36 – Molsheim 12 – Obernai 4 – Rosheim 3.
A village on the wine route with its theater square, fine Renaissance houses and riot of flowers in season.

 RESTAURANTS

● Le Châtelain

41, rue Monseigneur-Barth.
Tel. 03 88 95 83 33. Fax 03 88 95 80 63.
contact@lechatelain.com
Closed Mon., Tue. lunch, Thu. lunch,
3 weeks end Jan.–mid-Feb.
Prix fixe: 22€, 48€, 22–24€ (*winstub*).

In this 1722 cellar, Désiré Schaetzel, winegrower and owner of the Clos des Délices hotel in Ottrott, organizes wine tastings and serves polished meals. Next to the dining room, where we savor foie gras carpaccio or pan-tossed jumbo shrimp, a little corner of a *winstub* allows one to snack, at a reasonable price, on blood sausage with apples or tête de veau. The house red is readily drinkable.

BOUXWILLER

67330 Bas-Rhin. Paris 447 – Saverne 15 – Bitche 34 – Strasbourg 42.
tourisme.bouxwiller@wanadoo.fr.
Once witches celebrated their Sabbath on Batsberg hill. Today, the city hall has acquired a stately air. As a bonus, the village boasts two museums, one of them devoted to Judaism in Alsace.

 HOTELS-RESTAURANTS

■ La Cour du Tonnelier

84, Grand-Rue.
Tel. 03 88 70 72 57. Fax 03 88 70 95 74.
www.courdutonnelier.com
Closed 2 weeks Christmas–New Year's,
3 weeks Aug.
Rest. closed Sun. dinner, Mon.
16 rooms: 52–97€.
Prix fixe: 8,50€ (weekday lunch), 24–28€.
A la carte: 45€.

Jérôme Veit has taken over this modern establishment with gusto, equipping it with comfortable rooms, a busy bar and a decent restaurant. Thomas Kapp charms his guests with duck foie gras terrine, the house-prepared escargots, a poached cod filet with chervil sauce, an Argentinian sirloin steak with slow-cooked leeks and the frozen berry soufflé. The swimming pool and garden are bonuses.

In Imbsheim (67330). 3 km sw via D6.
● S'Batsberger Stulwel   SIM

25, rue Principale.
Tel.-Fax 03 88 70 73 85.
Closed Mon., Tue. dinner, 1 week Sept.,
1 week Jan., 3 weeks June.
Prix fixe: 14€, 18€, 35€.

Anny Reixel offers a keen welcome in her country *winstub*. With its profusion of flowers and plants, paintings and inscriptions, the house has plenty of character, as do the local dishes, presented with zest. Regional flat savory tarts called "tartes flambées", slow-simmered beef and noodles and the stuffed pork trotter are monuments of popular art.

▼ SHOPS

CHARCUTERIE

▼ **Lorch**

39, Grand-Rue.

Tel. 03 88 71 35 26.

Jean-Louis Lorch makes knacks, country bacon, old-fashioned liver sausage, garlic sausage, jambonneau (cured pork knuckle) and selects quality farmhouse meats.

PASTRIES

▼ **Rodolphe Isenmann**

28, Grand-Rue.

Tel.-Fax 03 88 70 70 50.

The father, Rodolphe Isenmann, is quietly handing over the reins of this temple to Lady Tartine to his son. The bredele (small Alsatian cakes, baked in a variety of flavors) and charbon de Bouxwiller are appealing indeed.

BRUMATH

67170 Bas-Rhin. Paris 470 – Haguenau 11 – Strasbourg 17 – Saverne 30.

The 1870 war took its toll here, but the town still has its ancient houses, signs of a rich past evinced by the Gallic-Roman archeological digs.

■ HOTELS-RESTAURANTS

● **L'Ecrevisse**

4, av de Strasbourg.

Tel. 03 88 51 11 08. Fax 03 88 51 89 02.

www.hostellerie-ecrevisse.com

Closed 2 weeks end July–mid-Aug.

Rest. closed Mon. dinner, Tue.

17 rooms: 50–85€. 2 suites: 100€.

Prix fixe: 45€, 75€.

A la carte: 65–70€.

This typically Alsatian inn with its swimming pool has been in the Orth family for seven generations. Tradition rhymes with quality here. The delightful welcome, comfortable guest rooms and elaborate cuisine concocted by Michel (possibly a touch too ornate on occasion, but perfectly in line with local tradition) attract

our attention here. Foie gras served three ways, crayfish tail cassolette, individual fresh and smoked fish terrines, the game (in hunting season) and the pretty chocolate dessert board are fine, classical fare, generous and carefully prepared. The luxurious dining room has style and the extensive wine list of 120 vintages is well worth perusing.

● **Krebs'tuebbel** SIM

4, av de Strasbourg.

Tel. 03 88 51 11 08. Fax 03 88 51 89 02.

www.hostellerie-ecrevisse.com

Closed Mon. dinner, Tue., 1 week at end July, 2 weeks beg. Aug.

Prix fixe: 9,50€ (lunch), 17,50€, 31€.

A la carte: 33–42€.

Michel Orth's inn (an adjunct to the Ecrevisse) serves traditional Alsatian dishes. Apart from the shrewd regional tapas, these include shrimp soup, poached Fontaine salmon, slow-simmered chicken in creamy white sauce and a frozen apple nougat dessert. A fine selection of wines and beers.

In Mommenheim (67170). 6 km nw via D421.

● **Castel San Angelo** SIM

53, rte de Brumath.

Tel. 03 88 51 61 78. Fax 03 88 51 59 96.

Closed Sun. lunch, Mon. dinner, Wed. dinner.

Prix fixe: 30€ (Sun. lunch).

A la carte: 40€.

Angelo Bulone and his Sicilian family run this very neo-rustic Castel with great good humor. We dine pleasantly on Provençal-style frog legs, stuffed squid, a Sicilian meat dish and the tiramisu.

● **Chez Clément** SIM
"à la Gare"

1, rue de la Gare.

Tel. 03 88 51 61 17. Fax 03 88 51 69 61.

restclement67@aol.com

Closed Tue. dinner, Wed. dinner.

Prix fixe: 10€ (weekday lunch), 12€, 15€, 28€, 32€, 8€ (child). A la carte: 45€.

Joséphine and Clément Gilbert's eatery provides a pleasant welcome and efficient service. The check is modest and the cuisine well crafted. We reserve a table to feast on a marbled duck foie gras with fig chutney, a veal filet with morels and the fruit gratin served with vanilla ice cream. Amiable set menus at lunchtime.

 | SHOPS

BREAD AND BAKED GOODS

▼ **André Herzog**
77, rue du Gal-du-Port.
Tel.-Fax 03 88 51 13 71.
Just the place to enjoy almond kouglof, special breads, brioches, bredele (small, flavored cakes) and onion tart.

BUSCHWILLER

68220 Haut-Rhin. Paris 482 – Mulhouse 29 – Altkirch 26 – Colmar 64 – Saint-Louis 6.
A corner of Sundgau with flowers, orchards and verdant countryside a stone's throw from Basel and Saint-Louis.

 | RESTAURANTS

● **La Couronne** `SIM`
6, rue du Soleil.
Tel. 03 89 69 12 62.
Closed Mon.
Prix fixe: 8,50€ (lunch). A la carte: 40€.

This large village house converted into a rustic brasserie in green, brown and beige tones is energetically run by Anne-Rose Oser. A young veteran of the Armes de Bâle in Gewenheim, she performs a light repertoire that has its charms. A chanterelle gratin, sirloin steak with morels, frozen kouglof and a house mille-feuille dessert strike the right note.

CLIMBACH

67510 Bas-Rhin. Paris 474 – Strasbourg 63 – Bitche 38 – Haguenau 30 – Wissembourg 9.
A crossroads community on the border of the Palatinate, at a meeting of ways that run through the forest village of Wingen and the Col du Pigeonnier to the lost trails of the Northern Vosges.

 | HOTELS-RESTAURANTS

■ **Le Cheval Blanc**
2, rue de Bitche.
Tel. 03 88 94 41 95. Fax 03 88 94 21 96.
Closed Sun. dinner (mid-Nov.–mid-Mar.),
Tue. dinner, Wed., mid-Jan.–mid-Feb.,
1 week July.
12 rooms: 45–51€.
Prix fixe: 15,50€, 25€, 36€,
8,50€ (child).

The Freys' charming family inn has discreetly changed hands. We are planning a quick visit to find out more. The last we heard was that both the neat rooms with their modern furniture and the Alsace cuisine were looking good.

COLMAR

68000 Haut-Rhin. Paris 447 – Strasbourg 73 – Bâle 68 – Fribourg 51 – Nancy 142.
info@ot-colmar.fr.
With its fine chefs throughout the surrounding winegrowing district, restaurants in the town itself, pleasant stores and appealing market, Colmar welcomes visitors with a smile. As its reputation dictates, "the most Alsatian of Alsace towns" —proud of the illuminations that shift and change as we stroll, its Unterlinden museum and the canals of its Little Venice—remains faithful to the postcards by "Hansi," Jean-Jacques Waltz, the town's native portraitist. When we visit Colmar, we look upwards and count the picture book signs he painted before we sit down to eat at the Rendez-Vous de Chasse, JY's, the Neuland, Brenner's or the Maison des Têtes.

■ HOTELS

■ Hôtel les Têtes
19, rue des Têtes.
Tel. 03 89 24 43 43. Fax 03 89 24 58 34.
les-tetes@calixo.net
www.maisondestetes.com
Closed Feb.
17 rooms: 91–175€.
3 suites: 209–245€.

This hotel owes its name to the hundreds of sculpted heads decorating its facade. Dating back to 1609, it has an enchanting interior courtyard. The passages that lead to its typically Alsatian rooms were decorated by a local artist. In the dining room, we are charmed by the regional specialties (see Restaurants: La Maison des Têtes).

■ Le Colombier
7, rue Turenne.
Tel. 03 89 23 96 00. Fax 03 89 23 97 27.
www.hotel-le-colombier.fr
Closed Christmas vac.
28 rooms: 70–190€. 3 suites: 150–190€.

The décor here successfully reconciles the Renaissance components of this 15th-century establishment with the contemporary, neo-art nouveau furniture that equips the rooms. The bar is delightfully relaxing and the welcome wonderfully attentive.

■ Grand Hôtel Bristol
7, pl de la Gare.
Tel. 03 89 41 10 10 / 03 89 23 59 59.
Fax 03 89 23 92 26.
www.grand-hotel-bristol.com
92 rooms: 65–145€. 15 suites: 99–145€.
Half board: 85–185€.

The rail station just opposite was built in 1900, like the hotel. Inside, the comfortable rooms are undergoing renovation. The brasserie is popular, the restaurant renowned and the welcome highly professional. (See Restaurants: L'Auberge and Le Rendez-Vous de Chasse.)

■ Mercure Champ-de-Mars
2, av de la Marne.
Tel. 03 89 21 59 59. Fax 03 89 21 59 00.
h1225@accor-hotels.com
www.mercure.com
75 rooms: 107–127€.

A park provides the setting for this seventies chain hotel with all the functional aspects provided by establishments of that period.

■ Le Maréchal
4, pl des Six-Montagnes-Noires.
Tel. 03 89 41 60 32. Fax 03 89 24 59 40.
www.hotel-le-marechal.com
28 rooms: 80–215€. 2 suites: 245€.
Prix fixe: 35€, 55€, 75€, 11€ (child).
A la carte: 70€.

These 16th- and 17th-century Alsatian houses with their view of the Lauch form a delightful hotel complex run by Romantik Hotels. The old-fashioned rooms look out on the canal and the regional cuisine is up to the same high standard in the Echevin restaurant with its smart terrace.

■ L'Amiral
11b, bd du Champ-de-Mars.
Tel. 03 89 23 26 25. Fax 03 89 23 83 64.
www.hotel-amiral-colmar.com
47 rooms: 49–95€. 1 suite: 110€.

This former malting plant opposite a park in the town center provides modern rooms in warm tones, a fitness center and WiFi, as well as a snug bar.

■ Mercure-Unterlinden
15, rue Golbery.
Tel. 03 89 41 71 71. Fax 03 89 23 82 71.
h0978@accor-hotels.com / www.mercure.com
76 rooms: 97–107€. 4 suites: 135€.

The main attraction here is the immediate proximity of the Unterlinden museum and a shopping mall. A professional welcome, smiling service, modern rooms and a wine bar with a hushed ambiance.

■ Novotel 🏛

At the airdrome, 49, rte de Strasbourg.
Tel. 03 89 41 49 14. Fax 03 89 41 22 56.
h0416@accor.com
www.novotel.com
66 rooms: 78–107€.
Prix fixe: 15€, 8€ (child).

This chain hotel built in the seventies is still a headquarters for business visitors. The rooms are functional, the swimming pool and garden pleasant places to relax and the cuisine honest.

■ Saint-Martin 🏛

38, Grand'Rue.
Tel. 03 89 24 11 51. Fax 03 89 23 47 78.
colmar@hotel-saint-martin.com
www.hotel-saint-martin.com
Closed beg. Jan.–beg. Mar.
40 rooms: 89–129€. 2 suites: 149€.

The Louis XVI facade, turret, Renaissance stairway, meticulously decorated rooms and warm welcome have an immediate appeal. A charming address to remember.

■ Le Turenne 🏛

10, rte de Bâle.
Tel. 03 89 21 58 58. Fax 03 89 41 27 64.
turennecol@aol.com
www.turenne.com
82 rooms: 47–68€.

Not far from "Little Venice", this half-timbered hotel with a very Alsatian touch is an agreeable place to stay.

In Horbourg-Wihr (68180). 3 km e

■ L'Europe 🏵🏛

15, rte de Neuf-Brisach.
Tel. 03 89 20 54 00. Fax 03 89 41 27 50.
reservation@hotel-europe-colmar.fr
www.hotel-europe-colmar.com
111 rooms: 125–156€. 10 suites: 168–700€.
Prix fixe: 25€, 64€. A la carte: 45€.

This vast hotel complex with its imposing neo-Alsatian architecture and spacious, comfortable rooms offers a range of facilities (swimming pools, tennis court, meeting rooms). The Jardin d'Hiver serves local dishes and the Eden a more sophisticated cuisine. Duck foie gras with fig chutney, pike-perch medallions with Pinot Noir sauce served on a bed of sauerkraut, organic steak tartare with tomato, white wine, Cognac and butter sauce are splendid.

In Sainte-Croix-en-Plaine (68420). 10 km se via N422 and D1.

■ Le Moulin 🏵🏛

Rte d'Herrlisheim.
Tel. 03 89 49 31 20. Fax 03 89 49 23 11.
www.aumoulin.net
Closed beg. Nov.–31 Mar.
Rest. closed lunch, Sun.
17 rooms: 45–70€.
A la carte: 40€.

A stone's throw from the town, this old mill lost in the countryside offers large rooms at bargain prices, some of them renovated this year. Its little museum of rural items and regional restaurant serving residents only are first-rate.

● | RESTAURANTS

● Le Rendez-Vous de Chasse ◉ V.COM

At Grand Hôtel Bristol, 7, pl de la Gare.
Tel. 03 89 23 15 86. Fax 03 89 23 92 26.
reservation@grand-hotel-bristol.com
www.grand-hotel-bristol.com
Prix fixe: 42€, 69€, 80€.
A la carte: 85€.

A native of Westphalia in Germany who trained at the Armes de France, Valet de Coeur and Auberge de l'Ill, Michaela Peters presides over the kitchens of this institution with its luxurious décor, tables set well apart, elite staff and splendid wine list. The boss, Richard Riehm, has an eye to every detail, but even so, little Michaela has successfully imposed her style and marked her territory. Her lightly Alsatian manner is subtle and free of frills and frontiers. We like the foie gras degustation, the sautéed frog legs with chanterelles or the tender veal roast ("Cousin" Michaela's Alsace is a trove of energy and charm).

There follow the fish prepared with finesse (a cod filet served with herb-seasoned jumbo shrimp or the monkfish medallions stuffed with truffles and served with spaghettini and arugula) and the game in season (sautéed venison medallions with a delicate cherry sauce). References to local culture, which we felt were lacking here two years ago, now feature on the changing menu, even among the fine desserts, which include the splendid Alsatian-style plums in Pinot Noir with pain perdu ice cream.

● **La Maison des Têtes**

At Hôtel les Têtes, 19, rue des Têtes.
Tel. 03 89 24 43 43. Fax 03 89 24 58 34.
les-tetes@calixo.net
www.maisondestetes.com
Closed Sun. dinner, Mon., Tue. lunch,
Feb. vac.
Prix fixe: 65€, 12,50€ (child).
A la carte: 60–65€.

Behind the 105 sculpted heads that grace the facade of this fine Renaissance residence lies a dining room of character where Marc Rohfritsch enthralls his audience with tasteful classical dishes. Riesling-seasoned goose foie gras, frog legs in a parsley cream sauce, sea bream roasted skin-side down with braised fennel and a balsamic vinegar jus, roasted pigeon breast with potatoes slow-roasted in goose fat or a crème brûlée with brown sugar perfumed with Marc de Gewurz are a keen tribute to regional tradition. The remarkable Carmen's service is spirited and there are 150 fine wines to discover. (See Hotels.)

● **JY'S**

17, rue de la Poissonnerie.
Tel. 03 89 21 53 60. Fax 03 89 21 53 65.
www.jean-yves-schillinger.com
Closed Sun., Mon., mid-Feb.–beg. Mar.
Prix fixe: 29€ (lunch), 49€, 67€.

In the heart of the "Little Venice" district, Jean-Yves Schillinger's restaurant stuns and startles. Behind the facade decorated with a neo-Gothic fresco by Edgar Mahler, the cuisine in the contemporary dining room designed by Olivier Gagnère is apposite indeed. Jean-Yves plays on contrasting textures and flavors with never a slip. Ginger-marinated red tuna tartare, the steamed scallops and shrimp, roasted pigeon breast served with ceps and an aligot wine foam and the cherry gazpacho and caramelized pistachios over an orange sablé cookie conjure up visions of distant climes and set heads spinning.

● **L'Arpège**

24, rue des Marchands.
Tel. 03 89 23 37 89. Fax 03 89 23 39 22.
restaurant.arpege@wanadoo.fr.
Prix fixe: 27€, 32€, 52€, 10€ (child).
A la carte: 50–55€.

Patrice Kayser concocts succulent dishes that reflect both his inspiration and especially the changing produce available at the market. Potato gratin with foie gras, scallops with orange, coriander and olive oil, milk-fed veal chops simmered with garlic and preserved lemons or the Alsatian squab with cumin-infused carrot jus and pain d'épice tiramisu with salted-butter caramel ice cream are proof that this fine technician (who trained here with Alberto Bradi) has not lost his touch.

● **Bartholdi**

2, rue des Boulangers.
Tel. 03 89 41 07 74. Fax 03 89 41 14 65.
restaurant.bartholdi@wanadoo.fr
Closed Sun. dinner, Mon.,
end Jan.–beg. Feb., 2 weeks June–July.
Prix fixe: 18,50€, 21€, 49€.
A la carte: 40–50€.

Roland and Thierry Foit tend with gusto to the dining room in this gourmet brasserie, and Bernard Schwartz's reliable bistro fare is up to the same high standard. Washed down with wines produced by the place's owners—including the rosy cheeked Jacky Cattin—the goose and duck foie gras, duck breast in salad, pike-perch braised in red wine, tête de veau served with vinaigrette and a frozen meringue dessert with whipped cream fail to disappoint.

● Meistermann   `COM`

2a, av de la République.
Tel. 03 89 41 65 64. Fax 03 89 41 37 50.
info@meistermann.com
www.meistermann.com
Closed Sun. dinner, Mon., Feb. vac.
Prix fixe: 17€.
A la carte: 40–45€.

Gino Di Foggia breathes life into this central brasserie with her singsong accent, while Jean Vandredeuille cooks judiciously. Chicken oysters and foie gras over mixed greens, pike-perch filet over choucroute with a smoked bacon cream sauce, the famous choucroute garnished with five meat cuts and the pears caramelized with licorice charm the gourmand clientele here.

● Aux Trois Poissons   `COM`

15, quai de la Poissonnerie.
Tel.-Fax 03 89 41 25 21.
Closed Sun. dinner, Tue. dinner, Wed.,
Nov. 1 vac., 1 week Christmas–New Year's,
2 weeks July.
Prix fixe: 21€, 27€, 45€, 8€ (child).
A la carte: 55€.

After training in England, Gilles Seiler eagerly took up the reins of his father Jean's establishment. On a bank of the Lauch, he focuses on both land and sea produce with equal attention to detail. Pan-seared foie gras served over an autumn salad, catfish filet with crisp vegetables in an herb-seasoned butter, pike-perch served over a bed of sauerkraut with a beurre blanc sauce and the honey and Sichuan peppercorn–seasoned duck make an excellent impression before we move on to the ritual kouglof glacé.

● Auberge du Neuland   Ⓝ🍴SIM

2, chemin du Neuland.
Tel. 03 89 23 49 37. Fax 03 89 41 56 95.
Closed Tue. dinner, Wed.,
Thu. dinner (Nov.–Easter).
Prix fixe: 8,40€ (lunch), 11,50€ (lunch),
19€. A la carte: 30€.

Lost in the countryside, this modern establishment, unremarkable in appearance, is worth a detour. Muriel Jamm, a lively blonde, elegantly attends to the guests, while her husband Joël concocts lively, well-crafted dishes. This fine technician (who trained at the Chambard in Kaysersberg, then the Schoenenbourg in Riquewhir) has chosen a studiedly modest style here. Escargots in their parsley and garlic butter, wild boar terrine served with a quince purée, fried carp with an onion, herb, caper and mustard mayonnaise, tête de veau served with a cocotte of sautéed potatoes, puff pastry with blood pudding and apples (fleischkiechke) almost eat themselves. The prices are affable, the desserts blameless (kouglof glacé and a charlotte made with pain d'épice) and the local wines well chosen.

● Jules   Ⓝ🍴SIM

5, rue Conseil-Souverain.
Tel. 03 89 24 42 21.
Closed Sun., Mon., 2 weeks Nov.
Prix fixe: 18€ (lunch), 28€, 36€.

In the shadow of the Koifhus, this is a restaurant to try. Julien Spiegel made quite a career for himself (Schillinger, Haeberlin, Bocuse, Dutournier, Savoy and the Elysée) before opening this refined establishment. The harmony of the décor, where rusty steel melts into subtle off-white shades, offers a charming contrast. The innovative cuisine takes the form of shrewd set menus. A foie gras Tatin, sea bream with a ginger seasoned cannelloni, pike-perch cooked skin-side down with cabbage and cumin, yakitori-style duck brochettes and variations on theme of strawberry (cappuccino, marinated in balsamic vinegar and sorbet) are well crafted. The service is smooth and the genuine mastery of produce and deft touch are surprising.

● Wistub Brenner   🍴SIM

1, rue Turenne.
Tel. 03 89 41 42 33. Fax 03 89 41 37 99.
Closed Tue., Wed., 1 week Nov., Christmas–New Year's, 2 weeks Feb., 1 week June.
Prix fixe: 8€ (child). A la carte: 33–47€.

Gilbert Brenner, a former pastry chef by trade with a passion for all good things, presents the ne plus ultra of tradition in a burlesque cloak. His tripe in Riesling sauce are a wonderful thing. Gilbert, who prepares pork shank, pork shoulder, the tourte de la vallée (an Alsatian pastry baked with Munster cheese and ground pork), the choucroute, the hanger steak seasoned with garlic as happily as smoked salmon served with green lentils, refreshes his traditional repertoire (aimed at preserving good local recipes) on an ever-changing blackboard. In a lively *winstub* setting open to the outside world, we delight in the marbled veal and parsley and the herb-seasoned chicken, pâté in a pastry crust with Riesling aspic or a delicately pressed zucchini, tuna and feta terrine, which give an idea of the contribution this traditional *winstub* with its Southern French leanings is making to the rejuvenation of the genre. All the local winegrowers come to savor the delights on offer here.

● L'Auberge　🏠SIM

At Grand Hôtel Bristol, 7, pl de la Gare.
Tel. 03 89 23 59 59. Fax 03 89 23 92 26.
reservation@grand-hotel-bristol.fr
www.grand-hotel-bristol.com
A la carte: 40€.

This brasserie opposite the rail station has remained loyal to the region's cuisine. The 1900 setting with its wall frescos, antique woodwork and old stove breathes its charm. The house terrine with prunes, vineyard-keeper's salad, fish filets over a bed of choucroute, tête de veau with vinaigrette sauce and a chilled mousse with kirsch slip down smoothly.

● Anadolu　SIM

31, rue Vauban.
Tel. 03 89 23 71 71.
gurbuz.t@wanadoo.fr
www.anadolu.fr
Closed Sun. lunch, Mon., Sept.
Prix fixe: 30€, 24€.
A la carte: 35€.

This small Turkish tavern with its terrace on a pedestrian street is efficiently run by Talat Gurbuz. The appealing cuisine

includes delicious mezzé (assorted Lebanese appetizers), lamb in many forms, chicken brochettes and a mild kadaïf (honey- and almond-seasoned angel hair pastry with fresh lemon). The short wine list completes our journey to the East with a few Ottoman vintages. The cost of the fare for this change of air (and fare) remains modest.

● Caveau Saint-Pierre　SIM

24, rue de la Herse.
Tel. 03 89 41 99 33. Fax 03 89 23 94 33.
Closed Mon., Jan.
Prix fixe: 17€.
A la carte: 35€.

Tourists are fond of the exposed stone and beam décor and "Little Venice" surroundings, but the cuisine here also has its charms: foie gras, herb-encrusted cod, grilled beef tenderloin and the vacherin dessert slip down effortlessly.

● Chez Hansi　SIM

23, rue des Marchands.
Tel.-Fax 03 89 41 37 84.
Closed Wed., Thu., Jan.
Prix fixe: 18€, 44€. A la carte: 40–50€.

In his typical Old Colmar cellar, Marc Gautier makes a fine ambassador for his region. The woodwork, Alsatian furniture, waitstaff in traditional costume and local dishes go together perfectly. An onion tart, goose foie gras, pike-perch in Riesling sauce, choucroute with smoked sausage, bacon and pork and a frozen kouglof with kirsch are models of their genre.

● Au Cygne　SIM

15-17, rue Edouard-Richard.
Tel. 03 89 23 76 26. Fax 03 89 24 39 31.
Closed Sat. lunch, Sun., Mon. dinner,
1 week Christmas–New Year's, 1 week at
Easter, 15 Aug.
Prix fixe: 10€, 16€, 6€ (child).
A la carte: 35–40€.

The tarte flambée (a thin-crusted savory tart with cream, onions and bacon), fish simmered in red wine, sirloin steak served with marrow and pear croustillant here are neatly crafted, vibrant traditional dishes. Kathy and Bertrand Roth uphold the *winstub* spirit.

● Hammerer   SIM

3, pl Hastinger.
Tel.-Fax 03 89 41 52 43.
Closed Sun., Wed. dinner, Bank holidays, end July–beg. Aug.
Prix fixe: 9,50€ (lunch), 27€ (lunch).
A la carte: 30€.

Francis Staub, the dandy of cookware, is an admirer of this paneled dining room where we savor the classic dishes concocted by Jean Warth. The presskopf (a head cheese and aspic terrine) as well as a steak with "real" house made French fries are monuments of their kind. The set menus are a bargain.

● Au Koïfhus   SIM

2, pl de l'Ancienne-Douane.
Tel. 03 89 23 04 90. Fax 03 89 23 66 00.
Prix fixe: 18€, 19,50€, 23,50€, 7€ (child).
A la carte: 35€.

The salad gourmande (duck breast, gizzards and foie gras), salmon in puff pastry over sauerkraut, beef tenderloin with shallots and with bone marrow and a Strasbourg-style veal steak with spätzle followed by a delicious kouglof glacé are good indeed. Eric Libbra's charming, wood-trimmed *winstub* attracts plenty of customers.

● Le Restaurant du Marché   SIM

20, pl de la Cathédrale.
Tel. 03 89 24 93 88.
f.kurtz@libertysurf.fr
www.restaurantdumarché.fr
Closed Sun., Mon., 1 week Nov. 1, Feb. vac., 2 weeks Aug.
Prix fixe: 14,50€ (weekday lunch).
A la carte: 45€.

Frédéric and Laurence Kurtz provide a charming welcome and serve a healthy market-based cuisine that strikes just the right note. Ginger-seasoned crisp breaded pork trotters, orange spotted flounder with endives, veal roast with slow-roasted potatoes, crisp bacon and ceps and the

frozen bittersweet chocolate truffles are pleasant indeed.

● Le Temps des Délices   SIM

23, rue d'Alspach.
Tel. 03 89 23 45 57. Fax 03 89 23 82 95.
angelsteraneo@aol.com
Closed Sun., Mon., 1 week beg. Jan., 1 week beg. Aug.
Prix fixe: 19€ (lunch), 35€ (dinner).
A la carte: 50–55€.

Although Michelangelo Straneo is somewhat neglecting the fine Italian cuisine that used to delight us so much in his wood trimmed chalet, his foie gras terrine with spiced aspic, sautéed cod filet, tender veal medallions and a suave tiramisu are still tasteful classics. The dining room has its charm with its yellow walls, wood banquettes and library.

● La Ville de Paris   SIM

4, pl Jeanne-d'Arc.
Tel. 03 89 24 53 15. Fax 03 89 23 65 24.
Closed Mon. dinner, Tue.
Prix fixe: 21€. A la carte: 40€.

This central *winstub* had its moment of glory under Gibert Brenner. It continues on an even keel with Claudine Bartholomé at the helm. We still enjoy the escargots, foie gras, salmon in a Riesling sauce, tête de veau, liver quenelle and the caramel flan, all reliably prepared by Steve Mergenthaler.

In Sigolsheim (68240). 6,5 km nw via N 83 then D10.

● Auberge du Pont de la Fecht   SIM

Tel. 03 89 41 48 12. Fax 03 89 24 51 44.
Closed Mon., Tue., Bank holidays.
Prix fixe: 9€ (lunch), 12€ (lunch), 18€, 28€. A la carte: 25–30€.

The Wiss' inn is worth a foray into the forest. Visitors young and old enjoy the garden, terraces and dining rooms. Monique at the tables and Hubert in the kitchen gratify their regular guests with presskopf (a local head cheese and aspic terrine) vineyard-keeper's salad, pork shank stuffed with horseradish, braised pork shank, beef served with sea salt and a frozen vacherin dessert.

 | SHOPS

BREAD & BAKED GOODS
▼ Jean-Pierre Bechler
4, rue Charles-Marie-Widor / 8, rue du Nord.
Tel. 03 89 41 07 34 / 03 89 41 81 84.
Splendid breads with sesame, rye, poppyseed, beer, bacon, walnuts, cheese or organic grains are the masterpieces purveyed by Jean-Pierre, who does so much for gastronomy in his region.

▼ Boulangerie Colle
5, pl Saint-Joseph.
Tel. 03 89 79 05 05.
Eric and Isabelle Colle provide wholegrain, hazelnut-raisin, organic, or pumpernickel bread, and cinnamon cake.

▼ Helmstetter
11-13, rue des Serruriers / 4, rue de Turenne.
Tel. 03 89 41 27 78 / 03 89 24 59 10.
In his picturesque store and tearoom, Frédéric Helmstetter prepares quality Vosges baguette; sourdough boule; bread with sesame, poppyseed, wheat-rye, walnuts or bacon, and bredele (small, flavored cakes).

BUTCHER
▼ Herrscher
1, pl des Six-Montagnes-Noires.
Tel. 03 89 41 27 80.
At Michel Herrscher's store, there is never a shortage of veal from Corrèze. Montbéliarde breed of beef raised in the Ried and wild game in season. Superb prepared dishes, too.

CHARCUTERIE
▼ Tempé
43, rue des Clefs.
Tel.-Fax 03 89 24 50 41.
Milk-fed veal, flank steak, entrecôte, bacon, knackwurst, pâté baked in a pastry crust, raw-cured ham and beer sausages, all appetizing, at the Tempé store.

CHEESE
▼ Fromagerie Saint-Nicolas
18, rue Saint-Nicolas.
Tel. 03 89 24 90 45.
www.fromagerie-st-nicolas.com
Jacky Quesnot seeks out the best farm cheeses and matures them in his new vaulted brick cellars, which visitors can tour on request. Munsters from Orbey de Chaize in Basses-Huttes or from Modion in Pré-Vareth, Runtzenbach tomme and Bambois chèvres make an impression.

COFFEE
▼ Les Cafés au Bon Nègre
9, rue des Têtes.
Tel. 03 89 20 61 10.
www.districafes.com
Estelle Petitdemange's store opposite the Unterlinden Museum offers a remarkable selection of coffees (Kenya, Colombia, Jamaican Blue Mountain) and striking Darjeeling and Ceylon teas and infusions.

IMPORTED PRODUCTS
▼ Enopasta Bradi
14, rue des Serruriers.
Tel. 03 89 23 58 01.
We were fond of Alberto Bradi when he ran Alsace's number one Italian restaurant and we continue to trust in his judgment at this quality store, which offers pastas of all shapes; wines from Piedmont, Tuscany or Sardinia; balsamic vinegar, and fine olive oils.

PASTRIES
▼ Chez Thierry et Annabelle
25, rue des Têtes.
Tel. 03 89 41 27 67.
Annabelle and Thierry Mutzig delight food lovers with their bread with anise or raisins, kouglof, Linzer torte, apple streusel or chocolate cake.

▼ Jean
6, pl de l'Ecole.
Tel. 03 89 41 24 63.
Michel Casenave and Christian Dosch's reputation is built on their "black pearl" cake, ganaches, hazelnut pralines, "golden

sun" or "créole". They also supply an excellent gray d'Albion (chocolate mousse, coffee, caramel) and a Cointreau flambé. A splendid 1900 vintage store.

▼ Richon

8, rue Stanislas.
Tel. 03 89 41 26 84.

Laurent and Claude Richon prepare splendid streusel, langhopf, kouglof, Sévigné (hazelnut sponge cake with chocolate mousse and pralines), Saint-Honoré (a choux pastry ring, with caramel and kirsch cream), chestnut torche and quality traditional chocolates (truffles, nougat cream).

TABLETOP & KITCHENWARE

▼ Arts et Collections d'Alsace

1, rue des Tanneurs.
Tel.-Fax 03 89 24 09 78.

The kelsch tablecloths, engraved carafes, beer mugs, milk jugs and fine prints here make excellent, authentic gifts.

WINE

▼ Maison Pfister

11, rue des Marchands.
Tel. 03 89 41 33 61.

Dominique Dauce eagerly extols the virtues of his meursault from Coche-Dury, Jacques Sélosse or Billecart-Salmon Champagnes, châteauneuf-du-pape from Château Rayas and Alsatians made by Muré.

▼ La Sommelière

19, pl de la Cathédrale.
Tel. 03 89 41 20 38.
www.lasommeliere.fr

Anne-Marie Tempé rigorously selects the region's best vintages and also offers carafes and glasses from Riedel and the Cristallerie Royale de Champagne. A delicatessen section.

◆	RENDEZVOUS

BEER BAR

◆ La Krutenau

1, rue de la Poissonnerie.
Tel. 03 89 41 18 80.

With its excellent atmosphere, this Little Venice tavern is just the place for a properly served beer.

BRASSERIE

◆ Les Dominicains

1, rue Reiset.
Tel.-Fax 03 89 23 68 21.

The service here is prompt and the beers (Adelscott, Bitburger, Guinness) are deftly poured.

TEA SALONS

◆ Au Croissant Doré

28, rue des Marchands.
Tel. 03 89 23 70 81.

This art nouveau establishment between the Bartholdi museum and Pfister delights us with its fine fruit tarts, chocolate fondant, tortes, quiches, hot chocolate and choice teas.

◆ Richon

8, rue Stanislas.
Tel. 03 89 41 26 84.

We enjoy apple streusel, Saint-Honoré and chestnut torche in the chic tearoom behind the elegant store.

COLROY-LA-ROCHE

67420 Bas-Rhin. Paris 407 – Sélestat 31 – Strasbourg 67 – Molsheim 38 – Lunéville 70. A step away from the industrious Bruche and Ban de la Roche valleys, here is a Vosges village surrounded by forest, full of thickets where the inhabitants gather wild berries and hunt in the autumn. The last thing you might expect to find here is a luxury hotel, but …

	HOTELS-RESTAURANTS

■ La Cheneaudière

3, rue du Vieux-Moulin.
Tel. 03 88 97 61 64. Fax 03 88 47 21 73.
www.chenaudiere.com
25 rooms: 90–260€. 7 suites: 255–420€.
Prix fixe: 45€, 49€ (lunch, wine inc.), 110€.

Mireille François is the charming hostess of this Vosges Relais & Châteaux establishment. We come here for the relaxing atmosphere, indoor swimming pool, forest walks and cozy, paneled rooms. Chef Roger Bouhassoun meticulously prepares the house standards, served in a vast, luxurious dining room with bay windows looking out on the surrounding greenery. Fresh Scottish salmon tartare prepared tableside, a pairing of goose and duck foie gras, lobster fricassée with thick basil pasta, salmon trout baked in salt, simmered veal sweetbreads with morels and cream in sauce and the warm soufflé flavored with plum eau-de-vie from Lorraine are all in very good taste.

In 67130 Bellefosse. 9 km ne.

● **Auberge de la Charbonnière** ⚙SIM

Col de la Charbonnière, Champ du Feu.
Tel. 03 88 08 31 17. Fax 03 88 08 31 38.
col-charbonniere@aol.com
Closed Mon. dinner, Tue., 2 weeks Nov.,
2 weeks Mar.
Prix fixe: 14€, 18€, 21€.

Christian Brüls and Michel Felden run this easygoing chalet a step away from the ski trails. Michel manages the dining room with gusto, while Christian prepares his unfussy cuisine. Fondues, raclettes and chapeaurade (meat in bouillon with grated vegetables) are served in the evening. At lunchtime, we make short work of escargots, cervelas sausage with vinaigrette, pork cheeks with Pinot Noir sauce and large grilled pork ribs served with a caramelized Chinese sauce.

In 67420 Ranrupt. 2 km sw.

● **Ferme-Auberge Promont** SIM

37, Hauts-des-Près, col de Steige, toward
Champ-du-Feu, forest road on left off D214.
Tel.-Fax 03 88 97 62 85.
Closed dinner, Fri., 1 Dec.–26 Dec.
Prix fixe: 16€, 18€.

In this friendly, panoramic Vosges farmhouse, Maryse and Corine Schymnoll champion their region's cuisine at unbeatable prices. Covered meat pies, roasted duck or veal and kirsch-flavored mousse are washed down with a well-chosen Pinot Noir.

▼ | SHOPS

JAMS

▼ **Les Confitures du Climont**

In Ranrupt. 2 km sw.
Hameau de la Salcée (near the col de Steige).
Tel. 03 88 97 72 01.
www.confituresduclimont.com

Agnès and Fabrice Krencker prepare their sublime jams with pear and ginger, mirabelle plum with cinnamon, sour cherry, blueberry, hazelnut-plum and the mysterious "*bicolore*" in copper kettles.

D

DACHSTEIN

67120 Bas-Rhin. Paris 476 –
Saverne 28 – Sélestat 41 – Strasbourg 23 –
Molsheim 6.
With its ramparts, château and church, this trim
village by the Bruche is well worth a detour.

 RESTAURANTS

● **Auberge de la Bruche** COM
1, rue Principale.
Tel. 03 88 38 14 90. Fax 03 88 48 81 12.
www.auberge-bruche.com
Closed Sat. lunch, Sun. dinner, Wed.,
12 days at end Dec.–beg. Jan.,
mid-Aug.–end Aug.
Prix fixe: 26€, 64€. A la carte: 52–60€.

Hubert Raugel has turned his fine inn on
the bank of the Bruche into a charming little gourmet halt. These days, the service
has slipped a tad, but we cannot fault the
schniederspätle (local stuffed dumplings)
with foie gras, pike-perch with morels
in ravioli nor the beef filet medallions
served with gnocchi, which all carry the
hallmark of true skill. The fleur d'oranger
parfait with chocolate sauce is well crafted
and the Alsatian wines by the glass very
palatable.

DAMBACH-LA-VILLE

67650 Bas-Rhin. Paris 426 –
Obernai 19 – Sélestat 9 –
Strasbourg 46 – Saverne 61.
otdlv@netcourrier.com.
The main square is splendid indeed with its bear
fountain and Renaissance houses. The best view
of the village's old roofs is to be had walking from
the Saint-Sébastien chapel in the heart of the
vines to the foot of the Vosges mountains.

 HOTELS-RESTAURANTS

■ **Au Raisin d'Or** ⌂
28 bis, rue G.-Clemenceau.
Tel. 03 88 92 48 66. Fax 03 88 92 61 42.
au-raisin-dor@wanadoo.fr
www.au-raisin-dor.com

Closed 20 Dec.–20 Jan., Mon.
Rest. closed Mon., Tue. lunch.
8 rooms: 42–46€.
Prix fixe: 8€, 28€, 8,50€ (child).
A la carte: 40€.

This Alsatian-style guesthouse stands
on the wine route. The rooms are rustic and neat, and Michel's welcome does
justice to Anne Imbs' cuisine. With the
house vintages, we wash down monkfish
medallions with ham, frog legs in puff
pastry and the pigeon filet with orange-
seasoned mustard sauce.

■ **Le Vignoble** ⌂
1, rue de l'Eglise.
Tel. 03 88 92 43 75. Fax 03 88 92 62 21.
Closed Jan.
7 rooms: 54–74€.

A step away from the church, this converted barn dating back to 1765 offers
trim little rooms. The atmosphere is rustic, Caroline Martin's welcome warm,
the breakfast generous and the prices
restrained. WiFi.

▼ SHOPS

PASTRIES

▼ **Kamm**
80, rue du Maréchal-Foch.
Tel.-Fax 03 88 92 40 65.
Jean-Paul Kamm's delicious ice creams,
cakes, warm pastries, kouglofs, chocolates and petit fours are of unfailingly
high quality.

◆ RENDEZVOUS

BAR

◆ **Caveau Nartz**
12, pl du Marché.
Tel. 03 88 92 41 11.
Michel Nartz's cellar occupies an exquisite, narrow 17th-century building. Visitors taste the wines he produces himself,
along with a slice of kouglof or a few
escargots.

DANNEMARIE

68210 Haut-Rhin. Paris 448 – Mulhouse 25 – Belfort 24 – Altkirch 10.
A traditional halt on the Sundgau fried carp route.

●	RESTAURANTS

● Ritter

5, rue de la Gare.
Tel. 03 89 25 04 30. Fax 03 89 08 02 34.
Closed Mon. dinner, Tue., Thu. dinner,
Christmas–New Year's vac., Feb. vac.,
1 week July.
Prix fixe: 9,50€ (lunch), 15€, 22€, 30€,
9,50€ (child). A la carte: 40€.

Richard Enderlin reliably runs this fine 1900 residence with its farm museum décor of tankards and tools. We savor the duck foie gras medallion, duckling with mirabelle plum sauce and the frozen Kirsch mousse. A pleasant choice of wines by the glass.

DIEFMATTEN

68780 Haut-Rhin. Paris 536 – Mulhouse 21 – Colmar 49 – Belfort 23 – Thann 14.
This is where gourmet Sundgau begins, in a simple, neat village that seems to have been transported from another age.

▉/●	HOTELS-RESTAURANTS

● Le Cheval Blanc

17, rue de Hecken.
Tel. 03 89 26 91 08. Fax 03 89 26 92 28.
patrick@auchevalblanc.fr
www.auchevalblanc.fr
Closed Mon. (exc. lunch Bank holidays),
Tue. (exc. lunch Bank holidays),
2 weeks mid-Jan., 2 weeks end July.
8 rooms: 54–99€.
Prix fixe: 23€ (weekday lunch), 52€, 34€,
39€. A la carte: 70€.

This former farm in pastel blue has been converted into a modern hostelry. Patrick Schlienger, son of the family and disciple of Bocuse, Jung and Willer, presides over the stove. His parents tend to the dining room with a smile, while sommelier Daniel Gresser recommends fine wines from Alsace and elsewhere. Savoring the foie gras confit, grilled sole with a saffron-seasoned foam, guinea hen breast in caramelized cream, cherry soup with almond milk ice cream and the strawberry profiteroles with pistachio ice cream, we wish we could eat here on a regular basis. A terrace, pleasant grounds and eight trim rooms for an overnight stay.

DOSSENHEIM-SUR-ZINSEL

67330 Bas-Rhin. Paris 452 – Saverne 8 – La Petite-Pierre 16.
A gateway to the Northern Vosges with hidden, ruined châteaux, as in Hunebourg nearby. The Petite-Pierre and its forest are just a step away.

●	RESTAURANTS

● Chez Clauss

154, montée des Tilleuls.
Tel. 03 88 70 00 81. Fax 03 88 70 05 27.
www.restaurant-clauss.com
Closed Sat. lunch, Mon.
Prix fixe: 14,90€ (lunch, weekdays), 20,90€ (weekdays), 30€ (Sun.).

Roby Clauss has been running this affable inn with its woodwork, sandstone and fine paintings for many a year now. Guests have long gathered there on weekends to enjoy the loggers' plate with grilled sausage, tartes flambées and the flambéed fruit brochette, a traditional repertoire enthusiastically performed by this expert tennis timekeeper. But now his son, Philippe, has returned from a tour of duty with the greats (Arnsbourg, Crocodile, Palme d'Or) and revolutionized the house style. His set menus are bargains, the wines well chosen and the dishes too sophisticated for the setting: marinated sardines added to tomato gazpacho in a glass, chanterelle risotto with green vegetables and the sea bream with Coppa ham and slow-cooked caramelized fennel. To be continued.

EBERSMUNSTER

67600 Bas-Rhin. Paris 508 – Strasbourg 40 – Obernai 23 – Saint-Dié-des-Vosges 55 – Sélestat 9.

This Ried village is famous for its magnificent abbey church in the Austrian baroque style. The Ill runs serenely through the village.

●	RESTAURANTS

● Les Deux Clés

72, rue du Général-Leclerc.
Tel. 03 88 85 71 55.
Closed Mon., Thu.
Prix fixe: 30–33€. A la carte: 40€.

This old-style inn opposite the abbey church is friendliness incarnate. One comes here for the family welcome, the neat dining room with its curved ceiling and the cozy atmosphere. Add to this a poultry liver terrine, the breaded and fried eel, Mère Baur's wine-simmered fish, pike-perch with cream sauce, the roasted stuffed breast of guinea hen, the "almond mount" dessert and the frozen Vielle Fine soufflé. Fine choice of local wines.

● Restaurant de l'Ill

52, rue du Général-Leclerc.
Tel. 03 88 85 75 40.
Closed Mon., Tue.
Prix fixe: 8,50€ (lunch), 25,50€, 27€.

An amusing kitsch décor with souvenirs of the 1870 war, antique furniture, Betschdorf pots and art nouveau lamps. There is a small terrace and a smiling reception from Josiane. The chef, an ex-antiques dealer, cooks up in exquisite fashion frog legs wrapped in greens and a tasty fried carp with spicy mayonnaise. The day's special (crunchy vegetables, stuffed chicken) is generous. In short, this is a lively place that should be sought out.

EGUISHEIM

68420 Haut-Rhin. Paris 445 – Rouffach 10 – Mulhouse 39 – Colmar 7.
info@oteguisheim.fr.

Ancient ruins seem to show that this is the "cradle" of vineyards. In addition there is the site at the foot of the Husseren towers, the route through the old houses and the high-quality winemaking.

	HOTELS-RESTAURANTS

■ Hostellerie du Château

2, rue du Château.
Tel. 03 89 23 72 00. Fax 03 89 41 63 93.
www.hostellerieduchateau.com
10 rooms: 65–114€. 1 suite: 115–155€.

Modern, and in the heart of the village, this hotel has cheerful rooms with bright colors.

■ Hostellerie du Pape

10, Grand-Rue.
Tel. 03 89 41 41 21. Fax 03 89 41 41 31.
www.hostellerie-pape.com
Rest. closed Mon., Tue., 3 weeks Jan.,
10 days beg. Feb.
33 rooms: 65–95€.
Prix fixe: 17€, 48€, 10€ (child).

Maurice Huber is the professional manager of this modern hotel with functional rooms situated at the edge of the town, while Jean-Marie Boucheseche gives a heartfelt rendition of traditional dishes. The pan-seared duck foie gras with ceps, pressed pheasant with hazelnuts, pike-perch in thin slices with potatoes and the venison medallions with red cabbage are extremely well prepared. Local wines are on the program.

■ Auberge Alsacienne

12, Grand-Rue.
Tel. 03 89 41 50 20. Fax 03 89 23 89 32.
www.auberge-alsacienne.net
Closed 20 Dec.–10 Feb.,
1 week at end June–beg. July.
Rest. closed Sun. dinner, Mon.
17 rooms: 55–64€. 2 suites: 70€.
Prix fixe: 20€, 27,50€, 7,50€ (child).

An inn like they used to be. Sweet rooms and serious cuisine are on offer from Thierry Peter, relieved in the kitchen by

Stéphane Laurent. Local dishes have their voice here, but one that has been vigorously reinterpreted. The escargots and mushrooms in a crêpe pouch, pike-perch with leek cream, goose breast with raspberry vinegar and the apple and raisins marinated in Gewurz, served in streudel, are finely done.

● Le Caveau d'Eguisheim COM

3, pl du Château.
Tel. 03 89 41 08 89. Fax 03 89 23 79 99.
Closed Mon., Tue., 3 weeks Feb.–mid–Mar.,
1 week July.
Prix fixe: 37€, 59€, 20€.
A la carte: 65€.

The serious chef of the village is Jean-Christophe Perrin. The man we knew from La Galupe in Urt and Toiny in Saint-Barth has transformed this winemaker's house on two floors into a quality establishment. His fine handling of themes based on pork (a wonderful presskopf), his carp ravioli in white wine bouillon, the tuna on a tarte flambée (a flat savory tart), the "squab in a woodcock's nest" and the beautiful Salers beef in glossy Bordelaise sauce are spirited exercises in style that highlight the produce. The wines labelled Beyer and Wolfberger, both shareholders in the restaurant, follow suit.

● La Grangelière COM

59, rue du Rempart-Sud.
Tel. 03 89 23 00 30. Fax 03 89 23 61 62.
lagrangeliere@wanadoo.fr
www.lagrangeliere.com
Closed Sun. (off season), Thu. (off season),
3 weeks Mar.
Prix fixe: 22€ (wine inc.), 29€, 65€,
10€ (child). A la carte: 60€.

Discreet but very correct, Alain Finkbeiner, who was chef at the Château d'Isenbourg in Rouffach, has not forgotten the great lessons he learned on the Côte d'Azur, principally with Chibois in Cannes. Duck carpaccio with soy sauce vinaigrette, fennel seed–seasoned John Dory, the foie gras mille-feuille served hot, the veal tenderloin medallion as well as the pan-simmered pêche de vigne with

house ice cream make a very good showing. Ad hoc wines suggested by Karine.

● Au Vieux Porche COM

16, rue des Trois-Châteaux.
Tel. 03 89 24 01 90. Fax 03 89 23 91 25.
vieux.porche@wanadoo.fr
Closed Tue., Wed., 1 week Nov., end Feb.–
end Mar., 10 days end June–beg. July.
Prix fixe: 23€, 8,50€ (child).
A la carte: 45€.

This 18th-century winemaker's house is run with dynamism by Pascal and Betty Feuermann. Both he, a former sommelier with Chambard, and she, daughter of an owner-grower, cannot be pried from the surrounding vineyards. On the cuisine side, their chef Eddy Fischer produces the goods. The rustic dining room with stained glass windows, beams and wooden fittings is the scene for classic feasts. A marbled foie gras terrine, pike-perch simmered in Riesling and a frozen kirsch-flavored dessert look very good.

● Pavillon Gourmand SIM

101, rue du Rempart-Sud.
Tel. 03 89 24 36 88. Fax 03 89 23 93 94.
http//perso.orange.fr/pavillon.schubnel/
Closed Tue., Wed., Christmas.
Prix fixe: 16€, 25€, 30€, 60€, 9€ (child).

Pupil of star establishments (Bocuse, Vergé, Haeberlin and Tantris), Pascal Schubnel, former chef of Le Caveau, now succeeded in the kitchen by his son David, serves regional cooking modestly but efficiently. His onion tart, his pike-perch and Riesling soufflé, his choucroute and his Gewurz sorbet are models of their kind.

▼	SHOPS

BREAD, BAKED GOODS & PASTRIES

▼ Marx

39, Grand-rue.
Tel. 03 89 41 32 56.
The Roesches (Roger Marx's son-in-law and daughter) supply quality artisanal pretzels, plum tarts, kouglofs and sweet pastries.

TABLETOP & KITCHENWARE

▼ Au Château Fleuri

5, pl du Château.

Tel.-Fax 03 89 24 13 41.

The Bintz family enthusiastically present floral tablecloths, glassware and Betschdorf and Soufflenheim pottery. Happy memories.

▼ Aux Trois Cigognes

45, Grand-rue.

Tel. 03 89 23 30 31.

Browse through the typically Alsatian tableware and tablecloths in this charming emporium.

ELSENHEIM

67390 Bas-Rhin. Paris 449 – Colmar 18 – Sélestat 14 – Strasbourg 61.

In an otherwise anonymous village consisting of several houses planted in the Ried, just above Illhaeusern on the route to Marckolsheim, sits one stately home with wrought-iron balconies.

 | RESTAURANTS

● Le Cottage `SIM`

22, rue Principale.

Tel. 03 88 92 51 59. Fax 03 88 74 98 00.

lecottage@evc.net

Closed Mon., Tue. dinner, Wed. dinner, 2 weeks Feb., 2 weeks Aug.

Prix fixe: 12€ (lunch), 35€. A la carte: 50€.

Gilbert and Dominique Zeyssolff run this village inn with professionalism, offering a smiling welcome, quality produce and traditional dishes, without forgetting the wines of their vinicultural friends. Fish in red wine sauce, scampi cassolette, pikeperch simmered in Riesling, veal kidneys in mustard sauce and frozen cherry parfait are eaten with pleasure.

ENSISHEIM

68190 Haut-Rhin. Paris 467 – Mulhouse 15 – Colmar 24 – Guebwiller 14.

This former capital of the Austrian *landgraviat*, decimated by the last world war, is proud of its town hall with arched vaults and its Jesuits' church, and a little less of its sadly famous prison.

 | HOTELS-RESTAURANTS

■ La Couronne ◐⬚

47, rue de la 1er-Armée.

Tel. 03 89 81 03 72. Fax 03 89 26 40 05.

la-couronne@wanadoo.fr

9 rooms: 65–99€. 4 suites: 65–165€.

Prix fixe: 30€, 42€, 72€, 10€ (child).

A la carte: 70€.

Jean-Marc Pflimlin is the spirited newcomer to this establishment with a good reputation. Housed in a building dating from medieval times, the rooms mix modern comfort and old-fashioned charm, while the seasonal fare is precisely designed. Jumbo shrimp and escargot ravioli served with small vegetables, spiceglazed Atlantic sea bass with three-rice ratatouille, squab breast with "flavors of the forest", chocolate and acidulated cream soufflé served hot are finely-crafted dishes that manage to blend with one of the 1,000 wines in the cellar.

● Le Thaler `SIM`

47, rue de la 1er-Armée.

Tel. 03 89 26 43 26. Fax 03 89 26 40 05.

la-couronne@wanadoo.fr

Closed Sun. dinner.

Prix fixe: 12€ (lunch). A la carte: 35€.

This friendly drinking place is the inexpensive annex to La Couronne. Tête de veau with vinaigrette, Munster cheese in puff pastry served in salad and a slice of herb-seasoned kidneys are peasant dishes in the best taste. Good choice of wines by the glass.

ERSTEIN

67150 Bas-Rhin. Paris 418 – Strasbourg 24 – Colmar 49 – Molsheim 27 – Sélestat 25.

grandried.oterstein@wanadoo.fr.

This is the homeland of Alsace sugar, the road between Ried and Vosges with a cuisine awaiting discovery.

HOTELS-RESTAURANTS

■ Crystal Hôtel

41, av de la Gare.
Tel. 03 88 64 81 00. Fax 03 88 98 11 29.
baumert@hotelcrystal.info
www.hotelcrystal.info
Hotel closed 1 week Aug.
Rest. closed Fri. dinner, Sat. lunch, Sun.,
1 week Christmas–New Year's, 3 weeks Aug.
Prix fixe: 30€.

This hotel marries functionality and charm. The renovated rooms are comfortable, the garden welcoming, the bar friendly and there are meeting rooms for seminars. The cuisine is not lacking in daring or character. A pressed shrimp and vegetable terrine, roasted Atlantic sea bass with whole grain mustard sauce, duckling served with kumquat and foie gras and the frozen mandarin orange mousse are among our good memories.

● Jean-Victor Kalt

41, av de la Gare.
Tel. 03 88 98 09 54. Fax 03 88 98 83 01.
jean-victor.kalt@wanadoo.fr
Closed Sun. dinner, Mon., 1 week at end July,
10 days beg. Aug.
Prix fixe: 28€, 45€, 65€. A la carte: 75€.

The surroundings of this business district are hardly enchanting but Jean-Victor Kalt's restaurant deserves the detour. This disciple of Pierre Gagnaire serves up a cuisine balanced between peasant and aristocratic produce, tradition and modernity. In the dining room with its nineties setting, marbled terrine of smoked sausage and two types of foie gras, veal tenderloin medallion with morels and the raspberry and Bourbon vanilla-seasoned tiramisu give great joy, as does the cellar, rich in wines from all over France.

68480 Haut-Rhin. Paris 529 – Altkirch 19 – Colmar 79 – Mulhouse 37 – Bâle 27.
infotourisme@jura-alsacien.net.
Enchanting and dreamy, this is the former capital of Sundgau, with the château of the Counts of Ferrette, little streets that cascade down, greenery everywhere and wanton vegetation.

HOTELS-RESTAURANTS

● Au Cheval Blanc   SIM

3, rue Léon-Lehmann.
Tel. 03 89 40 41 30. Fax 03 89 40 49 08.
Closed Mon., 1 week at end Dec., June.
Prix fixe: 22€, 23€, 25€.
A la carte: 25–30€.

Local dishes, a rustic, simple atmosphere and sensible prices are the assets of this unpretentious village restaurant. Munster cheese in puff pastry, fried carp filet, fried lamb and the apple streudel are delicious.

● Le Jura   SIM

33, rue du Château.
Tel.-Fax 03 89 40 32 09 .
restdujura.dietlin@laposte.net
www.restdujura-dietlin.com
Closed Tue. dinner, Wed. dinner, Christmas,
1 week July.
Prix fixe: 15€, 28€, 7,50€ (child).
A la carte: 35€.

Alsace is on the program with Jean and Mireille Dietlin: well-laid tables, décor of a neat inn with wood fittings, yellow and green colors and a classic but light cuisine. One enjoys the autumn salad, escargots, pike-perch sautéed in oil with white wine, brandy, garlic, shallots and tomatoes, the veal kidneys flambéed in Cognac and the house chocolate charlotte and seasonal fruit tarts.

In Ligsdorf (68480). 4 km s via D432.

■ **Le Moulin Bas** ❀ ⌂

1, rue de Raedersdorf.
Tel. 03 89 40 31 25. Fax 03 89 40 37 15.
info@le-moulin-bas.fr
www.le-moulin-bas.fr
Rest. closed Tue.
8 rooms: 65–85€.
Prix fixe: 12€, 32€, 60€.
A la carte: 50€.

Right on the Swiss border, this 18th-century mill deserves a stop as much for the place as for the cuisine. The refined rooms in a rustic style, the two tennis courts and the terraces, one of them new, are an invitation to true relaxation. The classic cuisine impresses: a fine carpaccio, tuna croustillant with tomato, roasted pigeon with yellow peaches and the strawberry mille-feuille are extremely well conceived.

In Lutter (68480). 8 km se via D23.

■ **Auberge Paysanne** ❀ ⌂

1, rue Wolschwiller.
Tel. 03 89 40 71 67. Fax 03 89 07 33 38.
aubergepaysanne2@wanadoo.fr
www.auberge-hostellerie-paysanne.com
Closed 2 weeks Feb., 2 weeks beg. July,
Christmas, Mon. (exc. by reserv.). Rest.
closed Mon., Tue. lunch.
16 rooms: 49–69€.
Prix fixe: 9,50€ (weekday lunch), 18€, 23€,
29€, 9,50€ (child).
A la carte: 45€.

With the arrival of Carmen Guérinot, this 17th-century village farm is experiencing a second youth. The repainted exterior, smart breakfasts and renovated rooms on a rustic theme are all seductive. The guesthouse cuisine (salmon crêpe, jumbo shrimp with preserved lemons, pork tenderloin medallion in an herb crust, floating island) created by Andréas Andréou has the merit of being reasonably priced.

In Moernach (68480). 5 km w via D473.

■ **Au Raisin** ⌂

85, rue des Tilleuls.
Tel. 03 89 40 80 73. Fax 03 89 08 11 33.
contact@auraisin.com
www.auraisin.com
Open daily. Rest. closed Mon.
8 rooms: 36–44€.
Prix fixe: 15€, 36€, 7€ (child).

The Schneiders have for three generations offered both regulars and tourists the comfort of their rooms, their smart dining room and the seriousness of their regional, traditional cuisine, currently created by Robert.

▼	SHOPS

CHEESE

In Vieux-Ferrette. 1 km N. via D432.

▼ **Bernard Antony**

5, rue de la Montagne.
Tel. 03 89 40 42 22.
Bernard Antony, who travels the world extolling the virtues of matured cheese, offers Larzac tomme, Termignon bleu, saint-félicien, soft brie, goat milk tomme from the Ariège, authentic camembert, munster and vacherin from Bauges at the peak of their form. In the store, visitors can taste the season's best fresh cheeses, together with selected wines.

G

FOUDAY

67130 Bas-Rhin. Paris 408 – Strasbourg 62
– Saint-Dié 34 – Saverne 56 – Sélestat 37.
The Bruche valley road leads to Upper Vosges and
meanders through bucolic Ban de la Roche.

 HOTELS-RESTAURANTS

■ **Julien**
12, rue Nationale.
Tel. 03 88 97 30 09. Fax 03 88 97 36 73.
hoteljulien@wanadoo.fr
www.hoteljulien.com
Closed 2 weeks Jan. Rest. closed Tue.
36 rooms: 77–121€. 10 suites: 121€.
Prix fixe: 12€ (lunch), 15€, 18€, 22€,
9€ (child), 28€ (Sun.), 36€ (Sun.).
A la carte: 43–50€.

Modern and charming, with its wooded surroundings and flowers, this large building is situated in the middle of a park in the heart of the Bruche valley. The comfort of the rooms, the quality of the facilities (swimming pool, sauna, hammam and fitness center) and the sensible prices are golden assets. Gérard Goetz's menus draw on local sources. The pan-seared foie gras with apples as well as his variation on theme of the presskopf (with foie gras, a marvel!), the roasted scallops with lemon butter, the veal kidney and sweetbread fricassée with morels and the soft-centered Guanaja chocolate cake with vanilla ice cream make the hotel guests very happy. The large wine list is the domain of Bernard Heng, while reception and restaurant services are delivered with the warm personality of Hélène Goetz.

GRAND-BALLON

68760 Haut-Rhin. Paris 497 – Colmar 44 –
Guebwiller 20 – Mulhouse 37.
The most intoxicating of the Alsace mountain towns, reaching more than 1,424 meters, with its belvedere monument symbolizing, in the midst of peaceful Vosges, the end of the wars and European reconciliation.

 HOTELS-RESTAURANTS

■ **Chalet-Hôtel du Grand Ballon**
Rte des Crêtes,
at the summit of the Grand Ballon.
Tel. 03 89 48 77 99. Fax 03 89 62 78 08.
www.chalethotel-grandballon.com
25 rooms: 23,65–30,50€.
Prix fixe: 14,50€, 21,50€, 28€,
8€ (child). A la carte: 32€.

Lovers of nature like this place for its peace and quiet, gentle prices and very spruce rooms. Regional fare without any pretension has pride of place: the house-prepared country terrine, pork cuts and choucroute, and the house tarts are very authentic.

GRENDELBRUCH

67190 Bas-Rhin. Paris 476 – Strasbourg 42
– Molsheim 18 – Obernai 11 – Urmatt 6.
A mountain village that has retained the Old World charm of the Vosges.

 RESTAURANTS

● **L'Auberge de la Grenouille** SIM
26, rue de l'Eglise.
Tel.-Fax 03 88 95 52 27.
Closed Mon., Tue., mid-Feb.–end Feb.
Prix fixe: 27€, 35€, 8€ (child).
A la carte: 40–45€.

Goose foie gras in a covered pie, pepper-seasoned smoked herrings served cold, fennel-seasoned Atlantic sea bass, leg of venison and the crème brûlée: young Ludovic Hyolle, who has taken over a house in this mountain village,

29

has returned to a straightforward cuisine that enhances produce and avoids futile sophistication.

● **Ferme-Auberge du Pâtre** SIM

27, rue de la Victoire.
Tel.-Fax 03 88 97 55 71.
gross.andre@wanadoo.fr
www.bienvenue-a-la-ferme.com
Closed weekdays (exc. Fri. lunch July–Aug.),
Christmas–New Year's vac.
Prix fixe: 16€ (lunch), 22,50€ (lunch).

We visit the farm and have lunch at the inn. Céline and André Gross do all the work themselves, particularly with their goats, and produce menus at unbeatable prices: the house tourte served with salad, rabbit terrine, slow-simmered lamb shoulder and the house tart make merry feasting.

GUEBERSCHWIHR

68420 Haut-Rhin. Paris 452 – Colmar 11 – Mulhouse 42 – Strasbourg 86.
An adorable winegrowing village with a vast grand-place, a Romanesque bell tower and old houses open up each year for the Fête de l'Amitié (Feast of Friendship), not to mention the famous slopes (Goldert and Steinert) and the highly reputed Muscat in its cellars.

HOTELS-RESTAURANTS

■ **Relais du Vignoble**
& Belle Vue

33, rue des Forgerons.
Tel. 03 89 49 22 22. Fax 03 89 49 27 82.
relaisduvignoble@wanadoo.fr
www.hotelrelaisduvignoble.com
Closed 1 week Dec., Feb.
Rest. closed Wed. lunch, Thu.
30 rooms: 46–89€.
Prix fixe: 16€, 28,50€.
A la carte: 40€.

Situated next to the family cellar, the Roths' recent construction is a choice stopover on the wine route. The contemporary rooms, some with a balcony, promise rest and repose. The domain wines are served in the restaurant and on the terrace overlooking the vineyards and accompany the fine country dishes (pâté in pastry served hot, the fish choucroute, a duckling filet with pepper sauce and the frozen vacherin).

● **La Taverne Médiévale** SIM

11, rue Haute.
Tel. 03 89 49 20 79. Fax 03 89 49 28 62.
tavernemedievale@wanadoo.fr
Closed Tue., Wed., 1 week beg. Nov.,
3 weeks end Feb.–mid–Mar.,
1 week at end June.
Prix fixe: 20€, 35€, 8€ (child).
A la carte: 35€.

In their cheerful rose-colored sandstone tavern Jean-Michel and Sylvie Schmidt serve up food that is rooted in the local region. The proof is in the duck foie gras terrine, the house choucroute, beef filet Ganseliesel (a local specialty) and frozen kouglof, all washed down by local wines.

▼	SHOPS

FOIE GRAS
▼ **Boutique Canoie**

2, rue Haute.
Tel. 03 89 49 24 76.
Marcel Metzler, a veteran of Robuchon and the Bristol in Colmar, prepares irresistibly tempting foie gras with figs and gingerbread or with chestnuts, quail terrine with raisins, and foie gras—or "canoie"—(a blend of duck and goose foie gras in layers).

GUEBWILLER

68500 Haut-Rhin. Paris 475 – Mulhouse 23
– Belfort 51 – Colmar 26 – Strasbourg 104.
ot.guebwiller@wanadoo.fr.
An industrious town, a wine town with small
production vineyards, a sunny microclimate and
four grands crus: enough to make its reputation,
along with the Schlumberger dynasty and its
hardy winegrowers far from the beaten track.

 HOTELS-RESTAURANTS

■ **Château de la Prairie** ✿ 🏨

Allée des Marronniers.
Tel. 03 89 74 28 57. Fax 03 89 74 71 88.
info@chateau-prairie.com
www.chateau-prairie.com
15 rooms: 55–179€. 3 suites: 115–179€.

This 19th-century genteel residence in
the heart of its two-hectare grounds offers
peace and relaxation in functional rooms
and nicely appointed lounges. Cécile and
Franco Fancello welcome us with a smile.

■ **L'Ange** 🛆

4, rue de la Gare.
Tel. 03 89 76 22 11. Fax 03 89 76 50 08.
hoteldelange@wanadoo.fr
www.hotel-ange.com
Rest. closed Sat. lunch (exc. by reserv.).
36 rooms: 50–65€.
Prix fixe: 29€, 32€. A la carte: 35€.

Franco Fancello is again at the helm of
what used to be a maternity hospital. The
rooms are functional and Carl Jacquot's
cuisine is carefully crafted. The recipes
are true to tradition, with allusions to the
South of France. Arugula salad with parmesan, escargots prepared in the style
of Alsace (stuffed with spiced butter and
herbs and cooked in local wine), pike-
perch on a bed of sauerkraut, sea bream
in a salt crust, the house tiramisu and the
frozen Marc de Gewurztraminer mousse
all shimmer gently.

● **La Taverne du Vigneron** SIM

7, pl Saint-Léger.
Tel. 03 89 76 81 89. Fax 03 89 74 87 42.
Closed Mon., mid-Jan.–end Jan.
Prix fixe: 8,50€, 17,50€, 19,50€.
A la carte: 30€.

This tavern is true to a cheerful tradition.
Vineyard-keeper's salad, a head cheese and
aspic terrine, trout poached in Riesling, a
veal escalope with cream sauce, a frozen
kouglof and a slice of apple tart go down
pleasantly in a relaxing atmosphere.

In Berrwiller (68500). 9 km s.

● **A l'Arbre Vert** 🎥COM

96, rue Principale.
Tel. 03 89 76 73 19. Fax 03 89 76 73 68.
www.restaurant-koenig.com
Closed Sun. dinner, Mon., 3 weeks July.
Prix fixe: 20€, 28€, 45€.

A sterling reception, a floral atmosphere, a cuisine that is true to tradition
but enriched by contemporary influences; in short, everything is pleasing
here. Mathieu, the son, is precise when
he prepares breaded veal sweetbreads and
green asparagus served in salad, oven-
roasted scallops with whole vanilla beans,
a roasted squab breast in an herb and pine-
nut crust and the strawberry tiramisu with
rhubarb sorbet. The wine list, in the hands
of Robert, the father, offers carefully chosen bottles where Alsace, naturally, has
pride of place.

In Hartmannswiller (68500). 7 km se via D5.

■ **Meyer-l'Amphitryon** 🛆

49, rte de Cernay.
Tel. 03 89 76 73 14. Fax 03 89 76 79 57.
www.hotel-meyer-alsace.com
Closed Sun., 2 weeks Feb.
9 rooms: 47–70€.
Prix fixe: 23€, 7€ (child).

This rustic and (ahead of its time) strictly
non-smoking establishment has classic
and nicely appointed rooms. Jean Mayer,
who trained in the Fer Rouge in Colmar
and the Abbesses in Remiremont, serves
up regional cuisine that changes with the
seasons. Salad with crayfish Florentine

served in the cooking dish at the table, the fisherman's plate with an anise-seasoned beurre blanc, the hunter's plate and a pain d'épice crème brûlée all make a good impression.

In Soultz (68360). 3 km via D430.

● **Metzgerstuwa** **SIM**

69, rue du Maréchal-de-Lattre-de-Tassigny. Tel. 03 89 74 89 77. Fax 03 89 76 14 63. Closed Sat., Sun., Christmas–New Year's, end June–beg. July.
Prix fixe: 7,50€ (lunch), 22€. A la carte: 30€.

A discreet star of Alsace gastronomy, Gilbert Schluraff—our Charcutier of the Year in 2005—still works wonders in his cheerful and pleasant *winstub*. The charcuterie plate, generously carved pork cuts, variations on the pork trotter, the poached salmon, escalope with cream sauce and the frozen kouglof is healthy, simple and nourishing food. It reveals true know-how and the prices are heaven sent.

▼	SHOPS

BREAD & BAKED GOODS
In Soultz. 3 km via D430.

▼ **Schmidt**

4, pl. de la République. Tel. 03 89 74 11 17.
Since 1786 the Schmidt family has been baking, first in Merxheim, and, since 1894, in Soultz. Jean-Philippe upholds the family reputation, by way of his pretzels, breads (rye, whole-grain, walnut, sourdough, country white), kouglof and anise biscuits.

CHARCUTERIE
In Soultz. 3 km via D430.

▼ **Gilbert Schluraff**

69, rue du Maréchal-de-Lattre-de-Tassigny. Tel. 03 89 76 95 62.
This is the realm of artisanal charcuterie at the summit of its glory. Stuffed pork trotters, house choucroute, smoked salmon, fresh goose foie gras, country bacon, presskopf, leberwurst, blutwurst and other sausages of all genres make an impressive showing.(See restaurant Metzgerstuwa.)

CHOCOLATE & PASTRIES

▼ **Christmann**

8, pl de l'Hôtel-de-Ville.
Tel. 03 89 74 27 44.
www.henster.fr
Claude Henster crafts fine ganache with cardamom, Black Forest cake, manjari chocolates with pecans, Sacher cookies and a nice Opéra cake.

▼ **Husser**

135, rue de la République.
Tel. 03 89 76 94 69.
Daniel Husser delights gourmets with his Bartholdi (walnut biscuit, meringue base and caramel cream), as well as his range of 40 pure-cacao chocolates.

WINE

▼ **Cave des Grands Crus**

15, rue de la République.
Tel. 03 89 76 59 31.
www.cavedesgrandscrus.com
Denis Engel offers more than 1000 vintages, including 25 vintage bottles of Mouton-Rothschild and a number of Pétrus. Wines from Schlumberger, Schoffit and Trimbach, as well as 35 or so Alsatian eaux de vie and liqueurs are available.

GUEWENHEIM

68116 Haut-Rhin. Paris 459 – Mulhouse 21 – Altkirch 23 – Belfort 26 – Thann 9.
In the extreme south of Alsace, on the D466 linking the Aspach bridge to Masevaux, a choice stopover, a monument to wine.

●	RESTAURANTS

● **Restaurant de la Gare** **COM**

2, rue Soppe.
Tel. 03 89 82 51 29. Fax 03 89 82 84 62.
restaurant.gare@tv-com.net
Closed Tue. lunch, Wed., Feb. vac., 3 weeks July Aug.
Prix fixe: 27€, 30€, 42€, 65€, 8,50€ (child). A la carte: 55€.

Disregard the facade of this train station restaurant: the wine list is a monument!

The Seidel family has run this establishment for four generations and everything they offer is worth a visit. The cuisine: tender scallops, the pressed hen and goose foie gras, roasted Atlantic sea bass, truffle-seasoned pork trotter wrapped in a caul lace bundle and a fruit gratin with an island-style marquise are a testament to Michel's talent as he devotes himself passionately to his cuisine.

GUNDERSHOFFEN

67110 Bas-Rhin. Paris 464 – Strasbourg 48 – Haguenau 16 – Sarreguemines 62.
The gateway to the northern Vosges, the suburb of Niederbronn where passing visitors stop to admire the half-timbered houses and enjoy the gourmet eateries.

 HOTELS-RESTAURANTS

■ Le Moulin

7, rue du Moulin.
Tel. 03 88 07 33 30. Fax 03 88 72 83 97.
hotel.le.moulin@wanadoo.fr
www.hotellemoulin.com
Rest. closed Sun. dinner, Mon., Thu.,
1 week Feb., 3 weeks Aug.
10 rooms: 84–210€.
Prix fixe: 42€, 53€, 70€, 90€.
A la carte: 92€.

This renovated old grain mill has ten customized rooms in a chic rustic style that have been adapted to today's tastes by the painter Edgar Mahler. Grounds, a watercourse and a large breakfast buffet. Au Cygne is just 300 meters away.

● Au Cygne

35, Grande-Rue.
Tel. 03 88 72 96 43. Fax 03 88 72 86 47.
sarl.lecygne@wanadoo.fr
www.aucygne.fr
Closed Sun. dinner, Mon., Thu.,
mid-Feb.–beg. Mar., 3 weeks Aug.
Prix fixe: 42€, 53€, 70€, 88€.
A la carte: 95€.

Annie and François Paul have taken a village inn and transformed it into a major eatery in a region that is not lacking in such establishments. The half-timbered blue-ish facade, the warm colorful interior, the paintings by Walch and frescoes by Mahler, the beautiful Annie's charming welcome and the subtle cuisine of François—who trained with Mischler in Lembach—skillfully reworks tradition with refinement, modernity and a deliberate touch of the South but without abandoning the rich region of Alsace. The ham served with schniederspätle (local stuffed dumplings), lobster salad with crunchy vegetables seasoned with citrus zest, roasted John Dory with artichokes and sundried tomatoes, ginger-seasoned langoustine tails, the rack and tenderloin of lamb with curry-seasoned golden raisin sauce, roasted thick-cut pork tenderloin with pine nuts, olive oil and basil, as well as the chocolate dessert platter and the quetsche plum beignets with spice ice cream, are wonders of their kind. The wine list is full of delicious temptation, the menus are reasonable and the charming nearby mill is worth visiting.

● Le Soufflet

13, rue de la Gare.
Tel.-Fax 03 88 72 91 20.
lesoufflet@free.fr
www.lesoufflet.free.fr
Closed Sat. lunch, Mon. dinner, Wed. dinner.
Prix fixe: 26€, 54€. A la carte: 50–55€.

Facing the station and the town hall, Franck and Armande Chateauroux have opted for a dual vocation: serious and finely wrought cuisine in a stylish dining area and country cuisine in the *winstub* (Bahnstubel). Foie gras served three ways, pan-tossed jumbo shrimp, an orange roughy in cream sauce, ostrich filet, variations on the theme of wild woodruff and a frozen lime parfait are very good indeed.

H

<table>
</table>

▼	SHOPS

LOCAL PRODUCTS

In Mietesheim. 2 km s.

▼ Raifalsa

4, rue de la Gare.
Tel. 03 88 90 31 85.
www.raifalsa.fr
This store is a temple to horseradish in all its forms: in mustard, raw, in rémoulade or with mayonnaise.

68220 Haut-Rhin. Paris 480 – Mulhouse 40 – Altkirch 27 – Colmar 74 – Bâle 12.
One of the keys to the Sundgau region and a discreet gateway to Switzerland amidst the greenery of the orchards.

 HOTELS-RESTAURANTS

● Jenny

84, rue de Hegenheim.
Tel. 03 89 68 50 09. Fax 03 89 68 58 64.
reception@hotel-jenny.fr
www.hotel-jenny.fr
Rest. closed Sun., Christmas, end July–beg. Aug.
26 rooms: 60–140€.
Prix fixe: 13,50€, 26€ (lunch), 39€, 50€, 58€, 10€ (child).

Stay at Jenny's. You won't be disappointed by the bright, well-kept and functional rooms or by the extra attractions—a heated swimming pool, terrace, private lounge, two conference rooms, Internet, WiFi —nor by Monique Koehl's winning smile or Emmanuel Lambelin's vegetarian or gastronomic cuisine. He has worked with Westermann and is the ex-chef of the nearby Ancienne Forge. Not a vegetarian? In that case, go for the Landes duck foie gras prepared in house with pepper and fleur de sel, pan-seared Atlantic sea bass with mild spices served in a lovage-seasoned shellfish bouillon, venison medallions in a flavorful red wine sauce with crushed shallots with creamy cep polenta and a mango clafoutis with coconut and ginger ice cream; all are full of vigor.

▼	SHOPS

BREAD AND BAKED GOODS

▼ Marchand

32, av Souprosse.
Tel. 03 89 68 51 04.
Etienne Schoeffel is famous for his special breads: whole grain, rye, bran, sesame, poppyseed, walnut, sourdough or country style.

HAGENTHAL-LE-HAUT

68220 Haut-Rhin. Paris 481 – Mulhouse 36
– Altkirch 27 – Colmar 73 – Bâle 12.
Still in verdant Sundgau and the county gateway to Switzerland.

● | RESTAURANTS

● **A l'Ancienne Forge**
52, rue Principale.
Tel. 03 89 68 56 10. Fax 03 89 68 17 38.
baumannyves/a-lancienne-forge.html
Closed Mon. lunch, Tue., Wed. lunch.
Prix fixe: 28€, 38€, 48€.
A la carte: 40€.

The Baumanns made a judicious resolution to lower their prices and to offer every day a fixed-price menu and an à la carte menu with wine served by the glass. They also returned to fundamentals: creamy pumpkin soup, salmon with shrimp sauce, Brazillian beef, in addition to Sylvie Bauman's signature caramel panna cotta, are not to be sniffed at. Yves is attentive in the dining room and we gravitate towards peace in this old forge with its painted beams.

HAGUENAU

67500 Bas-Rhin. Paris 480 – Strasbourg 33
– Baden-Baden 42 – Karlsruhe 61.
tourisme.haguenau@wanadoo.fr.
A little Strasbourg with its shopkeepers, talented pastry chefs, a lively town center and, just on the edge of town, a view of the large local forest from above.

■/ | HOTELS-RESTAURANTS

■ **Les Pins**
112, rte de Strasbourg.
Tel. 03 88 93 68 40.
www.hotelrestaurantlespinshagueneau.com
Closed 24 Dec. dinner.
23 rooms: 68€.
Prix fixe: 17,50€ (lunch), 23,50€, 29€,
37€, 50€.

Eric Fuchs is a wine lover (his wine list is a monument) who takes this curious American-style motel, dating from the sixties, very seriously. The rooms are carefully appointed, the rear garden is a pleasure, the *winstub*-style wood-toned dining room is welcoming and the cuisine by Yannick Rosley, formerly of the Coq Hardi in Verdun, is very good. The house puff pastry, small herring in an old-style marinade, pike-perch with a meat stuffing, veal with chanterelles and a frozen Fleur de Bière-flavored soufflé look good.

■ **Europe** ⌂
15, av du Professeur-René-Leriche.
Tel. 03 88 93 58 11. Fax 03 88 06 05 43.
europe.hotel1@wanadoo.fr
www.europehotel.fr
Rest. closed Sat. lunch.
72 rooms: 48–75€.
Prix fixe: 10€ (weekday lunch), 19€, 35€,
6,50€ (child). A la carte: 40€.

Freddy Naegely and his daughter Sandrine gracefully manage this recent construction that is a bit from the center. Two swimming pools (indoors and out), a sauna, a veranda dining room overlooking the water and functional rooms all set the tone. In the restaurant, salmon carpaccio, pan-fried rouget with lemon tabouli and Aurélien Rust's signature berry soup make a good impression.

● **Le Jardin** V.COM
16, rue de la Redoute.
Tel.-Fax 03 88 93 29 39.
Closed Tue., Wed., Nov. 1 vac., Feb. vac.,
end July–beg. Aug.
Prix fixe: 17€ (weekday lunch), 18,50€,
29€, 34,50€, 46€.

The Jardin does not have a terrace but it does have a fine dining room with a caisson ceiling, colorful frescoes and nicely appointed tables. It immediately charms us with its painted facade and rich stained glass in the vestibule. The chadurée (an Atlantic version of bouillabaisse, this version seasoned with saffron), shrimp tartare served with guacamole and grilled Atlantic sea bass with a tropically inspired sauce prove that Damien Meyer, who trained with Mischler in Lembach, knows what he is doing when preparing fresh fish with art and originality. He serves up generous portions and then offers choice desserts: a rhubarb crème brûlée, praline-flavored frozen nougat and a strawberry pastilla. The service by his gracious wife lends charm and vibrancy to the house.

● L'Essentiel 🍴SIM

2, pl du Marché-aux-Bestiaux.
Tel. 03 88 73 39 47. Fax 03 88 73 29 48.
rlessentiel@wanadoo.fr
Closed Sat. lunch, Sun., Mon. dinner.
Prix fixe: 12€–13,50€ (lunch),
29–35€ (dinner).

The essential here is the red and brown décor, the atmosphere of a Parisian bistro and especially the seductive cuisine. Pierre Weller (La Source des Sens in Morsbronn) and his brother-in-law Laurent Ritter have succeeded in creating a style with eclectic influences and with the help of their chef Alexandre Rubler. The produce is of good quality and the preparations nicely inspired: a salad with smoked duck breast and foie gras, grilled tuna with olive oil and peppers, quick-seared veal kidney with mustard sauce and strawberries in their jus served with white chocolate ice cream. An interesting wine list includes some Spanish vintages.

● Chez Monique SIM

13, rue Meyer.
Tel. 03 88 93 30 90.
www.buerehiesel.com
Closed Sun., Mon., Bank holidays,
2 weeks beg. Sept., 1 week Christmas–New
Year's, 1 week at end May.
A la carte: 35€.

Monique Baumann knows how to receive us in her *winstub* next to the theater. We enjoy her good, family cooking that is typical of the region—things like the tourte, the braised pork shank served with Munster cheese sauce, the choucroute and the warm mirabelle plum gratin. Her many regular customers enjoy

the friendly atmosphere and the service fit for a king. The prices toe the line.

In Marienthal (67500). 6 km s via D48.

● Epices et Sens V.COM

1, rue du Rothbach.
Tel. 03 88 93 43 48. Fax 03 88 93 40 35.
contact@epicesetsens.com
www.epicesetsens.com
Closed Sun. dinner, Mon., 3 weeks Sept.,
2 weeks Mar.
Prix fixe: 32€, 42€, 48€. A la carte: 60€.

René Fieger, who trained with Mischler in Lembach, Outhier in La Napoule and also in Canada and Shanghai is a traveling chef who offers us a sophisticated Franco-Asian cuisine with its eyes "on the horizon". We are not sure that the baroque setting of this stopover near a hermitage suits the experimental dishes he prepares with gusto: a slice of head cheese and aspic terrine served "New Wave style" with foie gras ice cream and arugula, the jumbo shrimp with soba (Japanese buckwheat noodles), glazed duck served with vegetable spring rolls or the grilled thick-cut Iberian pork tenderloin served with a corn flan. The berry panna cotta is slightly gelatinous, but the melon simmered in Pineau is freshness itself.

In Niederschaeffolsheim (67500). 6 km s via N63.

■ Au Boeuf Rouge

39, rue du Général-de-Gaulle.
Tel. 03 88 73 81 00. Fax 03 88 73 89 71.
www.boeufrouge.com
Closed 2 weeks Feb. Rest. closed Sun. dinner,
Mon., Tue. dinner, 3 weeks July.
13 rooms: 64–68€.
Prix fixe: 25,50€ (weekday lunch), 34€,
47€, 57€, 68€, 10€ (child).
A la carte: 65€.

Since 1880, generations of Gollas have succeeded each other at this good inn. François, the latest in the line, is in charge of the kitchen and trained with Loiseau in Saulieu and Savoy in Paris. He is very good at playing with the produce of both land and sea. Foie gras served three ways, langoustines with vermicelli, pan-sizzled truffle-seasoned turbot and potatoes and meat layered in puff pastry look good. The game is well prepared in season and the pineapple refreshed with mint, served with piña colada sorbet, is an extremely cool way to finish off. Anne Golla recommends the great wines in the cellar.

In Oberhoffen-sur-Moder (67240). 7 km ne via D29.

● **Au Cerf**

2, rue Principale.
Tel. 03 88 63 22 64. Fax 03 88 53 88 94.
Closed Sun. dinner, Mon., Thu. dinner, end Jan.–beg. Feb., 3 weeks Aug.
Prix fixe: 10,80€ (lunch), 22,50€, 29,50€, 43,50€.

The Dorns have created a warm atmosphere in this cozy traditional establishment. The à la carte menu is generosity itself, offering us carefully prepared gastronomic dishes at moderate prices. The business menu offers (for 29,50€) shrimp and monkfish with Middle Eastern seasonings in puff pastry or foie gras served two ways, pike-perch with a crayfish coulis or duck breast with ceps and a mirabelle plum vacherin or a berry soup served with crème brûlée. Marie-José smiles as she welcomes us and serves while Francis concocts the generous cuisine. The wine list is a mine of good things. The overall impression is one of simplicity and authenticity and wins our affection.

▼	SHOPS

BREAD AND BAKED GOODS
▼ **Frédéric Bleichner**

35, Grand-Rue.
Tel.-Fax 03 88 93 82 64.
Crowds flock to Frédéric Bleichner's store for pretzels, kouglof and special breads (old-fashioned, or made with Alsépi flour).

▼ **Gilles Schoenahl**

156, Grand-Rue.
Tel. 03 88 73 20 39.
Gilles Schoenahl lovingly prepares pavé d'Haguenau, mixed-grain baguette,

molosse (a large bread weighting more than 1 kg), sourdough boule, old-fashioned loaf, sourdough brioche ("*l'étoile des neiges*"), Sundgau pound cake and orange-flavored hearts. The Kleins from the Arnsbourg are regular customers here.

CHOCOLATES & PASTRIES
▼ **Heitz**

62, Grand-Rue.
Tel.-Fax 03 88 93 92 78.
www.chocox.com
Guy Heitz's improvisations are based on the jams of France, chocolate sculptures, sandhaas (ganache with beer reduction), traditional salt-glazed Alsatian pitchers, kouglof, bredele (small Alsatian cakes, baked in a variety of flavors), berawecke (bread with dried fruit, kirsch and spices), pretzels or anise bread.

CHOCOLATES, PASTRIES & ICE CREAM
▼ **Pâtisserie Maxime**

25, Grand-Rue.
Tel. 03 88 93 94 72.
Tarts, pastries, petit fours and chocolates, all mouthwatering in their variety and subtlety.

◆	RENDEZVOUS

TEA SALON
◆ **Farandole**

11, rue du Général-Gérard.
Tel. 03 88 63 82 15.
This charming tearoom, where patrons enjoy fruit tarts, delicate mousses and sweet pastries, features fine, antique woodwork.

HANDSCHUHEIM

67117 Bas-Rhin. Paris 460 – Marlenheim 4 – Strasbourg 17 – Saverne 23.

A little commune in Kochersberg, not far from Strasbourg on the N4 and much appreciated by lovers of the tarte flambée.

| ● | RESTAURANTS |

● L'Espérance

5, rue Principale.
Tel. 03 88 69 00 52. Fax 03 88 69 10 19.
Closed lunch, Mon., Tue., Jan.
A la carte: 25€.

This temple of the tarte flambée offers us one of the most successful of the genre, with a thin and crunchy crust, creamy base and either onions and smoked bacon or mussels with garlic and parsley butter or perhaps Munster cheese or fresh goat cheese. They are cooked up in the wood-fired oven by the constantly moving Michel Schott. Two rooms, one old style with a patina and the other, more modern, in green pastel shades, with marquetry and Spindler engravings, have the charm of a friend's house. In addition, there are little *winstub*-style dishes like ham cooked over hay, served with exquisite grumbeerekiechle (potato cakes), bibeleskäs (garlic-, onion- and chive-seasoned fresh white cheese), and a presskopf (head cheese and aspic terrine).

HEILIGENSTEIN

67140 Bas-Rhin. Paris 437 – Strasbourg 38 – Colmar 36 – Barr 3.

One of the little-known capitals of Alsatian wine next to the Vosges Piedmont, this is where we find the rarity that bears the name of the commune: a Klevener, or the old Traminer made from pink Savagnin.

| ■ / ◐ | HOTELS-RESTAURANTS |

■ Le Relais du Klevener

51, rue Principale.
Tel. 03 88 08 05 98. Fax 03 88 08 40 83.
relaisduklevener@wanadoo.fr
www.alsacelogis.com
Closed Mon., Wed., Thu. lunch,
22 Dec.–mid-Feb.
29 rooms: 42–53€.
A la carte: 38€.

Olivier Meckert's inn makes a good impression. We savor game in season, perch filet with mushrooms, beef with chanterelles and an apple tart with almond cream. Rustic bedrooms for a well-deserved rest.

● Le Raisin d'Or

38, rue Principale.
Tel. 03 88 08 95 23. Fax 03 88 08 26 81.
auraisindor@wanadoo.fr
Closed Tue., Wed., Feb. vac.,
2 weeks beg. July.
Prix fixe: 19€, 24€, 27€, 8€ (child).
A la carte: 35€.

Olivier Heyd, who worked at l'Ami Fritz in Ottrott and at Beau Site in the glorious days of the Schreiber brothers, has taken over this roadside *winstub* where he plans to renovate the rustic dining room. For the moment, he delights his guests with a fairly spiced-up local cuisine, as we find with fleichschnacka (a local specialty, pasta stuffed with duck sausage), head cheese and aspic terrine served with crunchy vegetables, pike-perch poached in Riesling, crayfish cassolette with mushrooms and vegetables, a beef roast with Pinot Noir sauce and mushrooms and a frozen kouglof flavored with Marc. We only wish there were more of this prudent classicism around!

HINSINGEN

67260 Bas-Rhin. Paris 406 – Saint-Avold 35 – Strasbourg 90.
On the edge of the Moselle region, a village with an ambiguous profile. We see hilly Alsace here, but also the simple landscapes and farms of the Lorraine plateau.

●	RESTAURANTS

● La Grange du Paysan
8, rue Principale.
Tel. 03 88 00 91 83. Fax 03 88 00 93 23.
Closed Mon., 2 weeks winter, Good Friday, 1 week summer.
Prix fixe: 10 € (weekdays), 20€, 25€,, 28€, 32€, 40€.

Everything here—setting, décor, produce, cuisine—derives from peasant traditions. This old farmhouse offers essentially local produce that has been prepared with much finesse. Head cheese and aspic terrine (presskopf), smoked sausage, chitterling sausage, potato sausage and the white veal or blood sausage are happy to have the authentic smokey taste of bygone days. Jean-Luc Rieger cooks as naturally as a bird sings. The regional flat savory tart is a Rolls Royce of its kind, thin and crispy, with its naturally tart cream, its country bacon with a real smokehouse taste: it has a finesse that is rare and, moreover, it is sliced in the dining room and served on to the plate,, which is quite unusual. We don't regret the stuffed pork belly, the tête de veau, the braised ham, the liver quenelles served on a bed of sauerkraut or the cold aspic-glazed raspberries served over hot white chocolate.

HOCHFELDEN

67270 Bas-Rhin. Paris 466 – Strasbourg 23 – Saverne 15.
Beer is center stage in a brasserie that is a monument, the frontier with the Hanau region and Kochersberg, the route toward the North of the Vosges: Hochfelden offers all this.

●	RESTAURANTS

● L'Orchidée d'Asie
42, rue du Général-Lebocq.
Tel. 03 88 89 03 03.
Closed Sat. lunch, Mon.
Prix fixe: 31€ (for 2), 44€ (for 2).
A la carte: 25€.

The Trang family and chef Ding accomplish wonders in this roadside Vietnamese restaurant. We have to face the difficult task of choosing between Chinese, Vietnamese and Thai gastronomy and we enjoy stuffed crab claws, cod with spicy pepper or ginger sauce, glazed duck, beef with black mushrooms and the flambéed apple beignets.

◆	RENDEZVOUS

BRASSERIE

◆ Brasserie Météor
6, rue du Général-Lebocq.
Tel. 03 88 02 22 22.
www.brasserie-meteor.fr
The Haags have been running this model brewery since 1898. At the helm today, Michel and Yolande Haag brew light, clear, bitter Météor Pils; Ackerland lager; eight degree amber Mortimer; a rather mellower Wendelinus and a refreshing Blanche. Tours on request.

HOERDT

67720 Bas-Rhin. Paris 484 – Strasbourg 17 – Haguenau 16 – Molsheim 44 – Saverne 46.
This is the land of asparagus, in the Ried region on the banks of the Rhine with its fertile alluvial soil.

● **RESTAURANTS**

● **A la Charrue** SIM
30, rue de la République.
Tel. 03 88 51 31 11. Fax 03 88 51 32 55.
lacharrue@wanadoo.fr
www.lacharrue.fr
Closed Mon., Christmas–New Year's vac.,
3 weeks July.
Prix fixe: 9€ (lunch), 11€, 27€, 35€.
A la carte: 35–45€.

Asparagus has its temple in Fabienne Hae-gel's half-timbered Alsatian residence with its vast courtyard. We can enjoy the white vegetable in multiple preparations from April 1st to June 15th, after which the menu changes with the seasons. Excellent goose foie gras, head cheese and aspic ter-rine, pike-perch simmered in wine, veal medallions with wild mushrooms and fro-zen kouglof with macerated raisins make a nice impression.

HOHRODBERG

68140 Haut-Rhin. Paris 462 – Colmar 27 – Gérardmer 37 – Munster 8.
A nice setting overlooking the Munster valley, its gentle mountain decked with forests and its thatch roofs.

 HOTELS-RESTAURANTS

■ **Le Panorama**
3, rte Linge.
Tel. 03 89 77 36 53. Fax 03 89 77 03 93.
www.hotel-panorama-alsace.com
Closed 2 weeks Nov., 24 Dec.,
beg. Jan.–beg. Feb.
30 rooms: 44–71€.
Prix fixe: 16,50€, 19,80€, 26,50€, 37€.
A la carte: 40–50€.

Gilbert Mahler keeps an attentive eye on this establishment with its magnificent panorama overlooking the Munster val-ley. The modern rooms, heated swim-ming pool and carefully appointed dining room encourage us to stay overnight. In the restaurant, Arnaud Marschall serves

fresh new Munster cheese in puff pas-try, roasted pike-perch on a bed of sauer-kraut, grilled sandwiches, grilled rib eye steak and a streudel-style apple dessert. The local wines go down without diffi-culty and the prices are reasonable.

■ **Roess**
16, rte du Linge.
Tel. 03 89 77 36 00.
www.hotel-roess.fr
25 rooms: 35–62€.
Prix fixe: 19–31€.

This large 19th-century chalet was ren-ovated and enlarged in the sixties and is worth a visit for its friendly family atmo-sphere, welcoming interior, sumptuous view of the Upper Vosges and its very nice regional cuisine.

LE HOHWALD

67140 Bas-Rhin. Paris 430 – Sélestat 26 – Molsheim 33 – Strasbourg 53.
ot.lehohwald@wanadoo.fr.
A mountain resort in the heart of the fir forests: people come here in winter to go ski touring and all year round for the fresh air.

 HOTELS-RESTAURANTS

■ **Grand Hôtel**
16, rue Principale.
Tel. 03 88 08 36 00. Fax 03 88 08 36 01.
resa-hohwald@monalisahotels.com
www.monalisahotels.com
65 rooms: 65–110€. 7 suites: 90–140€.
Prix fixe: 16€, 54€, 7€ (child).
A la carte: 40€.

Samuel Moreau manages this hotel that has been completely renovated in a con-temporary designer style. In addition to its unassuming and carefully appointed rooms, this late-19th-century Grand Hotel offers all the usual spa features: a superb indoor swimming pool, sauna, Turkish baths and Jacuzzi. The modern restaurant in shades of beige, green and red serves a foie gras and potato mille-feuille, salmon trout filet, rack of lamb and a thin apple tart accompanied by French wines which may be served by the glass.

■ Le Clos Ermitage

34, rue du Wittertalhof.
Tel. 03 88 08 31 31. Fax 03 88 08 34 99.
info@clos-ermitage.com
www.clos-ermitage.com
19 rooms: 50–60€.
Prix fixe: 16€, 19€.

This fine 19th-century property is ideal for seminars or sports/health getaways. It has twelve conference rooms (two new ones added this year), a spa, two swimming pools (one of them heated), a sauna and a Jacuzzi. The rooms with their pastel shades are comfortable and the menus are light, particularly if we avoid the "chocolate temptation dessert".

■ Villa Mathis

Col du Kreutzweg, 2 km, in Breitenbach (67220)
Tel. 03 90 57 27 00. Fax 03 90 57 27 13.
www.villa-mathis.com
Rest. closed Mon.
Prix fixe: 12€ (lunch, weekdays), 25€.

Catherine Comau, who worked in the dining rooms for Julien at Fouday and in the Strasbourg Hilton, has transformed this thirties residence and its grounds, once the home of a famous automobile manufacturer and then a children's home, into a high-tech vacation resort. The rooms are bright and cheerful, looking out on the mountains, and we enjoy the cuisine in the spirit of the times. A citrus-marinated salmon carpaccio, rabbit terrine with a vinaigrette-seasoned beet and parsley duo, sirloin steak or hanger steak with mushrooms, veal kidney with mustard sauce and a frozen vacherin hit the spot.

■ La Forestière

10A, chemin du Eck.
Tel. 03 88 08 31 08. Fax 03 88 08 32 96.
http://laforestiere.fr.monsite.wanadoo.fr
Rest. closed lunch
3 rooms: 65–95€. 2 suites: 85–90€.
Prix fixe: 25€, 35€.

Catherine Marchal has put her heart into this new-look guesthouse that reminds us of a lodge in the Vosges. Exotic wood, slate, ceramic decoration and other fine materials have been used in a minimalist and restful style. In the restaurant, which is mainly reserved for guests, the chestnut soup, leg of wild boar and the chocolate brownies served with pan-simmered apricots hit the right spot.

■ Marchal

12, rue du Wittertalhof.
Tel. 03 88 08 31 04. Fax 03 88 08 34 05.
www.reperes.com/marchal
Closed 2 weeks Nov., 2 weeks Jan.
15 rooms: 45–68€. 2 suites: 75€.
Prix fixe: 17,40€, 23,30€, 26,60€.
A la carte: 35€.

Nelly Tastor has renovated this fine mountain inn. Each room is decorated to suggest a country. In the restaurant, Pierre Kazemi blends local produce with faraway flavors in the pike-perch filet served with cumin- and orange-seasoned carrots, the veal sauté with pomegranate and walnut sauce served with saffron-seasoned rice and the frozen pineapple mousse.

● La Petite Auberge

6, rue Principale.
Tel. 03 88 08 33 05. Fax 03 88 08 34 62.
www.lapetiteauberge-hohwald.com
Closed 1 week Nov., Jan.,
1 week at end June.
Rest. closed Tue. dinner, Wed.
7 rooms: 61€.
Prix fixe: 14,90€, 26,70€.

A little close to the road but charming, this country inn with duplex rooms with terraces is very welcoming. Assisted by his wife in the dining room, Robert Hubrecht concocts a cuisine that remains true to the Alsatian tradition, with smoked trout mousse, pike-perch filet with cream sauce, pork cuts and charcuterie served on a bed of sauerkraut and a generous dessert plate of good quality.

I

HUSSEREN-LES-CHATEAUX

68420 Haut-Rhin. Paris 482 – Colmar 9 –
Eguisheim 3 – Guebwiller 22.
The highest village in the vineyard (380 meters),
the proximity of the Vosges, tours of the ruined
château and neighboring Eguisheim: We almost
forgot to admire the winegrowers' signs.

 HOTELS-RESTAURANTS

■ Husseren-les-Châteaux

Rue du Schlossberg.
Tel. 03 89 49 22 93. Fax 03 89 49 24 84.
www.hotel-husseren-les-chateaux.com
Closed 10 days Jan.
37 rooms: 113–135€. 1 suite: 230€.
Prix fixe: 21€ (lunch), 28,50€, 39€, 53€.
A la carte: 55€.

Perched on a hill in the midst of trees this
contemporary hotel offers us an unbeatable view of the valley of the Rhine. After
exercising in the swimming pool, a round
of tennis or a sauna in the spa, we deserve
a break in one of the Scandinavian-style
duplex bedrooms. In the restaurant, Christophe Loche elaborates a classically artis-
tocratic cuisine such as the duck foie gras
escalope with berries, Cognac-flambéed
jumbo shrimp, beef filet medallions with
Port-enriched morel sauce and the crème
brûlée trilogy.

ILLHAEUSERN

68970 Haut-Rhin. Paris 439 – Sélestat 13 –
Colmar 17 – Strasbourg 60.
The most famous village in Alsace? In terms of
food, definitely. The houses were rebuilt after
the last war, as was the bridge over the Ill. The
tall church dates from 1957 and the stork has
returned to its nest.

 HOTELS-RESTAURANTS

■ Hôtel des Berges

4, rue des Collonges.
Tel. 03 89 71 87 87. Fax 03 89 71 87 88.
hotel-des-berges@wanadoo.fr
www.hoteldesberges.com
Closed Feb., Mon., Tue.
7 rooms: 252–287€. 6 suites: 342–497€.

The hotel annex to the Auberge de l'Ill
charms us discreetly with its garden. On
the banks of the river, and laid out like
a tobacco barn with a charming fisherman's hut, the residence has very finely
appointed rooms and suites with wood
furnishings. Breakfast is a real meal.

■ La Clairière

50, rte d'Illhaeusern.
Tel. 03 89 71 80 80. Fax 03 89 71 86 22.
hotel.la.clairière@wanadoo.fr
www.hotel-la-clairière.com
Closed Jan., Feb.
25 rooms: 78–202€. 2 suites: 240–260€.

Located next to the Forêt de l'Ill, this con-
temporary-styled Alsatian residence has
a heated swimming pool and a tennis
court. Peace and quiet are guaranteed.

■ Les Hirondelles

In the village.
Tel. 03 89 71 83 76. Fax 03 89 71 86 40.
hotelleshirondelles@wanadoo.fr
www.hotelleshirondelles.com
Closed 1 week at end Dec.,
beg. Feb.–20 Mar.
19 rooms: 62–80€.

Comfort and rustic authenticity are what
give this old village farmhouse its charm.

The open-air swimming pool is an added attraction in fine weather. WiFi.

● **L'Auberge de l'Ill** V.LUX

Rue de Collonges-au-Mont-d'Or.
Tel. 03 89 71 89 00. Fax 03 89 71 82 83.
aubergedelill@auberge-de-l-ill.com
www.auberge-de-l-ill.com
Closed Mon., Tue., 1 Jan.–8 Jan.,
Feb.–beg. Mar.

A fine setting, high-class service, great cuisine, an extensive wine list, a warm welcome and an atmosphere to match it: few establishments have all these assets together. The Haeberlins do, plus one more: the natural comeliness of a unique house anchored in its surroundings, proud of its roots and bringing together a well-bonded team (Michel Scheer, the master of the house, has been here for more than thirty years!). Ranging from Paul, who is over eighty years old and who extends a welcome and is in the kitchen every morning; to Jean-Pierre, who is elegance itself; to Danièle, who looks after guests in the dining room and in the garden; to the mother Marie, who comes round at the end of the meal to make sure that everything was just perfect; and of course Marc, the prodigy, son and chef who orchestrates more than twenty chefs. We conclude that this house is the manifestation of a family commitment. The Haeberlins don't work, they share a unique experience, as do their guests who anticipate their stay well in advance. They know that joy will come from the encounter with this unique place, the discovery of a new dish (the creamy Thai herb and shrimp soup garnished with a coconut emulsion) or from rediscovering an eternal classic (the famous salmon soufflé, the royal lobster Prince Wladimir with a bisque sauce), a wine discovered by accident among the immense listings or recommended by Serge Dubs, the exceptional *sommelier* who long ago won the title of best in the world in his category. A unique establishment? We were just about to say that. The other day, watching the majestic course of the Ill river, there was something fairy-tale-like about the bridge, the bank and all the flowers, the play of light and shade in the garden. There were the little toasts with foie gras, the little flat savory tarte flambée, with thick cream, the cool Muscat de Josmeyer à Wintzenheim. Then in an unassuming mother-of-pearl dining room with bay windows giving onto the exterior, walls lit up by Muhl's canvases, these unique moments were punctuated with splendid dishes: the terrine, served as an *amuse-gueule*, with the house-prepared sardines that are marinated, punctuated with a few grains of caviar and placed on a mound of ratte potato. Sublime in a rustic-yet-refined register, the tripe in a salad with broad beans and goose foie gras and, already a classic in the same mode, the pike-perch filet with a fine red wine sauce and fried eel with herb sauce; mouthwatering Atlantic sea bass and tomato-stuffed cannelloni, pesto and Jabugo ham—exotic and so fresh. The masterpiece disguised as a main dish: a reworking of a Rhône-Alps classic, the poached and truffled Miéral à Montrevel signature Bresse poultry with small stuffed cabbages, and the thighs cooked again with spring vegetables in truffle vinaigrette. Or the venison filet with a dried fruit compote, wild mushrooms and soft fromage blanc knepfles (similar to quenelles). On top of that, the desserts are always a sensation here because of our nostalgia for childhood (home-style frozen vacherin, an oven-baked crêpe with sour cherries served with Tahitian vanilla ice cream, the house ice creams). We wash it all down with a kirsch by Windholtz in Ribeauvillé, telling ourselves that we have not had a unique meal, a sublime experience but rather that we have quite "simply" lived through something completely exceptional.

● **A la Truite** SIM

17, rue du 25-Janvier.
Tel. 03 89 71 83 51. Fax 03 89 71 88 15.
Closed Tue. dinner, Wed.,
3 weeks mid-Feb.–beg. Mar.
Prix fixe: 18€, 26€, 39€. A la carte: 35–45€.

Jean Louis and Christophe Poujol form a twosome to cook up dishes that are reasonably priced and are anchored in the

```

local region, as witnessed by head cheese and aspic terrine (prepared in house), the fish stew made by Marie-Louise, the fried carp filets, the capon simmered in Riesling and the frozen kouglof (also prepared in house), all served in the warm and friendly atmosphere of an inn with a pleasant terrace on the banks of the river bordered with willow trees.

## INGERSHEIM

68040 Haut-Rhin. Paris 443 – Colmar 4 – Turckheim 3.
This suburb of Colmar with its high-quality winegrowers and gourmet artisans is the starting point for hikes through the Vosges.

### ● RESTAURANTS

#### ● Taverne Alsacienne

99, rue de la République.
Tel. 03 89 27 08 41. Fax 03 89 80 89 75.
tavernealsacien@aol.com
Closed Sun. dinner, Mon., Thu. dinner,
1 week Jan., 1 week at end July,
2 weeks beg. Aug.
Prix fixe: 11€ (lunch), 15€ (lunch), 18€, 53€.

Jean-Philippe Guggenbuhl runs the family tavern with an expert hand. The cuisine is based on local produce: foie gras with mango and passion fruit coulis, braised pike-perch with truffle-seasoned vegetable purée, the beef in Alsatian Pinot Noir sauce and the raspberry croustillant dessert delight us. A nice wine list with the comments of Béatrice Groell.

### ▼ SHOPS

#### CHARCUTERIE
#### ▼ Sigmann

44, rue de la République.
Tel. 03 89 27 01 75.
Bernard Sigmann, champion of Alsace charcuterie, meticulously prepares cervelas, blood sausage, goose foie gras, knackwurst, pâté in a pastry crust and liver sausages. Delivery throughout France.

67340 Bas-Rhin. Paris 469 – Haguenau 25 – Sarre-Union 39 – Saverne 23 – Strasbourg 45.
tourisme@pays-de-hanau.com.
This town, a crossroads in the Northern Vosges with its famous onion-domed synagogue and old houses, is at the heart of a fine region that seems to have emerged from one of Hansi's dreams.

### HOTELS-RESTAURANTS

#### ■ Aux Comtes de Hanau

139, rue du Général-de-Gaulle.
Tel. 03 88 89 42 27. Fax 03 88 89 51 18.
www.aux-comtes-de-hanau.com
Rest. closed Mon. dinner, Wed. dinner,
Feb. vac.
11 rooms: 38,50–71,50€.
Prix fixe: 10€, 50€, 9,50€ (child).
A la carte: 25–35€.

Since 1848 the Futterer family has welcomed guests to this inn situated at a corner on the road to the Northern Vosges. The rooms are clean and tidy. In the kitchen Louis Futterer cooks up traditional dishes that are served in the three dining rooms. The house-prepared head cheese and aspic terrine, the seafood pizza, enormous oven-roasted pork shank, delicately sautéed veal kidneys and a rum-raisin frozen kouglof are not to be sniffed at.

### ▼ SHOPS

#### CHARCUTERIE
#### ▼ Lorch

91, rue du Général-Goureau.
Tel. 03 88 89 48 15.
Potato sausages, presskopf, hure de langue (potted tongue in aspic), blood sausage, various smoked and stuffed hams and sausages, all prepared in accordance with local tradition, are the star products at Eric and Elisabeth Lorch's store.

#### REGIONAL PRODUCTS
#### ▼ Les Epices d'Ingwiller

Rue de la Brasserie.
Tel. 03 88 89 45 47.
```

Bernard Loch and Guido Massmann specialize in spices, from the commonest to the rarest, packaged in sachets. Chocolates, dried or candied fruit too.

ITTERSWILLER

67140 Bas-Rhin. Paris 429 – Sélestat 14 – Molsheim 24 – Strasbourg 40.
The location between the vines and Vosges is worthy of a postcard. The grand rue looks toward the slopes that are heavy with grapes and the *winstub* inn has sprouted annexes across the town.

 HOTELS-RESTAURANTS

■ **Arnold**
98, rte du Vin.
Tel. 03 88 85 50 58. Fax 03 88 85 55 54.
arnold-hotel@wanadoo.fr
www.hotel-arnold.com
Closed 2 days at Christmas.
Rest. closed Sun. dinner (Nov.–May),
Mon. (Nov.–May).
29 rooms: 77–110€. 1 suite: 120–315€.
Prix fixe: 23€, 32€ (Sat., Sun., lunch),
46€, 58€, 11€ (child).
A la carte: 55€.

Comfortable rooms with a view of the vineyards. The boutique selling local produce and Simon Bruno's cheerful *winstub* attract an increasingly large public. All appreciate Yves Fritsch's happy knack in the kitchen in the form of the goose foie gras, pike-perch in Riesling, mushroom-stuffed poultry breast and the frozen pain d'épice mille-feuille.

JUNGHOLTZ

68500 Haut-Rhin. Paris 475 – Colmar 32 – Mulhouse 23 – Belfort 62 – Guebwiller 6.
Close by the Notre-Dame de Thierenbach place of pilgrimage with its onion-domed church, a village surrounded by the forest. Famous also for its very moving Jewish cemetery.

 HOTELS-RESTAURANTS

● **Les Violettes**
Thierenbach.
Tel. 03 89 76 91 19. Fax 03 89 74 29 12.
lesviolettes2@wanadoo.fr
www.les-violettes.com
Rest. closed Mon., Tue., 2 weeks beg. Jan.
19 rooms: 70–195€. 3 suites: 210–300€.
Prix fixe: 28€ (weekday lunch), 47€, 63€,
12€ (child). A la carte: 67€.

On the edge of the forest, facing the pilgrims church, this chic *table d'hôte* looks good. The red sandstone building, polished up by the wonder boy of home hairdressing, Philippe Bosc, marks his return to his birthplace. Rooms with wood furnishings give it a rustic mountainy feeling, the dining rooms are decorated with good paintings and the terrace is panoramic: all dedicated to the glory of Alsace. Sébastien Sattler's food alternates between simplicity and sophistication: fresh foie gras trio (one marinated in Port, another rolled in smoked duck breast and the last one breaded in crushed hazelnuts), rockfish- and basil-stuffed cannelloni with tapenade and the roasted duckling served with stir-fried vegetables, bulgur risotto and a sweet pepper sauce make us want to travel and remind us that Jean-Yves Schillinger established the house cuisine. For dessert, the soft-centered Cuban chocolate cake with pralines and almond milk ice cream is a wonder. A post-prandial stroll along the neighboring woodland paths is *de rigueur*.

● Biebler `COM`

Thierenbach.
Tel. 03 89 76 85 75. Fax 03 89 74 91 45.
la-roseraie-biebler@wanadoo.fr
www.biebler.com
Closed Jan. Rest. closed Tue., Wed.
5 rooms: 46–70€. 2 suites: 75€.
Prix fixe: 22€, 25€, 30€, 36€,
10€ (child). A la carte: 45–50€.

Fabrice Biebler, alone at the helm, cooks good quality classic cuisine in this roadside inn: a puff pastry cup filled with meat in creamy white sauce, a rabbit terrine, a pike-perch and salmon duo, beef in sauce made with local wine and the plate of house dessert specialties, all washed down with nice local wines. Three renovated rooms for a well-deserved siesta.

● La Ferme des Moines `SIM`

Across from the church in Thierenbach.
Tel. 03 89 76 93 01. Fax 03 89 74 37 45.
www.lafermedesmoines.fr
Prix fixe: 12,90€ (weekday lunch), 20€,
8€ (child). A la carte: 35€.

This old farmhouse that once belonged to the Thierenbach monks has now become a large inn with Philippe Bosc watching over it and his wife Francine and Daniel Florenc in the kitchen. The dishes are best enjoyed with family or friends. Duck foie gras, head cheese and aspic terrine, fish simmered in Riesling, tête de veau with vinaigrette and apple streudel with vanilla ice cream are amazing. Watch out for the hustle and bustle on Sundays!

KATZENTHAL

68230 Haut-Rhin. Paris 441 – Munster 18 – Saint-Dié 48 – Colmar 7.
At the foot of Wineck castle, which gives its name to the local grand cru, this welcoming winegrowing village with its white bell tower was entirely rebuilt after the last war.

 HOTELS-RESTAURANTS

■ A l'Agneau

16, Grand-Rue.
Tel. 03 89 80 90 25. Fax 03 89 27 59 58.
www.agneau-katzenthal.com
Closed 1 week Nov., 1 week at end Dec.,
2 weeks at end Jan., 1 week July
Rest. closed Wed., Thu.
12 rooms: 45–60€. 1 suite: 80–110€.
Prix fixe: 19€ (lunch), 21€, 45€, 8€ (child).

Patricia and Christophe Munch are very serious about this little modern hotel with its cozy rooms. The welcome is friendly and reassuring, the regional *winstub*-style cuisine combined with wines from René Meyer's nearby vineyard make it a very Alsatian stopover. Riesling-seasoned pâté in pastry crust, sturgeon filet with sauerkraut, a stuffed quail and the kirsch dessert are good standards.

KAYSERSBERG

68240 Haut-Rhin. Paris 436 – Colmar 12 –
Sélestat 26 – Guebwiller 35.
ot.kaysersberg@calixo.net.
How beautiful Doctor Schweitzer's city is!
With its houses on the banks of the Weiss,
its deposed château, time-worn cobblestones,
flamboyant sandstone, comely *auberges* and
the call of the Vosges flirting with its vines.

 HOTELS-RESTAURANTS

● Le Chambard

9-13, rue du Général-de-Gaulle.
Tel. 03 89 47 10 17. Fax 03 89 47 35 03.
info@lechambard.fr
www.lechambard.fr
Rest. closed Mon., Tue. lunch, Wed. lunch.
20 rooms: 96–114€. 3 suites: 195€.
Prix fixe: 29€ (lunch), 47,50€, 64€, 75€,
15€ (child). A la carte: 75–100€.

The Nasti brothers' house at the entrance
to the village with its vast "zebra-colored"
rooms, modern-style suites and most of
all its choice cuisine make it a "must"
on the wine route. In the kitchen, Olivier
adds touches of the south to Alsatian culinary tradition. The dishes? Foie gras and
country bacon, a vegetable and potato
dish presented with style at the tableside,
Atlantic sea bass, the lemon-seasoned lobster in its shell or the pike-perch served
on a bed of julienned white and red radishes and with a beer vinegar- infused
jus: in short, food that is lively, tasteful,
sharp and that leaves your palate clean
and fresh and ready to taste the cheeses
matured by Jacky Quesnot in the Ferme
Saint-Nicolas in Colmar, followed by then
the amazing desserts, like the Victoria
pineapple served with rum grog, the exotic
fruits served with matcha tea sorbet and
the cherry compote (savory) with a Piedmont pistachio cream … Nice work! (See
also La Winstub du Chambard.)

■ A l'Arbre Vert

1, rue Haute-du-Rempart.
Tel. 03 89 47 11 51. Fax 03 89 78 13 40.
hotel-restaurantarbrevert@kaysersberg.com
Closed beg. Jan.–mid-Feb. Rest. closed Mon.
20 rooms: 59–73€.
Prix fixe: 23€, 27€, 10€ (child).

Eliane Wittmer extends a warm welcome
while Gaspard Batista produces good solid
food in this beautiful regional establishment. House terrine, oven-roasted half
quail with foie gras, pike-perch served on
a bed of sauerkraut, the honey-, Marc de
Gewurztraminer- and lemon-seasoned
duck breast and a crème brûlée close fine
meals that take their inspiration from the
local region. The charming setting, the
flowery facade, the reasonable prices, the
winstub-style dining room and the wood
furnishings are all extra attractions that
explain the success of the house.

■ Hôtel Constantin

10, rue du Père-Kohlmann.
Tel. 03 89 47 19 90. Fax 03 89 47 37 82.
www.hotel-constantin.com
20 rooms: 50–71€.

Denis and Christine Kohler are the driving force behind this tastefully appointed
winegrower's house. The rooms swing
between the Alsatian and the modern
style. Breakfast is served in the luminous
glass-roofed dining room enhanced by a
superb earthenware stove. Reasonable
prices.

■ Les Remparts

4, rue de la Flieh.
Tel. 03 89 47 12 12. Fax 03 89 47 37 24.
www.lesremparts.com
41 rooms: 66–84€.

On the edge of the old city this modern
hotel situated in a residential district
offers functional rooms. Ask for a room
with a terrace or balcony. A sauna and
game room to help us relax. WiFi.

● Au Lion d'Or `COM`

66, rue du Général-de-Gaulle.
Tel. 03 89 47 11 16. Fax 03 89 47 19 02.
auliondor@wanadoo.fr
www.auliondor.fr
Closed Tue. dinner, Wed., mid-Jan.–end Feb.
Prix fixe: 18€, 25€, 36€. A la carte: 38€.

An affordable Alsace: that's what this goodly inn dating from 1521 offers us. The Ancel brothers run this house that has been in their family since 1764. Daniel is at the reception, Jean-Marc serving and Jean-Joseph in the kitchen: duck foie gras, fish choucroute, tripe simmered in Riesling and regional flat savory tarts called "tarte flambée", plain or with cheese. A dining room with a large open fireplace and courtyard garden.

● La Vieille Forge `P` `SIM`

1, rue des Ecoles.
Tel. 03 89 47 17 51. Fax 03 89 78 13 53.
Closed Wed. (exc. Bank holidays), Thu. (exc. Bank holidays), Feb. vac., 2 weeks July.
Prix fixe: 19€, 20€, 25€, 32€, 9€ (child).

There is no room for frills in this old 15th-century forge transformed into a beige and rose-colored inn with exposed stonework and wood. The charming Marie Gutleben welcomes us while Christophe Grivel cooks up a cuisine that is both generous and finely crafted, anchored in the Alsatian countryside. Salad with soft mountain cheese and smoked ham, mushroom and escargot cassolette, pike-perch filet with crispy crêpes, served with sauerkraut, slow-cooked venison and onion stew with house spätzle and the frozen terrine dessert with pain d'épices delight the guests. The menus are a blessing.

● La Winstub du Chambard `SIM`

9-13, rue du Général-de-Gaulle.
Tel. 03 89 47 10 17. Fax 03 89 47 35 03.
info@lechambard.fr
www.lechambard.fr
Closed Mon., Tue. lunch, Wed. lunch, beg. Jan.–beg. Feb.
Prix fixe: 24€, 10,50€ (child).
A la carte: 40€.

We also find the Nastis in this *winstub* with yellow and pine décor right next to their gastronomic restaurant. They delight their customers with suckling pig presskopf, foie gras terrine with dried fruits similar to the Alsatian holiday cake called beraweke, pike-perch simmered in wine, the house choucroute and the frozen vacherin, all accompanied by a judicious selection of smart wines in which Alsace has pride of place.

● Flamme & Co `N` `SIM`

4, rue du Général-de-Gaulle.
Tel. 03 89 47 16 16.
Closed lunch, Mon., Tue. (off season).
A la carte: 20€.

They created a sensation in their village by opening this modern "tarte flambée" eatery. From 6:00 pm to midnight, the Chambard Nastis serve twenty-five sorts of "flammeküche" in an old *winstub* that has been modernized. Oven-browned with cheese, but also with fresh herbs, tomatoes and parmesan or with smoked salmon and herbs, these classic garnished pies are deservedly famous.

● Le Château `SIM`

38, rue du Général-de-Gaulle.
Tel. 03 89 78 24 33. Fax 03 89 47 37 82.
Closed Wed. dinner, Thu., 1 week at end Nov., 2 weeks Jan., 1 week at end June.
Prix fixe: 16,50€, 18€, 19€, 26€, 32€, 8€ (child).
A la carte: 30–35€.

The Kohlers, who own the Hotel Constantin, are also the driving force behind this rustic establishment with white and wood shades. Faithful gourmets come to savor Jean-Yves Bill's dishes. An onion tart, escargots prepared in the style of Alsace (stuffed with spiced butter and herbs and cooked in local wine), smoked trout with horseradish sauce, the coq au Riesling and the crème caramel are delightful and reasonably priced.

SHOPS

BREAD & BAKED GOODS

▼ **Au Péché Mignon**
67, rue du Général-de-Gaulle.
Tel. 03 89 47 30 40.
Jeanne Loewert delights sweet-toothed customers with her kouglofs, berawecke (bread with dried fruit, kirsch and spices), ice creams and sorbets, fruit tarts and delicious brie with kirsch.

CHARCUTERIE

▼ **Chez Daniel**
107, rue du Général-de-Gaulle.
Tel. 03 89 78 23 19.
Daniel Dotti has an expert eye for superb charcuterie: smoked filet mignon, country sausage with beer, "*fagot du vigneron*" (small, flat, cured beef and pork sausages with raisins), ham baked in pastry, kassler, bacon, foie gras, choucroute and smoked ham.

KEMBS-LOECHLE

68680 Haut-Rhin. Paris 493 – Colmar 60 – Mulhouse 25 – Altkirch 26 – Bâle 16.
On the edge of Alsace's Petite Camargue, an old commune of boatmen that is famous for its dam.

RESTAURANTS

● **Les Ecluses**   SIM
8, rue de Rosenau.
Tel. 03 89 48 37 77. Fax 03 89 48 49 31.
restaurant.les.ecluses@freezbee.fr
Closed Sun. dinner, Mon., Wed. dinner (Oct.–Apr.), Nov. 1 vac., Feb. vac.
Prix fixe: 14,50€, 39€, 8,50€ (child).
A la carte: 38€.

The dining room is unassuming and contemporary with red-orange cherrywood furnishings. Bertrand Welte delights his clients with crayfish salad seasoned with citrus and coriander, the Bismarck herring served on salad with green apples, mushrooms and sherry- seasoned cream sauce, Alsatian-style fish simmered in wine, venison shoulder with chestnuts and currants and frozen nougat with a berry coulis.

KIENTZHEIM

68240 Haut-Rhin. Paris 433 – Colmar 13 – Munster 28.
At the foot of the Sigolsheim cemetery, this historic village whose château is home to the Saint-Etienne fraternity and a wine museum, deserves a visit and some tasting.

HOTELS-RESTAURANTS

■ **Hôtel de l'Abbaye d'Alspach**
2/4, rue Foch.
Tel. 03 89 47 16 00. Fax 03 89 78 29 73.
www.abbayealspach.com
Closed beg. Jan.–mid-Mar.
28 rooms: 68–105€. 5 suites: 140–180€.

The charm of the old blends with modern comfort in these outbuildings of a 13th-century convent converted into a hotel. Rustic furniture, sauna, conference rooms.

■ **Hostellerie Schwendi**
2, pl Schwendi.
Tel. 03 89 47 30 50. Fax 03 89 49 04 49.
www.hotel-schwendi.com
Rest. closed Wed., Thu. lunch,
Christmas–10 Mar.
25 rooms: 65–98€.
Prix fixe: 22€, 30€, 36€, 46€, 9€ (child).

On a charming cobblestone square in the heart of the winegrowing village, Anita and René Schillé have transformed an 18th-century wine cellar into a charming stopover with a half-timbered facade, exposed stonework and wooden beams. The rooms are rustic and finely appointed and the dishes prepared by their son Fabien are good quality. Pan-seared foie gras with sour cherries, onion tart, trout and vegetable soufflé, breast of guinea hen with mushrooms and beer-macerated berries over shaved ice meet with no resistance.

KIFFIS

68480 Haut-Rhin. Paris 541 – Altkirch 31
– Colmar 90.

On the Swiss frontier the village stands as a sentinel overlooking the gently sloping hillsides of the Jura.

●	RESTAURANTS

● Le Cheval Blanc   SIM

21, rue Principale.
Tel. 03 89 40 33 05. Fax 03 89 40 36 66.
agnes.walther@tiscali.fr
Closed Mon., 2 weeks Jan., 2 weeks July.
Prix fixe: 13,50€, 22€, 30€,
45€, 8,50€ (child).
A la carte: 35€.

A warm eggplant and goat cheese dish, pheasant terrine with baby vegetables, herb-stuffed trout, a veal steak with Munster sauce and the frozen kouglof make a good impression in this old-style inn. André Walther pampers his guests in this welcoming house with solid oak parquet floor and massive wooden beams. We slip easily into the sheer pleasure of eating.

KILSTETT

67840 Bas-Rhin. Paris 489 – Strasbourg 14
– Haguenau 23 – La Wantzenau 5.

The silt from the Reid and the banks of the Rhine.

■/●	HOTELS-RESTAURANTS

■ Oberlé

11, rte Nationale.
Tel. 03 88 96 21 17.
www.hotel-oberle.fr
Closed 2 weeks Feb., mid-Aug.–beg. Sept.
Rest. closed Thu., Fri. lunch.
31 rooms: 30–51€.
Prix fixe: 10€ (weekdays), 21€, 36€,
10€ (child).

Modern but old style, a large family inn with practical rooms, a warm welcome,

table d'hôte cuisine and the *plat du jour* attracting lots of people for lunch.

● Le Cheval Noir   COM

1, rue du Sous-Lieutenant-Maussire.
Tel. 03 88 96 22 01.
Closed Mon., Tue., 10 days end July,
10 days beg. Aug.
Prix fixe: 12€ (weekday lunch), 25€, 45€.

A fine 18th-century half-timbered Alsatian house with its carefully appointed dining room decorated with a fresco representing a hunting scene, a welcoming family that has received people for five generations and a regional cuisine that has adapted to the tastes of today.

KINTZHEIM

67600 Bas-Rhin. Paris 432 –
Sélestat 5 – Colmar 22.

At the foot of Haut-Koenigsbourg castle, Monkey Mountain and the Eagle Park, this spirited winegrowing village offers a hearty welcome.

●	RESTAURANTS

● Auberge Saint-Martin   SIM

80, rue de la Liberté.
Tel. 03 88 82 04 78. Fax 03 88 82 26 20.
Closed Wed. (exc. July–Aug.),
1 week at end Nov., 3 weeks Jan.
Prix fixe: 9€ (weekday lunch), 19€, 21€,
8,50€ (child).
A la carte: 35–45€.

People used to stop here in days gone by for the tartes flambées. Patrice Blutzer set up shop in this roadside inn on the wine route and delights his customers with the house-prepared duck foie gras, the Tomme du Ried cheese salad, pike-perch in Pinot Noir sauce, oxtail braised in red wine and a sweet version of the regional tarte flambée, with apples and Grand Marnier. A fine wine list with 100 listings.

KOENIGSMACKER

57970 Moselle. Paris 349 – Thionville 9 –
Metz 39 – Luxembourg 41.
Near the valley of the Moselle, a village waiting to be discovered, a church with baroque furniture.

■	HOTELS

■ Moulin de Méwinckel
Tel. 03 82 55 03 28.
5 rooms: 40–70€.

In what used to be the stable of a peasant mill where the paddle wheel still turns, five quiet and brightly decorated rooms. A warm welcome.

KRAUTERGERSHEIM

67880 Bas-Rhin. Paris 492 –
Strasbourg 25 – Obernai 9 – Molsheim 16.
The name of the commune literally means "Cabbagetown", so we are not surprised that cabbage is the star vegetable in the neighboring fields.

●	RESTAURANTS

● Le Chou'Heim `SIM`
2, rue G.-Clemenceau.
Tel.-Fax 03 88 48 18 10.
eric.ivens@hotmail.fr
www.lechouheim.com
Closed Sat. lunch, Mon., Wed. dinner.
Prix fixe: 33€, 7€ (child).

Eric Ivens who took over this picturesque residence welcomes us while Jean-Marie Albrecht, who is in charge of the kitchens, is respectful of regional traditions, as we can see with escargots prepared in the style of Alsace (stuffed with spiced butter and herbs and cooked in local wine), smoked duck breast served on a bed of julienned cabbage, a salmon and pike-perch duo, the Cordon Bleu with morels and a house-prepared chocolate mousse. The prices are reasonable. A new stone cellar has opened.

KRUTH

68820 Haut-Rhin. Paris 453 –
Gérardmer 31 – Mulhouse 40 – Thann 20.
The high valley of the Thur at the southern end of the Alsatian Vosges. Don't miss the Saint-Nicolas waterfall.

■◢	HOTELS-RESTAURANTS

■ Auberge de France
20, Grand'Rue.
Tel. 03 89 82 28 02. Fax 03 89 82 24 05.
aubergedefrance@wanadoo.fr
www.aubergedefrance.fr
Closed beg. Jan.–beg. Feb., 2 weeks June.
Rest. closed Wed. dinner, Thu.
16 rooms: 46–53€.
Prix fixe: 11€ (weekday lunch), 17€, 39€, 8,50€ (child).

A pleasant old-style inn, with billiards, a bowling pitch, tidy rooms, a rustic dining room and Alsatian dishes with the colors of the mountains.

LABAROCHE

68910 Haut-Rhin. Colmar 14 –
Gérardmer 51 – Munster 25 – Saint-Dié 52.
One of France's largest townships. Hamlets
tucked into the landscape, thatched roofs, woodland paths can all be found at a height of 750m
right in the heart of the Vosges.

	HOTELS-RESTAURANTS

■ Au Tilleul ⬧
385, La Place.
Tel. 03 89 49 84 46. Fax 03 89 78 91 88.
au-tilleul@wanadoo.fr
www.hotel-tilleul.fr
Closed Jan.
30 rooms: 37–70€.
Prix fixe: 15€ (weekday lunch).

Martine and Christiane Munier's benevo-
lent gaze watches over this family *pension*
boasting lots of charm in its cozy rooms.
Taste tranquillity as well as Christiane's
cooking, whose treats include her individual chicken liver terrine, pâté in a short
crust with assorted raw vegetables, leg of
venison and her house-made éclair.

■ La Rochette ⬧
Rte des Trois-Epis.
Tel. 03 89 49 80 40. Fax 03 89 78 94 82.
www.larochette-hotel.fr
Closed 2 weeks Nov., mid-Feb.–mid-Mar.
Rest. closed Mon. dinner (exc. hotel clients),
Tue.
6 rooms: 52–55€. 1 suite: 58€.
Prix fixe: 16€, 28€, 37€, 43€.
A la carte: 38€.

Pretty rooms in a verdant setting with
breakfasts served on the veranda. The
dining room with its large French windows giving on to the garden lends a
final touch of charm. You won't tire of
the individual escargot and potato casserole (baekeofe), filet of turbot served
over risotto and the layered casserole of
pork tail and potato.

LANDERSHEIM

67700 Bas-Rhin. Paris 462 – Saverne 13 –
Strasbourg 25.
The rich and fertile countryside between Stras-
bourg and Saverne is known as the Kochersberg.
This village, with its white church and timber-
framed houses, is typical of the area.

■	HOTELS

■ Auberge du Kochersberg ⬧⬧
2, rte de Saessolsheim.
Tel. 03 88 69 93 08.
18 rooms: 80–130€ (by reserv. only).

Following several changes of owner-
ship, a local group of investors has just
reopened this mythical landmark. Ten
rooms have been entirely renovated in a
very comfortable style to put this establishment back in the class it deserves. (It
once served as the luxurious "canteen" of
the Adidas group). Banquets and restaurants are run by Kieffer catering.

LANDSER

68440 Haut-Rhin. Paris 475 – Mulhouse 11
– Bâle 32 – Colmar 54.
This little town in the Sundgau, not far from
Mulhouse and its museums, has a great gas-
tronomic future before it.

●	RESTAURANTS

● Hostellerie Paulus ⬧⬧
4, pl de la Paix.
Tel. 03 89 81 33 30. Fax 03 89 26 81 85.
Closed Sun. dinner, Mon., 1 week Christmas–
New Year's, 2 weeks Aug.
Prix fixe: 25€ (weekdays) 44€, 59€, 69€.

Hervé Paulus now serves his wonderful,
small menu (at 25€) at lunch and dinner. He doesn't compromise on quality,
offering balanced menus which reflect
his daily market purchases, seasonal
ingredients, traditional Alsatian as well
as other influences. The chocolate-col-
ored interior has just been redone and
the teakwood terrace on the back is a
pleasure on fine days. Pan-seared slice

of foie gras, langoustine brochette with crunchy fresh sweet pea carpaccio, John Dory with broad beans and Serrano ham, pike-perch with a stir fry of bok choy and bacon, veal sweetbreads with small French peas and steak with buttered potatoes reveal a neoclassicist of stupendous talent who plays skillfully on a register of tastes while avoiding the chi-chi like the plague. His thyme-seasoned roasted peaches and poached apricots with almond cake are choice. Top Alsatian wines form part of the feast and blond, smiling Stéphanie Paulus' charming welcome warms the heart.

LAPOUTROIE

68650 Haut-Rhin. Paris 457 – Colmar 20 – Sélestat 35 – Saint-Dié 36 – Munster 24.
A welcoming craft village with all the charm of the Vosges, fresh air, thatched roofs, cheese makers, the scent of distilling and savory scents wafting from the inns.

 HOTELS-RESTAURANTS

■ Les Alisiers
Follow signs from the church, 3 km to the sw via secondary road.
Tel. 03 89 47 52 82. Fax 03 89 47 22 38.
hotel@alisiers.com
www.alisiers.com
Closed beg. Jan.–beg. Feb.,
4 days at Christmas. Rest. closed Mon., Tue.
15 rooms: 50–122€. 1 suite: 180€.
Prix fixe: 15€ (weekdays), 28€, 39€, 45€, 10€ (child).

This old farmhouse dating back to 1819 houses a charming inn. Under the watchful eye of Ella Degouy and with the help of her son Matthias, you can make the most of colorful, contemporary rooms, a hammam and a regional cuisine served in the luminous dining room or on the terrace overlooking the valley. The foie gras served hot, salmon filet with bacon-seasoned cream, Limousin lamb platter and Marcel Manthermann's kirsch-flavored iced mousse dessert put you right on track.

■ Le Faudé
28, rue du Général-Dufieux.
Tel. 03 89 47 50 35. Fax 03 89 47 24 82.
info@faude.com
www.faude.com
Closed 3 weeks Nov., 3 weeks Mar.
Rest. closed Tue., Wed.
30 rooms: 42–92€. 2 suites: 128–164€.
Prix fixe: 19€, 26€, 31€, 52€, 9€ (child).

A kindly welcome awaits you at Thierry and Chantal Baldinger's enlarged and modernized village house. Three dining rooms (one in green tones, the other in orange and the third in mauve) allow traditional gourmets a choice of venue. A garden runs along the river, and cozy rooms, a fitness center with a heated pool, hammam and sauna, make you want to move in. At the stoves, Thierry and his second-in-command José Di Luca are multi-faceted and do not fail to deliver: The foie gras and white wine, caramel and sauerkraut chutney, pike-perch filet over sauerkraut, trilogy of tuna with tomato reduction, tête de veau with sauce gribiche (caper and pickle mayonnaise). The frozen layered nougat and meringue house dessert is staggering, as is the 500-bottle wine list.

▼ SHOPS

CHARCUTERIE
▼ Roger Baradel
68-70, rue du Général-Dufieux.
Tel. 03 89 47 50 06.
Using traditional methods, Roger Baradel manufactures raw cured ham, smoked bacon, sausages, smoked duck breast and vacuum-packed choucroutes.

CHEESE
▼ Fromagerie du Pays Welche
18, rue du Général-Dufieux.
Tel. 03 89 47 50 76.
www.haxaire.com
Florent Haxaire has renamed her father's establishment and enlarged its range of quality munsters. Chatzely with the flavor of wine and gingerbread, the block of père Antoine with mirabelle plum and cheese with elderflower are splendid.

Educational offshoot the Graine de Lait reveals the secrets of cheese production.

EAUX DE VIE

▼ **Gilbert Miclo**

La Gayire.

Tel. 03 89 47 50 16.

www.distillerie-miclo.com

Michel Miclo has taken over at his father's distillery and produces fabulous *cœurs de chauffe* (the best, middle part of the distillate) high in fruit. His local raspberry, sorbe-apple or wild service berry are worth the trip.

▼ **René de Miscault**

"Musée des eaux-de-vie"

85, rue du Général-Dufieux.

Tel. 03 89 47 50 26.

www.musee-eaux-de-vie.com

The main residence of René de Miscault, who also has businesses in Nol, Ribeauvillé and Fougerolles, is this museum devoted to eaux de vie. All his products (pear, Quetsch plum, raspberry, kirsch and Marc de Gewurz) are well worth purchasing.

LAUTERBOURG

67630 Bas-Rhin. Paris 519 – Wissembourg 19 – Haguenau 41 – Strasbourg 63.

tourisme.lauterbourg@wanadoo.fr.

This border town with its demolished ramparts alongside the Rhine river is the town furthest from the sea in the whole of France.

 HOTELS-RESTAURANTS

● **La Poêle d'Or** `V.COM`

35, rue du Général-Mittelhauser.

Tel. 03 88 94 84 16. Fax 03 88 54 62 30.

info@poeledor.com

www.poeledor.com

Closed Wed., Thu., 3 weeks Jan., end July–beg. Aug.

Prix fixe: 26€ (lunch), 40€, 73,50€.

A la carte: 60€.

This half-timbered house is a village institution where François and Marie-Odile Gottar match a gourmet tradition with a faultless welcome. Four hands man the stove—those of Jean-Marc and his father François, who has had a stint with some of the greats (Cerf at Marlenheim, Buerehiesel at Strasbourg). Be it in the Renaissance dining room or on the flowered terrace, treat yourselves to truffled foie gras, classic Alsatian choucroute made with fish instead of charcuterie, veal kidneys with whole grain mustard, pigeon simply roasted and served in its own cooking dish and a strawberry and raspberry feuilleté. Jean-Claude Wendling is good at pairing dishes with local wines.

In Munchhausen (67470). 6 km s via D248.

● **A la Rose** `SIM`

35, rue du Rhin.

Tel. 03 88 86 51 86. Fax 03 88 86 15 99.

Closed Mon. (exc. Bank holidays),

Tue. (exc. Bank holidays), 2 weeks beg. Feb.,

2 weeks July.

Prix fixe: 9,50€, 11,50€, 22€.

A la carte: 45€.

Thierry Lehmann devises compact *terroir* dishes in this traditional inn. The house prepared goose foie gras, meat stew with onions, herbs and Riesling wine, a venison filet steak and the crème brûlée are accompanied by Alsatian wines at reasonable prices. The flowered terrace is highly popular in good weather.

LEMBACH

67510 Bas-Rhin. Paris 461 – Wissembourg
15 – Bitche 32 – Strasbourg 55.
info@ot.lembach.com.
A forest town at the tip of Northern Alsace
and an exquisite layover on the road to the
region's fortified castles. Do not miss the ruins
of Fleckenstein.

■ HOTELS-RESTAURANTS

■ Hôtel du Cheval Blanc & Rossel'Stub

3, rte de Wissembourg.
Tel. 03 88 94 41 86. Fax 03 88 94 20 74.
info@au-cheval-blanc.fr
www.au-cheval-blanc.fr
Closed 2 weeks end Jan.–10 Feb., 10 days at
end Aug., 1 week beg. Sept.
Rest. closed Fri. lunch, Mon., Tue.
Rossel'Stub closed: Wed., Thu.
3 rooms: 107–138€. 3 suites: 199€.
Prix fixe: 26€. A la carte: 35–40€.

An exquisite hotel with bright, cozy rooms
in a chic rustic style. On the ground floor is
a *winstub* offering great value for money.
There are wooden tables, an open kitchen,
prompt service and light versions of traditional home cooking. Sure-fire successes,
the boneless roast duck in wine sauce, a
salmon terrine with cured herring with
horseradish cream, a pike fish quenelle
with shellfish sauce, pork trotter wrapped
in caul lace and served with mustard sauce
and the rhubarb and strawberry soup are
models of their kind.

■ Le Relais du Heimbach

15, rte de Wissembourg.
Tel. 03 88 94 43 46. Fax 03 88 94 20 85.
www.hotel-au-heimbach.fr
16 rooms: 55–70€. 2 suites: 107€.

A kindly welcome from Martin Biehler
in this half-timbered house opposite the
Cheval Blanc. Well-tended, homespun
rooms and generous breakfasts make
you want to take up residence.

● Le Cheval Blanc

4, rte de Wissembourg.
Tel. 03 88 94 41 86. Fax 03 88 94 20 74.
info@au-cheval-blanc.fr
www.au-cheval-blanc.fr
Closed Fri., Mon., Tue., 10 days Aug.,
2 weeks beg. Sept.
Prix fixe: 34€ (lunch), 56€, 69€, 89€.
A la carte: 130€.

This 18th-century coaching inn is in full
renewal. Fernand Mischler, the father, and
Franck, his son, are committed to quality. They, more than anyone, know how
to work a product in traditional and innovative ways. Take the frogs legs: served
as soup, as a tiny canapé, or crispy, ham-
style served on a garlic flan with parsley
jus, they are enough to make you faint as
you lick the plate. The Mischler's plush,
grand dining room with its coffered ceiling and elaborate fireplace definitely has
a soul; here, everything is at the service of
good taste. Loiseau used to say that "the
star in the kitchen is the product", a sen-
tence which could easily be appropriated
by these outstanding artisans who, were
they able to, would wear their modesty
emblazoned across their front. With them
mussel stew with saffron cream sauce,
parsley and shallots and a langoustine tail
in its bouillon gives the impression of having just been pulled out of the water that
morning in a port in the Finistère. Everything else is just as pleasing. The hot duck
foie gras pan tossed with acidic melon,
grilled rouget served over polenta, turbot
in a pastry crust and its little oyster soup
seems to have just jumped out of the sea.
The product and nothing but the product:
that's what one thinks when tasting the
simply roasted lobster with salted butter, a
rack of milk-fed lamb from the Aveyron in
a crust of herbs, juicy venison with chanterelles and berry jelly and Cyrille Lhoro's
cheeses (ah the Gouda, the Abondance,
the Fougeru and the Munster!) with amazing breads introduced to us in the dining
room with gusto by a master baker wearing a beret (a symbolic innovation). Everything is followed by regal desserts: the soft
raspberry dessert with champagne jelly
and lemongrass sorbet, a peach variation

with a light saffron pastry cream and Muscat wine sorbet or a lemon cream under the guise of *"après-dessert"*. In short it's always "plus" for the Mischlers who are definitely the Haeberlins of the North.

In Gimbelhof (67510). 10 km n via D3 and forest road.

■ Ferme du Gimbelhof
Tel. 03 88 94 43 58. Fax 03 88 94 23 30.
info@gimbelhof.com
Closed 20 Nov.–26 Dec., Feb. vac.
Rest. closed Mon., Tue.
8 rooms: 45–55€.
Prix fixe: 11,50€ (lunch), 28€, 6€ (child).

Nothing has changed in these wooded surroundings. Not the view of the Fleckenstein ruins, nor the simplicity of this verdant inn. Simple rooms and *terroir* cooking make this a peaceful stop.

▼	SHOPS

CHARCUTERIE
▼ Muller
1, rte de Wissembourg.
Tel.-Fax 03 88 94 41 11.
Guido Muller's homemade artisanal knackwurst, presskopf, bacon, liver sausage and raw cured ham are well worth a visit.

PASTRIES
▼ Georges Ehrstein
2, rte de Woerth.
Tel. 03 88 94 40 70.
Georges Ehrstein devotes his skills to the baking of Black Forest cake, kouglof, chinois (brioche pastry, whipped cream, raisins), nid d'abeille (vanilla cream cake with toasted almonds), fruit tarts, streusel and biscuits, all to be enjoyed immoderately.

67480 Bas-Rhin. Paris 501 – Haguenau 22 – Karlsruhe 46 – Strasbourg 45 – Soufflenheim 5.
L'Outre Forêt with its flower-filled village and potters' houses.

●	RESTAURANTS

● Auberge du Vieux Couvent
Locale known as Koenigsbruck,
2 km nw via D163.
7, rue du Vieux-Moulin.
Tel. 03 88 86 39 86. Fax 03 88 05 28 78.
Closed Mon., Tue.,
1 week Christmas–New Year's,
1 week at end Feb.–beg. Mar.,
1 week at end Aug.–beg. Sept.
Prix fixe: 26€, 36€.

A hop, skip and a jump from some convent ruins stands a 17th-century house with a timber-covered terrace for outside dining and a dining room covered with inscriptions in dialect. This is the home of Catherine and Damien Hirschel, who once worked at the Crillon in Paris. Back on native soil they fell in love with the house. The locals have been right in heaping laurels on the two menus, which are a steal. Delicious beef in salad with an egg vinaigrette, rabbit terrine with aspic and a foie gras or crayfish *verrine*, tuna steak with peppers in filo, duck confit and the Charolais beef sirloin with red wine sauce slip down nicely, not forgetting to praise the exquisite strawberry tiramisu with berry sorbet and pan-tossed apricots in acidulated sauce and the spéculos ice cream. A good-natured atmosphere and prompt service by a trio of adorable waitresses gives this country manor an air of great civility.

LIEPVRE

68660 Haut-Rhin. Paris 422 – Colmar 34 – Ribeauvillé 20 – Saint-Dié 30 – Sélestat 15. ot.valargent@rmcnet.fr.

The forest of Vancelle and Frankenbourg castle mark the limits of the countryside in this industrial town along the road to the Vosges of Lorraine.

	RESTAURANTS

In Bois-l'Abbesse (68660). 2 km w.

● La Vieille Forge `COM`

13, Bois-l'Abbesse.
Tel. 03 89 58 92 54. Fax 03 89 58 43 58.
alavieilleforge@wanadoo.fr
Closed 2 weeks Feb., 2 weeks Aug.
Prix fixe: 20€, 32€. A la carte: 40€.

An old forge, transformed into a congenial stopover, offering regional specialities at bargain prices. In the cozy paneled dining room, you'll enjoy escalope of foie gras with chutney, pike-perch cooked in Sancerre with morels, pan-tossed veal sweetbreads and kidneys and the delicious lemon pastry.

MARLENHEIM

67520 Bas-Rhin. Paris 465 – Strasbourg 20 – Haguenau 35.

Rendezvous on August 15 for the feast of l'Ami Fritz to discover the joyful soul of this first town along the region's wine route. Otherwise all year round the Hussers at the Cerf show gastronomic Alsace at its very best.

	HOTELS-RESTAURANTS

● Le Cerf

30, rue du Général-de-Gaulle.
Tel. 03 88 87 73 73. Fax 03 88 87 68 08.
info@lecerf.com
www.lecerf.com
Rest. closed Tue., Wed.
12 rooms: 90–140€. 2 suites: 200€.
Prix fixe: 39€ (lunch), 85€, 98€,
23€ (child). A la carte: 105€.

Under the direction of Michel Husser and his wife, Cathy, the place has recently been given a facelift. The waiters are now dressed in black, like avant-garde chefs' assistants, there is modern lighting and new chairs which have brought a note of clarity and gaiety to the Alsatian-style paneled dining room with its marquetry work by Spindler and its huge canvas by Loux. The house, however, stays obstinately true to tradition. The best proof of the Hussers' attachment to old recipes is the *plaisir* menu at 39€, served at lunchtime, which distills everything one loves and is often forgotten by more trendy establishments. Thus the paté in a pastry crust (named *royale*, with veal sweetbreads and morels), the thick-cut smoked salmon with a horseradish mousse, then puff pastry cups filled with veal sweetbreads and served with poultry quenelles and a creamy mushroom sauce, the civet of venison, slow simmered with onions and red wine served with the house-made chestnut spätzle noodles. Nothing but good, serious classic dishes which can be accompanied—thanks to the good idea of a competent sommelier—by wines by the glass of winemaker friends and neighbors. Traditional desserts include ice creams according to season or the Alsatian-style baba, as well as daily meat and fish choices which allow for a reasonably priced meal for a high class establishment. But one could go on and on about the foie gras terrine with mango chutney, the eel and escargot brochette with lentils and local pesto (garlic and parsley in addition to basil), the grand duck liver ravioli in a pot-au-feu and the famous and wonderful suckling pig choucroute, with medallions of caramelized meat, fare full of character which manages to lighten up dishes without straying too far from tradition. The house desserts are as good as the rest: baba au Kirsch served with cherry compote and a vanilla-flavored whipped cream and the frozen vacherin with fine meringue cut into matchsticks, all of which are wonderful creations in the spirit of the region.

● **Au Tonneau** SIM
2, pl du Kaufhaus.
Tel.-Fax 03 88 87 75 02.
Closed Fri., Christmas–New Year's.
Prix fixe: 14,70€, 17,30€, 22€, 24€, 34€,
8,50€ (child). A la carte: 36€.

A *winstub* atmosphere, friendly welcome, generous little dishes and local wines contribute to the success of this genial address. The barrel-covered walls give you a hint of what it's all about so order a glass of wine and feast on foie gras, pike-perch over sauerkraut, sirloin steak with morels and chocolate mousse or crème caramel.

■ **Hostellerie Reeb** COM
2, rue du Dr-Schweitzer.
Tel. 03 88 87 52 70. Fax 03 88 87 69 73.
info@hostellerie-reeb.fr
www.hostellerie-reeb.fr
Closed 3 weeks Jan.
Rest. closed Sun. dinner, Mon.
26 rooms: 50€. 2 suites: 87€.
Prix fixe: 19,50€, 24,50€, 31€, 44€,
12€ (child). A la carte: 40€.

Fredy Reeb is a welcoming host in his half-timbered house at the entrance to the village. Be it in the rustic or classic-style dining rooms, his cooking should be tasted

with a good Alsatian wine. The foie gras with fruit chutney, the Munster cheese and bacon in puff pastry and pike-perch in paupillette served with sauerkraut have character. The neighboring *winstub* offers local specialities. The rooms are charming and quiet, worthy of this Alsace village and quality address.

In Furdenheim (67117). 5 km e via N4.

● **La Ferme des Trois Frères** SIM
15, rte de Strasbourg.
Tel. 03 88 69 00 86. Fax 03 88 69 14 20.
Closed Sat. lunch, Mon., 2 weeks Oct.,
2 weeks Jan.
A la carte: 25€.

Dominique Schmitt has transferred his Marmoutier farm to the ex-Feldfof and made it into a charming mountain refuge. Dominique, a true lover of Savoie (he used to work at the Totem in Flaine) is a proponent of cooking with cheese. In his perfect chalet, the fine pasta from the Savoie and other regions are proposed in cheese sauce, Provençal style, pan tossed, Italian style or rolled with meat. Add a few of the best tartes flambées, the local savory flat pastries with cream and bacon, including the whole wheat peasant version, and his success at week's end is clear.

▼ | SHOPS

CHARCUTERIE

▼ **Burg**
63, rue du Général-de-Gaulle.
Tel. 03 88 87 52 10.
Michel Burg has several strings to his bow and his meats, prepared foods and charcuterie are of the highest quality. Knacks, cervelas, bacon, white or smoked ham, black or white boudin sausage, beer sausage, liver sausage, pistachio galantine (cold, stuffed pork appetizer, molded in aspic) and presskopf are unfailingly delicious.

PASTA

▼ **Heimburger**
7, rue du Général-de-Gaulle.
Tel. 03 88 59 59 09.
This is Alsace's number one pasta manufacturer. You can visit the factory and

purchase genuine "grandmother's noodles", along with traditional spaetzle, fresh egg noodles and tagliatelli with Italian herbs.

MASEVAUX

68290 Haut-Rhin. Paris 441 – Altkirch 30 – Colmar 57 – Mulhouse 29.
ot.masevaux@wanadoo.fr.
At the gateway of the Territoire of Belfort, this peaceful town is one of the frontiers of the province. The ballon d'Alsace is not far nor is the Asfeld lake and its attractive walks in the nearby woods.

 | HOTELS-RESTAURANTS

■ Hostellerie Alsacienne
16, rue du Maréchal-Foch.
Tel.-Fax 03 89 82 45 25.
http://perso.wanadoo.fr
hostellerie.alsacienne
Closed 3 weeks Oct., 1 week Christmas–New Year's. Rest. closed Mon.
8 rooms: 44–53€.
Prix fixe: 12€ (lunch), 24€, 38€, 43€, 9,15€ (child). A la carte: 44€.

Philippe Battman takes you under his wing in order to help you discover his version of regional recipes. Pan-seared duck foie gras, fish choucroute, almond-crusted trout with shredded rutabaga salad, pork cheeks simmered in amber beer and the slow-cooked figs seasoned with star anise and served hot with pistachio ice cream make for a nice finish. A typically regional décor with carved paneling and well-balanced prices make this a choice address. Pretty rooms redone in 1930's Alsatian style.

 | RENDEZVOUS

TEA SALON
◆ Christian Blind
12, rue Foch.
Tel. 03 89 82 46 34.
Christian Blind's regular customers come specially for his fruit tarts, kouglofs, "*patates aux amandes*" (potato-

shaped almond sweets), "*jour et nuit*" and "*créole*" (with pineapple chunks), all mouthwateringly delicious.

MERKWILLER-PECHELBRONN

67250 Bas-Rhin. Paris 505 – Strasbourg 48 – Haguenau 16 – Wissembourg 22.
Once the oil capital of Alsace, now a museum city and more recently a gastronomic crossroads.

● | RESTAURANTS

● Auberge du Baechel-Brunn
3, rte de Soultz.
Tel. 03 88 80 78 61. Fax 03 88 80 75 20.
beachelbrunn@wanadoo.fr
Closed Mon., Tue., 2 weeks end Jan., 2 weeks end Aug.
Prix fixe: 26€ (lunch), 38€, 50€, 65€.
A la carte: 51–58€.

The old family barn has become a modern inn with a bright, elegant, welcoming dining room that can boast of being one of the gastronomic shrines of Alsace. The know-how of Jean-Paul Limmacher, who trained at the Cheval Blanc, and the imaginative verve of Thomas, his son, a pupil of Bueherhiesel, do wonders with the best local seasonal products. Variations on the theme of foie gras, the pike-perch in thin slices of potato, the Alpilles lamb with *garrigue* herbs and the chocolate and garden mint parfait are good examples of this successful partnership. Your enjoyment will be rounded out by wines from a fine list presented by daughter-in-law Esther and by the highly affable service.

In Kutzenhausen (67250). 1 km n.
● Auberge du Puits
20, rte de Lobsann.
Tel. 03 88 80 76 58. Fax 03 88 80 75 91.
www.auberge-puits-6.com
Closed Mon., Tue., Wed. lunch, Jan.
Prix fixe: 34€, 41€, 48€, 60€, 8€ (child). A la carte: 45€–50€.

He is young and talented, his name is Alexandre Fender and his cooking is a heartwarming delight. Marie and Norbert

Koehler have created a gastronomic restaurant in this old café where the miners from the potassium mine used to gather to play *boules*. No effort is spared to offer a friendly welcome and incomparable service. Fine products and seasonal offerings, ranging from the Alsatian *terroir* to the four corners of the world, are some of Alexandre's secret ingredients to which he adds a hint of intuition. The cold fresh fromage blanc and shrimp soup, the curry-seasoned swordfish and the rack of lamb seasoned with masala spices are masterpieces. A lemon filled with fresh garden lemon balm sorbet is a divine suprise. This wake up call to the senses can be enjoyed without fear of spending a fortune.

▼	SHOPS

EAUX DE VIE

In Lobsann. 1.5 km from Merkwiller-Pechelbronn.

▼ Jean-Claude Hoeffler

7, rue des Jardins
Tel. 03 88 80 45 79.
www.distillerie-hoeffler.com

Jean-Claude Hoeffler distills spirits and liqueurs, keeping only the *cœur de chauffe* (the highest quality distillate). His fruit is meticulously chosen and the liqueurs in flavors like peach, crème de cassis, *sorbier* (sorbe-apple), blackberry or sour cherry are superb. The *alisier* (service berry), madder, quince, rosehip, wild raspberry and Marc de Muscat eaux de vie are perfect too.

MITTELBERGHEIM

67140 Bas-Rhin. Paris 500 – Sélestat 17 – Strasbourg 37 – Sélestat 20.

This exquisite Renaissance village on a knoll has two clock towers as well as hillsides of vineyards, including the zippy Zotzenberg which makes a wonderful Sylvaner. Meander through its streets and go knocking on cellar doors.

■●	HOTELS-RESTAURANTS

● Winstub Gilg

1, rte du Vin.
Tel. 03 88 08 91 37. Fax 03 88 08 45 17.

info@hotel-gilg.com
www.hotel-gilg.com
Closed beg. Jan.–beg. Feb.
Rest. closed Tue., Wed.
15 rooms: 45–85€.
Prix fixe: 20€, 45€, 70€, 11€ (child).
A la carte: 40€–45€.

This typical dwelling where regional culinary traditions excel sings an ode to Alsace. Two generations, Georges Gilg and his son-in-law Vincent Reuschlé, are firmly and expertly in charge of this establishment: a good example of the transmission of tastes and know-how of the *terroir*. The well-devised recipes are always topical. The delicious foie gras with truffle-infused jus in aspic, the exquisite monkfish medallions with curry-perfumed sesame seeds and the lamb medallion served over a ratatouille seasoned with wild thyme leaves a delicate taste in the mouth. The meal ends with a light ring-shaped savarin yeast cake soaked in Kirsch, served with fresh fruit, which is zingy and fresh. The wine list merits a detour and there are some regional steals for less than 25€ a bottle. The price is right and the pleasure is intense.

● Am Lindeplatzel `COM`

71, rue Principale.
Tel. 03 88 08 10 69. Fax 03 88 08 45 08.
Closed Mon. lunch, Wed. dinner, Thu.,
10 days at end Nov., 3 weeks Feb.,
10 days at end Aug.
Prix fixe: 29€, 34,50€, 52€, 10€ (child). A la carte: 54€.

A bit of here and a bit of there is what Patrick Durot looks for from his region and the rest of the world in order to concoct well-crafted dishes. It's hard to choose, once you've had the mixed greens, between sautéed shrimp with Chinese noodles or rack of lamb with thyme-infused jus, the chocolate fondant or a berry vacherin, but everything is worth a detour.

MITTELHAUSEN

67170 Bas-Rhin. Paris 475 – Strasbourg 20
– Saverne 22 – Haguenau 18.
This is the Kochersberg, with its large farms,
its fertile fields and a village with its old houses
and inscriptions painted on their facades.

 HOTELS-RESTAURANTS

■ **A l'Etoile**
12, rue de la Hey.
Tel. 03 88 51 28 44. Fax 03 88 51 24 79.
www.hotel-etoile.net
Hotel closed 2 weeks beg. Jan.
Rest. closed Sun. dinner, Mon.,
2 weeks beg. Jan., mid-July–beg. Aug.
24 rooms: 42–53€.
Prix fixe: 9,50€ (lunch), 17€, 26€, 30€, 35€.

Life is so pleasant here that one would like
to stay forever at the Bruckmanns. Chantal's welcome is charming, the prices are
very reasonable, the rooms little havens
of peace and Jacques' cooking, a delight.
Trained at Mischler at Lembach, he inter-
prets Alsatian recipes with brio: rabbit and
beer aspic terrine, pike-perch pot-au-feu
with cream sauce, lamb tenderloin and
the soft-centered chocolate cake are irreproachable. The lovely painting *l'Alsacien*
by Luc Hueber presides over this venera-
ble establishment.

MOLLKIRCH

67190 Bas-Rhin. Paris 450 – Strasbourg 41
– Molsheim 12 – Saverne 35 – Mutzig 8.
Brisk Vosges air between the Bruche valley and
the Grendelbruch mountains.

 HOTELS-RESTAURANTS

■ **Fischhutte** ⌂
30, rte de Grendelbruch.
Tel. 03 88 97 42 03. Fax 03 88 97 51 85.
fischhutte@wanadoo.fr
www.fischhutte.com
Closed 2 weeks end Feb.–mid-Mar., 1 week at
end June–beg. July Rest. closed Mon., Tue.
14 rooms: 54–74€. 2 suites: 90€.

Prix fixe: 13€ (dinner), 16€ (dinner), 32€,
45€ (wine inc.), 12€ (child).
A la carte: 44€.

Bernard Schahl greets occasional customers and regulars with a smile. The rooms
are cute and the cuisine pleasing. His generous poultry salad, spicy duck foie gras,
pike-perch filet with spring cabbage choucroute, leg of venison with mushrooms
and fresh fromage blanc tart meet with
great success. Jacky Bossuet advises on
wines with authority.

MOLSHEIM

67120 Bas-Rhin. Paris 475 – Strasbourg 28
– Sélestat 34.
infos@ot-molsheimmutzig.com.
The cars (Bugatti is from here), the wine (Brud-
erthal grand cru), the beauty of the monuments
(Metzig is a major Jesuit church): all contribute
to the soul and charm of this city in the round.

 HOTELS-RESTAURANTS

● **Diana**
14, rue Sainte-Odile.
Tel. 03 88 38 51 59. Fax 03 88 38 87 11.
info@hotel-diana.com
www.hotel-diana.com
Rest. closed Sun. dinner, New Year's.
55 rooms: 78–93€. 1 suite: 170€.
Prix fixe: 26€, 58€. A la carte: 45€.

Swimming pool, sauna and mini-fitness
center all add to the pleasure of a stay at
Christine and Michel Baly's contemporary establishment. Set in a one-and-a-
half-hectare park, spacious comfortable
rooms await the guests. At mealtimes,
Michel Knipilaire's menu makes your
mouth water. His overtly French cuisine
is deftly handled and allows a few esca-
pades abroad. Serrano ham with melon,
sea bream tagine with mild peppers, spice-
rubbed duck breast with orange-infused
fennel are pleasant surprises. Olive oil
ice cream served with spiced lace cookies
form a delicate conclusion. These dishes
are washed down with fine wines from
Alsace, Bordeaux or Barsac like château

Coutet, owned by the Balys. Exemplary welcome and service.

■ Le Bugatti

Rue de la Commanderie.
Tel. 03 88 49 89 00. Fax 03 88 38 36 00.
info@hotel-le-bugatti.com
www.hotel-le-bugatti.com
Closed 24 Dec.–2 Jan.
45 rooms: 47–53€.

Annex of the Diana, this modern establishment bears the name of the nearby car manufacturer and offers pleasant, moderately priced rooms in a modern setting.

● La Metzig

1, pl de l'Hôtel-de-Ville.
Tel. 03 88 38 26 24. Fax 03 88 49 36 27.
Closed Tue. dinner, Wed.
Prix fixe: 7,50€ (child). A la carte: 41€.

In the gothic cellars of this Renaissance house, you will be glad to try escargots, potato cakes, pike-perch with almonds, ham and cheese-stuffed veal escalope and the frozen Marc-flavored kouglof. Local wines flow from the source.

▼	SHOPS

PASTRIES

▼ Schaditzki

3, rue de Strasbourg.
Tel. 03 88 38 11 42.
Schaditzki's success dates from 1911. The old-style pastry dough is still manufactured using grandfather's recipe, for tradition is the trademark of Jean-Marie's son Christophe. Taste the chocolates, ice creams and mousses (three chocolates, raspberry, passion fruit, etc.).

WINE

▼ Vinifera

13, pl de la Liberté.
Tel. 03 88 38 07 06.
Wine grower and cellar man Robert Klingenfus recommends the right wine for each dish and sings the praises of his special favorites from every winegrowing region.

MORSBRONN-LES-BAINS

67360 Bas-Rhin. Paris 499 – Strasbourg 46 – Haguenau 11 – Wissembourg 28.
A picture postcard village set in the outer forest to be visited for its restorative properties and, as of now, a good table.

■/	HOTELS-RESTAURANTS

● Hôtel de la Marne et La Source des Sens

19, rte de Haguenau.
Tel. 03 88 09 30 53. Fax 03 88 09 35 65.
info@hoteldelamarne.com
www.hoteldelamarne.com
Closed 1 week beg. Nov., end Jan.–mid-Feb., 2 weeks July.
Rest. closed Sun. dinner, Mon.
13 rooms: 50–85€.
Prix fixe: 13,50€ (lunch), 22€, 40€, 60€, 13€ (child). A la carte: 55€–60€.

We had discovered Pierre Weller after his return home from his various experiences: Ducasse in Monaco, Bateau Ivre at Courchevel, Cheval Blanc at Lembach, Buerehiesel before Brazil and Japan as advised by Emile Jung. Now he's turned the interior of this establishment upside down, creating a large, modern dining room where he has preserved the pretty wood paneling but added contemporary seating and a screen which shows you what's going on in the kitchen. This restaurant pulls out all the stops and an inquisitive clientèle is beating down the doors. The tuna sashimi with foie gras beignet is the *amuse-bouche*; cep fricassée with sautéed artichokes in an arugula and green lentil salad and the sea bream with potato gnocchi with sausage and a pepper coulis are edging towards greatness. We also love the thick wedge of calf's liver in a hazelnut and pesto crust served with ratte fingerling potatoes and a lemon thyme jus and finally the thick-cut Iberian pork tenderloin grilled pink and juicy, served with an *al dente* risotto are nearing perfection. One reproach: desserts seem keener to transgress tradition than to provide pure pleasure, *viz à viz* chocolate mille-feuille (without pastry) with berries and a pepper sorbet and an upside-down tart (with phyllo, no short crust, no puff pastry, nor sweet pastry crust) with apricots, cardamom and pistachio. But youth must have its way…

MUHLBACH-SUR-MUNSTER

68380 Haut-Rhin. Paris 461 – Colmar 24 – Gérardmer 38 – Munster 6.
The Munster valley with its bucolic byways, fresh air and its farms-turned-inns where cheese dishes are still lovingly cooked the old way.

 | HOTELS-RESTAURANTS

■ Perle des Vosges

22, rte du Gaschney.
Tel. 03 89 77 61 34. Fax 03 89 77 74 40.
www.perledesvosges.net
Closed beg. Jan.–beg. Feb.
40 rooms: 40–73€. 5 suites: 106–117€.
Prix fixe: 13€, 65€, 8,50€ (child).

Ernest André Benz, formerly of Chapel, Jung and Ducasse, has come home to roost in this charming Vosgesian chalet perched on a hill. The rooms give onto the woods and the cuisine does honor to the region. In the Louis XII-style dining room, hikers and cross-country skiers are treated to escargot ravioli, pan-tossed rouget with herb-seasoned minced artichoke hearts and a veal cutlet served in an individual cocotte with mushrooms and spinach. The anisette-flambéed strawberries are a flamboyant dessert. One wants to return.

 | SHOPS

CHEESE

▼ Jean Meyer

2, chemin de Sendenbach.
Tel. 03 89 77 63 53.
Jean Meyer produces excellent farmhouse munsters and mountain tommes with his 20 dairy cows. Every morning, he opens his farm to visitors.

▼ Martin Sengelé

17, rue Sendenbach.
Tel. 03 89 77 77 00.
www.sengele.fr
We cannot fault Christophe Mettauer's emmenthal or munster—whether farmhouse or dairy, or with or without cumin.

MULHOUSE

68100 Haut-Rhin. Paris 464 – Strasbourg 117 – Bâle 35 – Colmar 43 – Belfort 42.
ot@ville-mulhouse.fr.
Mulhouse is probably sick and tired by now of its has-been and antiquated image of an "Alsatian Manchester". Mulhouse not Alsatian? Come now, there are *winstub*s or *"wistuwa"*, taverns serving fleischnacka, wines by the pitcher and a smart atmosphere. There are also those stars of the gastronomic arts, worthy of the region, be they named Jacques or the Bouton d'Or. But the museums alone would justify a visit here. From fine tables to good hotels (the Parc and her art deco appearance), this great Southern city opens wide its doors to each passing gourmet.

 | HOTELS

■ Le Parc

26, rue de la Sinne.
Tel. 03 89 66 12 22. Fax 03 89 66 42 44.
contact@hotelduparc-mulhouse.com
www.hotelduparc-mulhouse.com
79 rooms: 95–170€. 7 suites: 250–450€.

This 1930's grand hotel, with its lovely facade, is just across from theater. With its characterful entrance hall, period furniture, well-appointed rooms and white-marbled bathrooms, it ranks high. Charlie's bar is cozy and the Steinbach restaurant fancy. (See Restaurants.)

■ La Bourse

14, rue de la Bourse.
Tel. 03 89 56 18 44. Fax 03 89 56 60 51.
www.bestwestern.com/fr/hoteldelabourse
Closed 24 Dec.–31 Dec. (exc. groups).
46 rooms: 39–115€. 2 suites: 120–212€.
Half board: 54–150€.

After a stroll along the nearby Rhin-Rhône canal, we like to end up here, pampered by a thoughtful team in the oh-so comfortable rooms (some are themed) or in the little bar. Delicious breakfast served in an interior garden.

■ Bristol

18, av de Colmar.
Tel. 03 89 42 12 31. Fax 03 89 42 50 57.
lebristol@clubinternet.fr
www.hotelbristol.com
73 rooms: 55–120€. 10 suites: 75–250€.

Comfortable and practical: this is how to define this hotel strategically situated near the historic center and the town's various points of interest. The rooms offer you the possibility of languishing in a jaccuzi bathtub, while the art deco lounge is a relaxing spot.

■ Mercure-Centre

4, pl du Général-de-Gaulle.
Tel. 03 89 36 29 39. Fax 03 89 36 29 49.
H1264@accor.com
www.mercure.com
96 rooms: 105–125€.

To judge this hotel only by its 1970's-style facade would be a mistake because the rooms are well-conceived, the service and welcome are agreeable and the proximity to the railway station and the modern town, a plus. The Torpedo bar is pleasant.

■ Kyriad Mulhouse Centre

15, rue Lambert.
Tel. 03 89 66 44 77. Fax 03 89 46 30 66.
kyriad@hotel-mulhouse.com
www.hotel-mulhouse.com
60 rooms: 53–90€.

The Place de la Réunion is right next door to this city center hotel. The business rooms are roomy and functional. Fitness center with sauna and hammam.

In Froeningen (68720). 7 km sw via D8.

■ Auberge de Froeningen

2, rte d'Illfurth.
Tel. 03 89 25 48 48. Fax 03 89 25 57 33.
www.alsanet.com/froeningen
Closed Sun. dinner, Mon., Tue., 3 weeks Jan., mid-Aug.–1 Sept.
7 rooms: 55–65€.
Prix fixe: 13€ (lunch), 58€.

This typically Alsatian inn has a few ad hoc rooms, some with a balcony and a view of the village, the garden or the Ill. In the restaurant, Christophe does the region proud with goose foie gras in terrine, poached white halibut served on a bed of chanterelles vinaigrette, the signature Klapperstein beef tongue and the fresh figs poached in Pinot Noir, served with a verbena sorbet.

In Sausheim (68390). 6 km ne via N422A.

■ Mercure-Sausheim

N 422.
Tel. 03 89 61 87 87. Fax 03 89 61 88 40.
h0556@accor.com
www.mercure.com
98 rooms: 107–135€. 2 suites: 305€.

Situated next to the Peugeot factories, this hotel offers all the usual benefits of the chain. Everything is unsurprisingly classical except for the Alsatian décor and the eiderdowns on the beds. The swimming pool and tennis court are very welcome. The restaurant serves a local, down-to-earth cuisine.

●	RESTAURANTS

● Le Steinbach `V.COM`

At Le Parc, 26, rue de la Sinne.
Tel. 03 89 66 12 22. Fax 03 89 66 42 44.
www.hotelduparc-mulhouse.com
Closed Sat. lunch, Sun., mid-July–end Aug.
Prix fixe: 18€ (weekday lunch), 23€.
A la carte: 60€.

Cindy Lachaux is a newcomer to the stoves of this pretty art deco hotel where she composes a classical yet tuneful score with a slice of duck foie gras, steamed cod, a little nest of veal sweetbreads and Marc de Gewurztraminer sorbet. The menus are a steal and the service irreproachable.

● Il Cortile ◎COM

11, rue des Franciscains.
Tel. 03 89 66 39 79. Fax 03 89 36 07 97.
www.ilcortile-mulhouse.fr
Closed Sun., Mon., 2 weeks Jan., 20 Aug.–
beg. Sept.
Prix fixe: 23€, 35€, 52€.
A la carte: 60–65€.

Stefano D'Onghia knows how to play host at his table and how to plunge us into the heart of gastronomic Italy. Tried and true dishes are craftily interpreted, like the monkfish carpaccio, a cool tartare with balsamic or a rouget mille-feuille with eggplant caponata accompanied by sweet potato and banana ravioli. Then there's the veal saltimbocca, an herb- and rosemary-seasoned pasta and the raspberry tiramisu, fresh and creamy. The décor of the contemporary dining room has been revamped with charm and restraint.

● Le Poincaré Deux & le Bistro COM

6, porte de Bâle.
Tel. 03 89 46 00 24 / 03 89 06 16 65.
Fax 03 89 56 33 15.
Closed Sat., Sun.
Prix fixe: 19€, 35€, 10€ (child).
A la carte: 42–60€.

The second of its kind, Laurence and Renaud Chabrier's new Poincaré is a quality table where traditional cooking takes pride of place. Next door, the bistro is aptly named, offering well-cooked classics: the signature Jean Ducloux poultry liver terrine, scallops with "a thousand" caravan spices, beef with Bordelaise wine sauce served with bone marrow and the timeless Grand Marnier soufflé. It's simple, good and it works. The 1950's red and beige décor is wearing well.

● Restaurant de la Tour COM
de l'Europe

3, bd de l'Europe.
Tel. 03 89 45 12 14. Fax 03 89 56 18 28.
restaurant@tour-europe.com
Closed Mon.
Prix fixe: 25€, 28€, 34€.
A la carte: 42€.

One comes to the top of the Tour de l'Europe primarily for the unbeatable view over the town. The menus—especially the *terroir* menu—are worth the detour. The sliced escargots flambéed in Cognac, salmon escalope roasted with slices of foie gras, tender beef tenderloin and a soft frozen nougat do not lack skill.

● La Table de Michèle COM

16, rue de Metz.
Tel. 03 89 45 37 82.
michele.brouet@wanadoo.fr
Closed Sat. lunch, Sun., Mon.,
end Dec.–beg. Jan., 2 weeks Aug.
Prix fixe: 17€, 10€ (child).
A la carte: 55€.

Michèle Brouet, whom we encountered at the l'Auberge du Canon at Zillisheim, has turned this corner house into a modern and gourmand chalet. All of Mulhouse rendezvous here to taste the market-based cooking of this self-taught chef who is assisted by an enthusiastic, all-female team. Duck foie gras, grilled Mediterranean sea bass, oven-roasted lamb shank and figs poached in Port with a pain d'épice ice cream deliver what they promised as do wines selected by Michèle's daughter.

● La Tour de Jade COM

3, rue de Metz.
Tel. 03 89 66 10 18. Fax 03 89 66 00 79.
tourdejade@free.fr
www.tourdejade.com
Closed Mon.
Prix fixe: 9,60€ (lunch), 17,40€ (lunch),
20€ (lunch).
A la carte: 22–35€.

Sam Nang welcomes you with a smile to this exquisite Asiatic table. Chef Bora Dham scientifically concocts imperial pâté, spring roll, monkfish with spicy sauce, pork ribs and the Jade Tower cup, dedicated to the imperial Hué tower. Alsatian red, white or *rosé* wines or tea are available.

● Le Petit Zinc   SIM

15, rue des Bons-Enfants.
Tel. 03 89 46 36 78.
Closed Sun., 3 weeks Aug.,
Christmas–New Year's.
Prix fixe: 8,50€ (lunch).
A la carte: 35€.

The neo-1900 setting is a bit dated but the Weills still welcome the hoards of night-owls with a smile. We love Alain and Myriam's welcome. We also appreciate Claude Gresser's traditional cooking. The creamy split pea soup, trout with Riesling sauce, slow-cooked pork cheek and the frozen kouglof are washed down with some keen little wines. Agreeable service and reasonable prices.

● Au Fourneau des Halles   SIM

6, rue des Halles.
Tel.-Fax 03 89 66 57 07.
Closed Sat. lunch, Sun. lunch, Mon. dinner,
Christmas, 2 weeks beg. Aug.
Prix fixe: 7,50€ (weekday lunch), 18€,
6,90€ (child).
A la carte: 32€.

A lot of people file through this center city brasserie between 11:30 pm and 1:30 am. People meet up over the vineyard-keeper's salad, pike-perch simmered in sparkling wine, sirloin steak with pepper and the apple tart. A dynamic atmosphere and a generous cuisine.

● Aux Caves du Vieux Couvent   SIM

23, rue du Couvent.
Tel. 03 89 46 28 79. Fax 03 89 66 47 87.
philippe-thuet@wanadoo.fr
www.cavesduvieuxcouvent.com
Closed Sun. dinner, Mon., Wed. dinner,
1 week Christmas–New Year's.
Prix fixe: 11€, 16€ (wine inc.), 26€ (wine inc.), 19€, 6€ (child).
A la carte: 35€.

Philippe Thuet pays homage to the city and its traditions in his cellars. The walls are decorated with frescoes detailing the history of Mulhouse. Typical dishes include country-style head cheese in aspic terrine, fish choucroute, veal kidneys with Pinot Noir sauce and Beerawecka-flavored ice cream, which are simple and delicious.

● La Bruschetta   SIM

1, rue de Mittelbach.
Tel. 03 89 45 22 62. Fax 03 89 56 49 57.
Closed Sun., Mon.
Prix fixe: 12,50€ (lunch), 14€ (lunch).
A la carte: 38–51€.

Lino Rodi runs this modern trattoria with verve, offering Italian cooking based on market availability. One is regaled with the octopus carpaccio, swordfish with honey and balsamic sauce, saltimbocca with risotto and tiramisu. The minimalist décor with its ivory and sky-blue tablecloths is very restful. Wines can be had by the glass and the bill is not hefty.

● Winstub Henriette   SIM

9, rue Henriette.
Tel. 03 89 46 27 83.
Closed Sun., Mon., Bank holidays, Christmas.
Prix fixe: 7,62€ (weekday lunch).
A la carte: 34€.

Marie-Christine Musslin is everywhere, from the dining room to the kitchen, from the cellar to the terrace. Her center city *winstub* attracts a cheerful clientèle with good appetites. Munster cheese in puff pastry with crunchy vegetables, salmon filet on a bed of sauerkraut, local potato and meat casserole served with green salad and the apple streudel breathe sincerity.

● Zum Mehlala   SIM

7, rue d'Illzach.
Tel. 03 89 59 41 32.
Closed Sun., Mon.
Prix fixe: 9€ (child). A la carte: 25–30€.

One loses track of time in this inn. Marie-Thérèse Reithinger knows how to please her clients who are mad for her tartes flambées (local flat pies, often with cream and bacon), fleischschnaka (meat-filled hand-rolled pasta), bibelekäs (fresh fromage blanc and herbs), not to mention sauerkraut, chicken liver salad and the broiled steak, all good ideas. The rhubarb soup is light after all those rich dishes. Reasonable prices.

● **Zum'Sauwadala** SIM

13, rue de l'Arsenal.
Tel. 03 89 45 18 19. Fax 03 89 46 16 09.
www.restaurant-sauwadala.com
Closed Sun., Mon. lunch.
Prix fixe: 9,40€ (lunch), 16€ (lunch), 25€.
A la carte: 35€.

An unpronounceable name but filled with humor. Jacques Serpin's place is warm and does honor to regional cooking. The tender onion tart, vineyard-keeper's salad, a three-fish choucroute, baeckeofe (a local meat and potato casserole), Fleur de Bière sorbet and the frozen kouglof are typical and well made. The atmosphere is convivial and the bill just right.

In Dornach (68200). 3 km nw
● **Au Canon d'Or** SIM

40, rue de Belfort.
Tel. 03 89 43 50 63. Fax 03 89 42 61 76.
Closed Sat. lunch, Sun. dinner, Mon. dinner,
1 week Christmas–New Year's, 3 weeks July.
Prix fixe: 11€ (weekday lunch),
21,50€ (weekdays).
A la carte: 55€.

Gilles Reeb leaves nothing to chance, supplying himself from producers he knows and preparing the classic recipes which have gained him his reputation. Along with his wife Marie-Laure, he breathes life into this old 1686 coaching inn with its pleasant boLudeis interior. Feast on the foie gras trilogy (with pain d'épice, with Sichuan pepper, pan-seared), the stuffed poached sole with white sauce, mushrooms, truffles and lobster, the pigeon with chanterelle and trumpet mushrooms and the vanilla crème brûlée. A smiling, sincere welcome.

In Illzach-Modenheim (68110). 5 km ne via
D422.
● **La Closerie** V.COM

6, rue Henry-de-Crousaz.
Tel. 03 89 61 88 00. Fax 03 89 61 95 49.
restaurant.closerie@wanadoo.fr
www.la-closerie.fr

Closed Sat. lunch, Sun., Mon. dinner, Christmas–New Year's, mid-July–beg. Aug.
Prix fixe: 35€, 40€, 50€, 12€ (child).
A la carte: 57€.

A bourgeois interior but full of fantasy, light and warmth. Hubert Beyrath offers some gourmet moments over serious dishes concocted by Bertrand Sicard. The goose foie gras terrine with slow-cooked pear, fresh pasta gratin with broad beans served with rolled lobster claw, beef filet with bone marrow and red wine sauce served with a potato cake and the delicious lemon mille-feuille show off a mastery of cooking times and skills. The wine list is hefty, the menus well-planned and the service diligent.

In Riedisheim (68400). 2 km.
● **Le Relais de la Poste** V.COM

7, rue du Général-de-Gaulle.
Tel. 03 89 44 07 71. Fax 03 89 64 32 79.
contact@restaurant-kieny.co
www.restaurant-kieny.com
Closed Sun. dinner, Mon., Tue. lunch, Feb.
vac., end July–mid-Aug.
Prix fixe: 27€, 37€, 57€, 80€.

The Kienys have been in this house since the middle of the 19th century. Jean-Marc, the latest of that name, offers a cuisine that is not afraid to be innovative. A vegetable tarte with pepper raspberry sorbet, the "local fair"-style waffle with potatoes and marinated minced salmon, the grilled John Dory served with an escargot, parsley and garlic ragout, catfish filet meunière served with butter, stir fried vegetables with fresh ginger, the slice of goose foie gras served hot, as well as the veal medallions in paupiette with peppercorn-seasoned jus, are artfully honed dishes. The chic, paneled tavern, decorated in coaching inn style, is warmly welcoming. The desserts, a "sweet version of Alsatian traditions" or a "revamped Black Forest cake", are tasty and thoughtful. The cellar tempts and Mariella Kieny is a fine hostess.

In Riedisheim.

● **Auberge de la Tonnelle** `COM`

61, rue du Maréchal-Joffre.
Tel. 03 89 54 25 77. Fax 03 89 64 29 85.
Closed Sun. dinner, Wed.
Prix fixe: 25€ (lunch), 38€, 45€, 78€.
A la carte: 65–70€.

Roland Burger has filled this famous establishment in a suburb of Riedsheim with warmth. You can feel the efforts being made so that customers will leave happy and contented. Business men have their lunch habits and there are lots of faithful clients at the weekend. Each and every one appreciates the variations on theme of foie gras, the catch of the day, a rack of Limousin lamb and a Tasmanian chocolate dessert. A convivial atmosphere and prompt and serious service. The menu prices are acceptable.

In Rixheim (68170). 6 km se via N66.

● **Le Manoir Runser** `V.COM`

65, av du Général-de-Gaulle.
Tel. 03 89 31 88 88. Fax 03 89 31 88 89.
info@runser.fr
www.runser.fr
Closed Sun., Mon.
Prix fixe: 20€, 40€, 50€, 70€.
A la carte: 55–68€.

This large, grand manor house set in the middle of parkland not far from Mulhouse is light and airy—a white facade on the outside and yellow tones on the inside—with a refined elegance that perfectly suits Eric Runser's cooking. This is a cuisine which, along with a great deal of precision and sincerity, depends on quality produce to express the best of itself. We praise the subtlety and richness of the flavors developed by the "Sentier des Saveurs" menu or à la carte, the salmon and lobster tartare, curry-seasoned scallops, the squab baked in a crust and the apricot streudel. This is meticulous work, good to look at as well as to eat, improved by a wine list which gives pride of place to Alsatian wines but also has other offerings fom France and elsewhere. Service is very attentive.

In Rixheim.

● **Le Petit Prince** `SIM`

100, rue de l'Aérodrome.
Tel. 03 89 64 24 85. Fax 03 89 64 05 21.
Closed Sun., Mon., 1 week Christmas–New Year's, end Aug.–beg. Sept.
Prix fixe: 32€, 42€, 52€.

You could stop by Laurent and Stéphanie Haller's every month and not find the same dish twice. Laurent regularly offers a new theme on which he imposes seasonal products. These can be the tartares, fresh hay, apple or chocolate, but there's always a surprise in the flavors. His work on the preparations, aromas, fruits, or vegetables, with recipes from here and elsewhere, is constant and works its charm. The sole served on a stone from the Rhine river, accompanied by a slice of seaweed-seasoned rice cake with oyster, hot wine and vinegar sauce, pan-roasted veal wrapped in a bamboo leaf with smoked tea, served with a shiitake noodle gratin and the fried ball of crème brûlée with wild blueberries refreshed with a yogurt sorbet reveal a huge overflow of ideas. Prices are measured and the welcome friendly.

In Zimmersheim (68440). 5 km s toward Bâle via rte du parc zoologique.

● **Jules** `V.COM`

65, rue de Mulhouse.
Tel. 03 89 64 37 80. Fax 03 89 64 03 86.
info@restojules.fr
www.restojules.fr
Closed Sat., Sun., 2 weeks Feb., 2 weeks Aug.
Prix fixe: 19€ (lunch).

The setting is warmly friendly and the dishes are written up in chalk on a blackboard. Juliette, aka "Jules" and Philippe Breitenstein run this village inn with energy and talent. They value fresh produce and follow the seasons. Bistro dishes (variety meat plate, wonderful tripe simmered in Riesling, chitterling sausage) find great favor.

▼	SHOPS

BREAD & BAKED GOODS

▼ Belépi

10, rue Wilson.

Tel. 03 89 45 49 68.

A range of pastries, including pain au chocolate, in unusual flavors such as chocolate-banana, chocolate-almond, raisin, chocolate chip or cinnamon are the star attractions here.

BREAD, BAKED GOODS & PASTRIES

▼ Diebold

18, pl de la Réunion / 9, rue de Provence.

Tel. 03 89 44 52 45.

Mathieu Diebold delights us with brioches topped with almonds, soft chocolate maréchal, "Rachel" (apple compote, streusel) and loaves with sesame, poppyseeds, walnuts and raisin, rye or beer.

BUTCHER

▼ Habegger

151, rue de Bâle.

Tel. 03 89 44 41 38.

The meats selected from the finest livestock farms (Limousin veal, beef from Charolais) and the homemade products here (smoked bacon, pork shoulder and sausages) are delicious and well chosen.

CHARCUTERIE

▼ Maurer Frères

24 et 42, rue du Sauvage.

Tel. 03 89 52 21 11.

Philippe Hazout and André Roth present dependably good pâté baked in pastry crust, smoked ham, sausages, foie gras and kassler.

▼ Tempé

16, rue de l'Ile-Napoléon.

Tel. 03 89 64 57 70.

www.tempe.fr

Smoked ham, knacks, country bacon, liver sausages, pistachio galantine and cervelas are accompanied by fine meats (veal from Corrèze, Charolais beef, Bresse poultry and lamb from Poitou).

CHEESE

▼ Au Bouton d'Or

5, pl de la Réunion.

Tel. 03 89 45 50 17.

Marc Schell selects young farm cheeses that he matures himself. Aged gruyère, fruity beaufort, reblochon, creamy saint-marcellin, saint-nectaire or munster are top quality.

CHOCOLATE

▼ La Chocothèque

7, pl de la Réunion.

Tel. 03 89 45 62 45.

Quality chocolates and homemade candies are the delicious sweet treats supplied by Camilla and Laurence Baldeck.

COFFEE

▼ Au Bon Nègre

22, rue du Sauvage.

Tel. 03 89 45 15 13.

Customers enjoy beverages and light dishes on the second floor, while the store purveys roasted coffees, teas and choice jams.

PASTRIES

▼ Carlos

26, rue Engel-Dollfus.

Tel. 03 89 42 16 06.

Christiane Ferragut and his bittersweet chocolates, lace cookies with rosemary or lavender, artisanal almond paste, fruit tarts and superb triple-chocolate cake never disappoint.

▼ Claude Helfter

27, passage Central.

Tel. 03 89 56 00 88.

The praliné feuillantine and the kouglof are still the star attractions here, but the panettone with dried fruit, chocolate panettone, pâté baked in a pastry crust, puits d'amour (small, round pastry filled with cream, jelly or fruit), Opéra (square, iced chocolate cake), guanaja chocolates and jams also feature in good place on the bill.

▼ Jacques
50-52, av d'Altkirch.
Tel. 03 89 44 27 32.
www.patisserie-jacques.com
The "Prince de Bollwerk", "*mini-suprême*", raspberry mille-feuille and manjari chocolate dessert are the specialties of this master confectioner. Montmorency cake (almond cream with kirsch-soaked cherries), raspberry tart, duchesse (nut and chocolate petit fours), peach-cinnamon dessert and the "*rêve noir*" hold few secrets for Michel Bannwarth.

In Riedisheim. 2 km.
▼ Laurent Kiény
3, rue du Général-de-Gaulle.
Tel. 03 89 54 04 99.
Laurent Kieny is a master of traditional pastry. His "diamant noir", his Black Forest cake, his ganaches, his Swiss apple tart and his kouglof are enchanting.

FRESH PRODUCE
▼ Les Petites Halles
22, rue du Sauvage.
Tel. 03 89 45 20 68.
The produce on display in this store is fresh and colorful: the papayas, pineapples, kiwis, mangos and other exotic fruits, chives, chervil and vegetables are at the peak of their form.

IMPORTED PRODUCTS
▼ Au Village Italien
34, rue Henriette.
Tel. 03 89 56 27 72.
In Mulhouse, Franka Sestito champions Italy and its finest produce (homemade fresh pastas, basil ravioli, ham, seafood or foie gras).

REGIONAL PRODUCTS
▼ Au Bretzel Chaud
176, rue de Belfort / 12, rue Mercière.
Tel. 03 89 46 65 22 / 03 89 66 93 23.
Paul Poulaillon, king of the pretzel, provides sublime moricettes (traditional savory pastries), Black Forest cake, duck mousse and Danish salami.

TABLETOP & KITCHENWARE
▼ La Boutique du Musée de l'Impression sur Etoffes
14, rue Jean-Jacques-Henner.
Tel. 03 89 46 83 01.
www.musee-impression.com
Tablecloths, doilies, handkerchiefs and other fine cotton creations are on offer in this store next to the museum.

▼ Muller-Ott
10, rue Henriette.
Tel. 03 89 45 30 93.
This town center emporium presents the finest tableware. The Haviland, Wedgwood and Mikasa china, Christofle, Erquis and Deetjen cutlery, and Baccarat and Sèvres carafes are competitively priced.

◆	RENDEZVOUS

BAR
◆ Le Charlie's Bar
In the Hôtel du Parc. 26, rue de la Sinne.
Tel.-Fax 03 89 66 12 22.
www.hotelduparc-mulhouse.com
In an art deco ambience opposite the theater, the city's chic set gathers for a cocktail in this piano bar.

BEER BAR
◆ O'Brian
5, pl des Victoires.
Tel. 03 89 56 25 58.
The paneled setting is warm in winter and cool in summer. Customers choose from the 15 beers on offer and enjoy a salad or light dish.

CAFES
◆ Le Guillaume-Tell
1, rue Guillaume-Tell.
Tel. 03 89 46 68 84.
As we sip a beer or an espresso, we soak up the charm of this historic former home, now a café on the most beautiful square in the city.

◆ Le Moll

6, pl de la République.
Tel. 03 89 66 59 23.
Opposite the square and its Charles X colonnades, the terrace of this café is the perfect place to enjoy a coffee or beer, or savor a fresh moricette (traditional savory pastry).

TEA SALONS

◆ Le Café Viennois

7, rue Henriette.
Tel.-Fax 03 89 66 07 54.
Aside from Jean-Marc Meyer's most flavorsome pastries (strudel, linzer torte, or tarte flambée), this polychromatic tearoom presents appealing dishes at lunch and dinner time.

◆ Claude Helfter

27, passage Central.
Tel. 03 89 56 00 88.
www.helfter.fr
The sweet delicacies served here make it well worth a visit. Chocolate panettone, old-fashioned pâté in pastry, "ducs d'Alsace" and feuillantine are meticulously prepared with an eye to tradition.

◆ Vertiges de Baalbek

6, rue des Trois-Rois.
Tel.-Fax 03 89 45 15 11.
Simon El Zoghbi's welcoming establishment offers a Middle Eastern décor and cuisine.

MUNSTER

68140 Haut-Rhin. Paris 443 – Colmar 19 – Mulhouse 57 – Strasbourg 89 – Saint-Dié 53.
tourisme-munster@wanadoo.fr.
This great Protestant town has risen from the ashes of World War II without sacrificing its austere style. Here is the gateway to nearby trails, the valley, pastureland and forests.

■ HOTELS-RESTAURANTS

■ Hôtel Verte Vallée

10, rue Alfred-Hartmann.
Tel. 03 89 77 15 15. Fax 03 89 77 17 40.

verte.vallee@wanadoo.fr
www.vertevallee.com
Closed beg. Jan.–beg. Feb.
100 rooms: 77–115€. 7 suites: 160€.
Prix fixe: 22€, 29€, 36€, 49€.

Set in tranquil parkland on the banks of the Fecht, this hotel near the city center has many assets: huge, light rooms, a fitness center, swimming pool, an aqua-gym course, hammam, Jacuzzi, conference rooms and WiFi. And if you want to get away from it all, two mountain chalets for six people each. The cooking highlights regional products and isn't half bad. On the menu, the duck foie gras with Port, smoked pike-perch served on a bed of choucroute, venison medallions served with a mushroom and foie gras cake and the lightly cooked cherry tartelette served with house ice creams are most pleasurable. Yvon Gauthier, who used to be a sommelier on the Côte d'Azur, presides over 400 different wines.

● L'Alsacienne `SIM`

1, rue du Dôme.
Tel. 03 89 77 43 49. Fax 03 89 77 58 52.
Closed Tue. dinner, Wed., 10 days Sept., 10 days Mar., 10 days June.
Prix fixe: 8,50€ (weekday lunch), 13,50€, 27,50€. A la carte: 30€.

A kindly house where—late into the night—you can enjoy typical Alsatian dishes lovingly cooked by Etienne Claude-Pierre. Inexpensive Munster quiche with salad, pike-perch filet, boneless pork trotter stuffed in the house style and the chocolate cake cut quite a dash.

● La Schlitte `SIM`

7, rue de la République.
Tel. 03 89 77 50 35.
bschlitte@hotmail.com
Closed Mon., Tue. dinner, 1 week beg. Jan., 2 weeks June July.
Prix fixe: 12,90€ (weekday lunch), 16€, 22,50€, 7,50€ (child). A la carte: 30€.

Delmina welcomes you with a smile while Bruno Savary cooks to please his guests. He delights them with Munster tourte, basil-seasoned salmon and braised ham shank with potato salad, a house specialty.

In Wihr-au-Val (68230). 6 km via D417 E.

● **La Nouvelle Auberge**

9, rte Nationale.
Tel. 03 89 71 07 70. Fax 03 89 71 08 97.
www.nauberge.com
Closed Sun. dinner, Mon., Tue., Nov. 1 vac.,
Christmas, Feb. vac., 1 week beg. July.
Prix fixe: 25€, 29,50€.

Simple fare has its merits. The proof: this old road stop run by Bernard Leray. In the rustic dining room, this former disciple of Bernard Loiseau puts his heart into a pigeon pâté in pastry, pike-perch with red wine sauce, braised kidneys with shallots and a vanilla cream dessert bursting with sincerity. These are well-cooked dishes, genuine and fresh.

▼	SHOPS

CHARCUTERIE

▼ **Daniel Jacquat**

44, Grand-Rue.
Tel. 03 89 77 90 65.
Daniel Jacquat keeps a close eye on production here. His baeckeofe, choucroute, local tortes, malkerbangel and traditional Alsatian charcuterie are well worth tasting.

CHOCOLATE & PASTRIES

▼ **Gilg**

11, Grand-Rue.
Tel. 03 89 77 37 56.
www.patisserie-gilg.fr
This store has been in the Gilg family for a long time, but Thierry, the son, has broken with tradition, offering "délice du marcaire" (shortbread, almond cream) and "le caprice du moine" (almond and hazelnut cream with blackberry compote on a shortbread biscuit).

68530 Haut-Rhin. Paris 470 – Strasbourg 103 – Colmar 28 – Mulhouse 26 – Guebwiller 5.
Secret paths through the Vosges forest: byways to stroll down, a Romanesque abbey in pink stone and a gourmet address.

	HOTELS-RESTAURANTS

■ **Saint-Barnabé**

53, rue de Murbach.
Tel. 03 89 62 14 14. Fax 03 89 62 14 15.
hostellerie.st.barnabe@wanadoo.fr
www.hostellerie-st-barnabe.com
Rest. closed Sun. dinner.
24 rooms: 56–150€. 3 suites: 183€.
Prix fixe: 13€ (lunch), 21€, 38€, 65€,
12€ (child). A la carte: 41–54€.

Right in the heart of the forest of the Vosges, Eric and Clémence Orban's hotel seduces one with its charm, the warmth of its welcome and the refined talent of the chef who has worked at the château d'Isenbourg at Rouffach. A thin vegetable tartelette with Scottish salmon, seafood platter with foamy butter mousseline and spiny artichokes, farm-raised quail with pan-tossed chanterelles and a gently spiced dessert with fennel seed-infused creamy caramel and raspberry sauce are scaling the heights. Not so the prices which remain reasonable.

■ **Domaine Langmatt**

Locale known as Domaine Langmatt.
Tel. 03 89 76 21 12. Fax 03 89 74 88 77.
info@domainelangmatt.com
www.domainelangmatt.com
Closed 1 week Apr.
Rest. closed Mon. lunch.
21 rooms: 96–190€.
Prix fixe: 28€, 63€. A la carte: 46–62€.

The *ballon* of the Vosges is the background of this hotel where you come to breathe the the air. Aside from the comfortable rooms, the swimming pool, sauna and fitness center will ensure you get into shape here. The table honors the region with mountain-cured ham, trout with almonds, sirloin steak with morels and the incontrovertible dessert made with Langmatt digestive liqueur.

MUTZIG

67190 Bas-Rhin. Paris 478 – Obernai 12 – Strasbourg 28 – Saverne 31.
A fortified gateway, the proximity of the Vosges and wine but no longer, alas, any beer. Only the name lives on.

 HOTELS-RESTAURANTS

■ Hostellerie de la Poste

4, pl de la Fontaine.
Tel. 03 88 38 38 38. Fax 03 88 49 82 05.
hostellerie.pfeiffer@wanadoo.fr
www.hostellerie-la-poste.com
Closed mid-Nov.–end Nov. Rest. closed Mon.
17 rooms: 44–55€.
Prix fixe: 8€ (weekday lunch), 18€, 30€, 9,50€ (child). A la carte: 36€.

This half-timbered Alsatian house with its tasteful rooms breathes authenticity. The local cuisine is one of quality: witness the duck terrine with crunchy spring vegetables, sea trout with crayfish, sirloin steak with Roquefort and the chocolate charlotte with coffee sauce. The local wines make good companions to the food.

■ L'Ours de Mutzig

Pl de la Fontaine.
Tel. 03 88 47 85 55. Fax 03 88 47 85 56.
hotel@loursdemutzig.com
www.loursdemutzig.com
47 rooms: 49–84€.
Prix fixe: 15€ (weekday lunch), 18€, 25€, 9€ (child). A la carte: 33€.

The rooms are charming and squeaky clean; the house is decorated around a bear theme. The cooking is faithful to the *terroir*. Escargots prepared in the style of Alsace (stuffed with spiced butter and herbs and cooked in local wine), pikeperch simmered in Riesling and served over noodles, beer-braised pork cheeks with fromage blanc quenelles and the

apple streudel with cinnamon ice cream are infinitely edible.

● Au Nid de Cigogne   SIM

25, rue du 18-Novembre.
Tel.-Fax 03 88 38 11 97.
Closed Sat. lunch, Wed.
A la carte: 36€.

Cédric Zimmermann is alone at the helm of this old tavern that was once the canteen of the workers from the local brewery. He is quality conscious and, seated next to the pretty green stove, you'll enjoy pork cheeks in aspic, grilled scallops and Atlantic sea bass with chanterelles, goose breast served on sauerkraut with pan-seared foie gras and the profiteroles served hot with vanilla ice cream. Saturday and Sunday night, tartes flambées take pride of place.

▼ SHOPS

PASTRIES

▼ Keller

33, rue du Maréchal-Foch.
Tel. 03 88 38 13 90.
His kouglof has won a regional award and the "*grès des Vosges*" chocolate, pear soufflé, Black Forest cake and streusel are much to Fernand Keller's credit.

▼ Oppé

29, rue du Maréchal-Foch.
Tel. 03 88 38 13 21.
Maestro of confection in its most elegant, traditional form, Jean-Pierre Oppé wins us round with his excellent soft kirsch cake, fruit tart, strawberry feuilleté, chocolate-caramel mousse, hazelnut "hedgehog", ice creams, sorbets and ganaches.

NEUF-BRISACH

68600 Haut-Rhin. Paris 464 – Colmar 16 –
Sélestat 31 – Mulhouse 39 – Bâle 62.
Built by Vauban, the walls remain intact, but
the town is new. The frontier still lies close by.

 HOTELS-RESTAURANTS

In Vogelgrün (68600). 3 km e via N415.
■ **L'Européen**
Ile du Rhin.
Tel. 03 89 72 51 57. Fax 03 89 72 74 54.
rene.daegele@wanadoo.fr
www.europeen-hotel.com
Closed mid-Jan.–mid-Feb.
40 rooms: 98–124€. 5 suites: 98–220€.
Prix fixe: 20€, 37€, 70€. A la carte: 55€.

On the Rhine, just a step away from the
German border, this motel belonging to
the Daegelé family has large, bright, modern rooms, a fitness center, swimming
pool, fine terrace and choice restaurant. In
the traditional dining room, foie gras, the
red wine stew with five varieties of fish, the
beef filet with a béarnaise sauce and the
crème brûlée are right on target.

In Vogelgrün.
■ **Le Caballin**
Ile du Rhin.
Tel. 03 89 72 56 56. Fax 03 89 72 95 00.
leranch@lecaballin.fr
www.lecaballin.fr
Closed Christmas–New Year's.
20 rooms: 53–73€.
Prix fixe: 18€, 25€, 34€, 10€ (child).
A la carte: 30–45€.

Set in a riding center, Roland Schmidt's
hotel has well-equipped rooms in orange
and burgundy tones. In the restaurant,
the view over the lake is delightful and
the regional cuisine is good. We enjoy the
frog legs, pike-perch poached in Riesling,
duck breast with pink peppercorns and
the frozen Kouglof.

NIEDERBRONN-LES-BAINS

67110 Bas-Rhin. Paris 451 – Saverne 39 –
Strasbourg 54 – Haguenau 22.
office@niederbronn.com.
The "Marienbad of Alsace" offers thermal
baths, pure springs and the delicious air of
the Northern Vosges mountains. Congeniality,
flowers and the fresh waters of the Steinbach
set the scene in this restful halt.

 HOTELS-RESTAURANTS

■ **Mercure Grand Hôtel**
16, av Foch.
Tel. 03 88 80 84 48. Fax 03 88 80 84 40.
H5548@accor-hotels.com
www.mercure.com
59 rooms: 75–95€. 4 suites: 114–130€.
Half board: 93–131€.

The fifties charm is a thing of the past:
this hotel now conforms to the chain's
codes: a professional reception, modern
rooms and suites and tennis courts.

■ **Muller**
16, av de la Libération.
Tel. 03 88 63 38 38. Fax 03 88 63 38 39.
hotel.muller@wanadoo.fr
www.hotelmuller.com
Closed 3 weeks Jan.
Rest. closed Sun. dinner, Mon.
43 rooms: 47–68,50€.
Prix fixe: 9,50€ (weekday lunch), 8€ (child).

This good, classical hotel appeals with
its woodwork, beige tones, warm welcome, swimming pool, fitness center
and spacious rooms. In a dining room
with veranda, we savor the escalope of
goose foie gras with apricot pain perdu,
house-smoked salmon, pike-perch with
sorrel, medallions of venison and frozen
kouglof.

■ Cully

35, rue de la République.
Tel. 03 88 09 01 42. Fax 03 88 09 05 80.
hotel-cully@wanadoo.fr
www.hotel-cully.fr
Rest. closed Sun. dinner, Mon., Feb. vac.
33 rooms: 46–65€. 2 suites: 65€.
Prix fixe: 11€ (weekday lunch), 20€, 30€,
8€ (child).

Located in a busy street, this hotel
housed in two buildings has an antique
charm. The rooms are simple and neat,
and offer a range of styles and colors. In
the paneled dining room, Daniel Cully
prepares an improvised regional cuisine. House goose foie gras, smoked
ham, fresh poached trout "*au bleu*", the
vineyard-keeper's guinea hen (wrapped
in grape leaves) and an iced vacherin
(a meringue and nougat dessert) are
shrewdly crafted.

■ Bristol

4, pl de l'Hôtel-de-Ville.
Tel. 03 88 09 61 44. Fax 03 88 09 01 20.
hotel.lebristol@wanadoo.fr
www.lebristol.com
Closed 2 weeks Nov., mid-Jan.–beg. Feb.
27 rooms: 45–80€. 2 suites: 70–90€.
Prix fixe: 9€ (weekday lunch), 15€ (weekday lunch), 20€ (lunch), 25€ (dinner), 8€
(child).

This year, Claude Foeller has opened
five new rooms in addition to the hotel's
older, efficiently soundproofed accommodation. Equipped with wooden furnishings, they offer an easy charm. In
the bright, beige-tinted dining room, we
savor Claude Foeller's cuisine. The dozen
escargots prepared in the style of Alsace
(stuffed with spiced butter and herbs and
cooked in local wine), vegetable-stuffed
pike-perch, lamb chops with rosemary
and honey and a frozen kouglof with
sauce are very honest.

● La Villa du Parc

At the Casino, 10, pl des Thermes.
Tel. 03 88 80 84 88. Fax 03 88 80 84 86.
www.casinodeniederbronn.com/events
Closed Christmas.
Prix fixe: 20€ (weekday dinner),
25€ (weekday dinner).
A la carte: 42€.

The casino's two restaurants provide
different options. The first serves exotic
dishes in neocolonial surroundings,
while the second offers a chance to sam-
ple regional recipes in a *bierstub* atmosphere. Clear consommé sprinkled with
coriander, a jumbo shrimp and vegetable stir fry, Mexican-style beef tenderloin with peppers and guacamole and
the Guauaquil chocolate truffle with
milk caramel ice cream offer an entertaining range of exotic flavors.

▼ SHOPS

BREAD & BAKED GOODS

▼ Marcel Vandhammer
32, rue de la République.
Tel. 03 88 09 02 73.
A baker's store where the special breads,
biscuits topped with fruit or pastry
cream and the sweet pastries are well
worth a visit.

PASTRIES

▼ Pascal Mary
31, rue du Général-de-Gaulle.
Tel. 03 88 09 74 68.
Sébastien Mary has taken over the family *pâtisserie*, where he offers a fresh take
on Black Forest cake, apricot nougat pastry, passion fruit dessert, hazelnut Santa
Maria, bûches and dacquoises.

NIEDERHASLACH

67280 Bas-Rhin. Paris 479 – Saverne 32 –
Strasbourg 39.
With the Gothic church and its 135-foot spire, the
Grand Ringelsberg crowning the village nearby
and the Nideck ruins that inspired Chamisso, a
rich tapestry lies at the end of the street.

HOTELS-RESTAURANTS

■ La Pomme d'Or

36, rue Principale.
Tel. 03 88 50 90 21. Fax 03 88 50 95 17.
lapommeniederh@wanadoo.fr
http://monsite.wanadoo.fr-lapommedor
Closed Sat. lunch, Sun. dinner, Mon.,
2 weeks Mar., 10 days July.
19 rooms: 32–47€.
Prix fixe: 10,70€, 20€, 25€.

Pierre Abelhauser's establishment is pleasant indeed. Its flowered facade and sober but neat, traditionally furnished rooms in blue and green tones go well with the market-based cuisine at gentle prices.

NIEDERMORSCHWIHR

68230 Haut-Rhin. Paris 444 – Colmar 7 – Les Trois-Epis 5.
Perched above the vines and clinging to the Vosges mountains, this winegrowing village is famous for its houses with oriel windows and inclined church bell tower, as well as its taverns and star confectioner.

HOTELS-RESTAURANTS

■ Hôtel de l'Ange

125, rue des Trois-Epis.
Tel. 03 89 27 05 73. Fax 03 89 27 01 44.
hotel-ange@wanadoo.fr
www.hotelange.fr
Closed 10 days Nov., Jan.–Easter.
20 rooms: 50–62€.
Prix fixe: 12€, 20€, 8€ (child).
A la carte: 35–45€.

In the heart of the village, the Boxler and Wiss families' half-timbered establishment is well worth a visit. Its rooms are inviting with their fine woodwork and antique furniture. There is no longer a hotel restaurant, but there are many *winstubs* nearby.

● Caveau Morakopf SIM

7, rue des Trois-Epis.
Tel. 03 89 27 05 10. Fax 03 89 27 08 63.
caveau.morakopf@wanadoo.fr
Closed Sun., Mon. lunch, 1 week Jan.,
1 week Mar., 1 week Nov.
A la carte: 40€.

This celebrated basement eatery on the wine route still has its appeal. Anne Guidat's smiling welcome, the cozy décor, the stained glass decorated with the Moor's head that gives the place its name, the rear terrace and the regional dishes prepared by Chantal Herque are enchanting. As we savor the tête de porc in aspic, salted pork tongue, steak with shallots, a real choucroute and the chocolate cake, we soon forget how tough it was to get a table.

● Le Caveau des Chevaliers de Malte SIM

127, rue des Trois-Epis.
Tel. 03 89 27 09 78.
c.malte@wanadoo.fr
Closed lunch (exc. Sun.), Tue.,
2 weeks beg. Jan., 2 weeks beg. July.
Prix fixe: 5,30€ (child). A la carte: 28€.

We are fond of this simple tavern with its pleasant atmosphere, rustic décor and tables and stools made from old barrels, run by Raymonde Wolff who watches over both kitchen and dining room. Carafes of amiable Alsatian wines accompany escargots, vineyard-keeper's salad, hot pâté in pastry crust, sautéed ham and potatoes and a frozen kouglof prepared with feeling.

● Caveau des Seigneurs SIM

124, rue des Trois-Epis.
Tel. 03 89 27 12 75.
Closed lunch, Thu.
A la carte: 28€.

Simple, enjoyable and easygoing, Liliane Hassenfrantz's eatery combines simplicity and good humor with a singular lack of fuss. The rustic cellar setting is ageless and the dishes honest rituals: we delight in the onion tart, tourte, pâté in a pastry crust and the ham and potato salad with fresh crunchy vegetables in season, all delightfully fresh.

pared: frog legs, pike quenelles, roasted quail with old-fashioned stuffing and the dessert cart do not disappoint. Thierry Leichtman tends to the generously stocked cellar.

▼ SHOPS

CHOCOLATE & PASTRIES

▼ Christine Ferber

18, rue des Trois-Epis.
Tel. 03 89 27 05 69.

Christine Ferber, queen of preserves, now has an international reputation. Her fine jellies have traveled the world. Raspberry-violet, black cherry, pear with vanilla or bitter orange are just some of her masterpieces. Pay a visit to her store in the heart of the Alsace winegrowing region and taste her chocolate macarons, her bûche with fruit, her iced vacherin and her fine pastries.

NIEDERSTEINBACH

67510 Bas-Rhin. Paris 453 – Bitche 24 – Strasbourg 64.
The castles of Northern Alsace, the course of the Steinbach, the sweet solitude of the fir forests and nothing more.

 HOTELS-RESTAURANTS

■ Le Cheval Blanc

11, rue Principale.
Tel. 03 88 09 55 31. Fax 03 88 09 50 24.
contact@hotel-cheval-blanc.fr
www.hotel-cheval-blanc.fr
Closed 1 week at end Nov.–beg. Dec.,
beg. Feb.–mid-Mar., 20 June–mid-July
Rest. closed Thu.
26 rooms: 49–69€. 1 suite: 100€.
Prix fixe: 25€, 35€, 45€, 53€,
8€ (child).

When you pay a visit to Michel Zinck, you enter an entertaining, refined world with the Vosges forest on the horizon. From the swimming pool to the giant chessboard, billiard table and *pétanque* ground, everything has been tailored for the enjoyment of guests. The cozy, invariably tasteful rooms and dining room are instantly relaxing. In the hands of the chef, who trained with Blanc, Lameloise, Bocuse and Robuchon, the flawless, quality produce is meticulously pre-

OBERHASLACH

67280 Bas-Rhin. Paris 426 – Strasbourg 40 – Molsheim 18 – Saverne 31.

The Nideck honored by Chamisso, waterfalls and ruins, the great forest of the Vosges, lively streams and an 18th-century chapel are the charms of this quiet village.

 HOTELS-RESTAURANTS

■ Saint-Florent

28, rue du Nideck.
Tel. 03 88 50 94 10. Fax 03 88 50 99 61.
hotel.stflorent@wanadoo.fr
www.hostelleriereeb.fr
Closed 28 Dec.–1 Feb.
Rest. closed Sun. dinner, Mon.
24 rooms: 40–56€.
Prix fixe: 16€, 25€, 31€. A la carte: 25–30€.

We heard he was leaving, yet Francis Reeb is still running this fine establishment, offering attractive rooms and very respectable dishes: house terrine, roasted pike-perch on a bed of Puy lentils, magret de canard seasoned with citrus and soft spices and the chocolate dessert.

● Ruines du Nideck   SIM

2, rue de Molsheim.
Tel. 03 88 50 90 14. Fax 03 88 50 93 58.
Closed Mon. dinner, Tue. dinner, Wed.,
3 weeks Jan., 2 weeks Aug.
Prix fixe: 18€, 34€, 8€ (child).
A la carte: 33–40€.

We visit Cyril Munch to taste his specialty (flambéed tarts), but he just as skillfully concocts pan-tossed frog legs with Riesling, crayfish in cassolette, veal kidney with mustard sauce, crème brûlée and a soft-centered chocolate cake. The menu changes regularly.

OBERLARG

68480 Haut-Rhin. Paris 470 – Mulhouse 49 – Colmar 90.

The Largue river meanders nearby through scenery peppered with green, wooded hills. The ruins of Lucelle Abbey and the Swiss border are excellent destinations for a walk.

● RESTAURANTS

● A la Source de la Largue   SIM

19, rue Principale.
Tel. 03 89 40 85 10. Fax 03 89 08 19 86.
Closed Tue., Wed., Thu.
Prix fixe: 19,80€ (lunch).
A la carte: 35€.

With great modesty, Jean-Marie Hirtzlin—who notably trained with Bocuse and Vergé—has returned from Riedisheim and the Tonnelle to the paternal inn and chosen to concentrate on a brilliantly simple regional cuisine. In the rustic dining room, his wife Martine extols his rabbit presskopf, fried carp, tête de veau and a frozen rhubarb parfait.

In Lucelle (68480). 3 km e.

■ Le Petit Kohlberg

Tel. 03 89 40 85 30. Fax 03 89 40 89 40.
petitkohlberg@wanadoo.fr
www.petitkohlberg.com
Rest. closed Mon., Tue.
35 rooms: 42–68€.
Prix fixe: 16€, 62€, 6,90€ (child).
A la carte: 26–50€.

The Meister family's inn continues to enchant us. Nestling in a magnificent park populated by roe deer and does, it offers a spectacular view of the Jura Mountains. The Swiss border is close by and there are fruit trees everywhere. The setting is genuinely delightful and can be enjoyed together with the Munster cheese in a crêpe pouch, garnished fried carp, ham and the frozen kouglof prepared by Jean-Pierre. The warm welcome at this fine establishment does it justice.

OBERMODERN

67330 Bas-Rhin. Paris 456 – Haguenau 19 –
Ingwiller 7 – Pfaffenhoffen 4.
The Pays de Hanau district with its orchards,
high houses featuring neat half-timbering and
North Vosges mountain route is almost a secret
country.

 HOTELS-RESTAURANTS

■ Ernenwein

11, rue de la Gare.
Tel. 03 88 90 80 08. Fax 03 88 90 86 62.
info@ernenwein.com
www.ernenwein.com
Closed 1 week beg. Mar., 2 weeks end Aug.
Rest. closed Thu.
12 rooms: 40–46€.
Prix fixe: 9€ (lunch), 27€, 40€,
6,50€ (child).
A la carte: 36€.

Roland Ernenwein brings his energy to
this inordinately charming hotel by the
rail station. The welcome is warm; the
rooms simple and well kept. The cuisine
pays tribute to the region and the dishes
are generous. Why deny ourselves the
pleasure of a duck presskopf with foie gras,
pike-perch, de-boned guinea hen stuffed
with foie gras? For dessert, the grapefruit
gratin is remarkable.

OBERNAI

67210 Bas-Rhin. Paris 485 – Sélestat 23 –
Strasbourg 30 – Colmar 45.
otobernai@sdv.fr.
Alsace in brief. With its shadow of Sainte-
Odile, place du Marché, belfry, town hall with
oriel windows and well at Six Seaux, this model
community proves that the image of Alsace as
pretty and gastronomic is no pipe dream.

 HOTELS-RESTAURANTS

■ La Cour d'Alsace

3, rue de Gail.
Tel. 03 88 95 07 00. Fax 03 88 95 19 21.
info@cour-alsace.com
www.cour-alsace.com
Closed 24 Dec.–25 Jan.
41 rooms: 119–179€. 2 suites: 159–279€.
Prix fixe: 29€, 48€, 13,70€ (child).
A la carte: 75€.

At the foot of the old walls in the heart
of town, this former tithe barn, refurbished with an ample helping of charm
by the Hagers, delights its guests. They
all appreciate its comfortable, hand-
some, neat rooms and there are no
complaints about Olivier Gerber's fine
cuisine. Served in the Jardin des Rem-
parts (the gourmet restaurant and terrace) and the Caveau du Gail (the chic
tavern), the carefully crafted dishes prepared by this Auberge de l'Ill veteran are
enchanting: pressed quail terrine with
a prune confit, turbot filet with sea salt
flakes, veal filet with chanterelles and
the raspberry gratin.

■ Le Parc

169, rte d'Ottrott, w via D426.
Tel. 03 88 95 50 08. Fax 03 88 95 37 29.
info@hotel-du-parc.com
www.hotel-du-parc.com
Closed 10 Dec.–mid- Jan.
Rest. closed Sun. dinner (exc. La Table),
Mon., dinner (exc. La Table).
56 rooms: 100–180€. 6 suites: 245–295€.
Prix fixe: 45€, 55€ (Sat., Sun., lunch), 60€
(Sat., Sun., lunch), 75€, 16€ (child).
A la carte: 80€.

Relaxation guaranteed in Marc Wucher's establishment! Say goodbye to stress in its comfortable, contemporary rooms (some with fireplaces), two swimming pools (summer and winter), fitness center, brand new Jacuzzi and spa with Moroccan-style massage rooms. In the Table restaurant, Jacky Schweighoffer serves up a modern take on local cuisine, including a fresh lobster and crab dish served with sisho sprouts, monkfish medallion with Iberian ham, veal sweetbreads and potato baeckeofe and variations on theme of the apricot. (See restaurant: Stub du Parc.)

■ Le Colombier

6-8, rue Dietrich.
Tel. 03 88 47 63 33. Fax 03 88 47 63 39.
info@hotel-colombier.com
www.hotel-colombier.com
36 rooms: 83€. 8 suites: 111–130€.

Michel Baly, also owner of the Colombier in Colmar and the Diana and Bugatti in Molsheim, has turned this old hotel into a pleasant port of call where we enjoy a workout in the fitness center.

■ La Diligence Résidence Bel Air

23, pl du Marché.
Tel. 03 88 95 55 69. Fax 03 88 95 42 46.
hotel.la.diligence@wanadoo.fr
www.hotel-diligence.com
25 rooms: 35–81€.

If you are looking for a traditional, practical hotel in the center of town, where each room is individualized and boasts an alcove, the Diligence is just the place. Or, you may prefer the Résidence Bel Air on the Obernai high corniche road, one kilometer from the center, in a relaxing, green setting.

■ Duc d'Alsace

6, rue de la Gare.
Tel. 03 88 95 55 34. Fax 03 88 95 00 92.
ducdalsace@ducalsace.com
www.ducdalsace.com
19 rooms: 53–95€.

Opposite the station, this fine, half-timbered establishment offers small but renovated rooms. The Fourchette des Ducs restaurant is on the first floor.

■ Les Jardins d'Adalric

19, rue du Maréchal-Koenig.
Tel. 03 88 47 64 47. Fax 03 88 49 91 80.
jardins.adalric@wanadoo.fr
www.jardins-adalric.com
44 rooms: 53–95€. 2 suites: 160–205€.

A dependably warm welcome and renovated, comfortable rooms, all in a setting where classical and modern styles meet.

● La Fourchette des Ducs

6, rue de la Gare.
Tel. 03 88 48 33 38. Fax 03 88 95 44 39.
Closed lunch (exc. Sun., Bank holidays), Sun. dinner, Mon., 10 days end Dec.–beg. Jan.,
1 week at end Jan.–beg. Feb.,
1 week beg. May, 3 weeks July–Aug.
Prix fixe: 75€, 95€, 12€ (child).

Twenty-five places and no more, three wait and five kitchen staff, two set menus, two dining rooms (one of them boudoir-style with a twenties Spindler fireplace), soft colors, no hullabaloo and reservations required with all tables taken. Oh, and did we mention that the restaurant is closed at lunchtime, except on Sunday? In short, we feel we are among a select few here. Serge Schall, who supervises the dining room, and Nicolas Stamm, master of the stoves, formerly at Haguenau, compete in the "enlightened amateurs" category. Having taken a look at what the best are doing elsewhere, they have decided to do better or do something else. In fact, their eatery is like no other… except the one run by their friends at the Arnsbourg, from whom they quietly "borrowed" the idea of successive succulent morsels to "rouse the palate" Parmesan and truffle cone, caramelized tomato and jumbo shrimp beignets with sesame, as well as the "appetizer trilogy" (truffles in scrambled eggs with a hazelnut mousse, crab and green apple tartare with apricot purée and oysters with balsamic vinegar) could be terribly affected, but are actually precise, fresh, easily digested and unpretentious. The rest of the food is in the same vein, including the langoustine duo (in a tart and in aspic) and the cauliflower mousse with caviar, suggesting one of the great Robuchon's famous creations, a sea-scented, tender recipe with an ambitious market garden touch (the cauliflower). The fine ravioli with young sweet peas or pumpkin in a frothy truffle butter and the lobster medallion with chanterelles and a foie gras emulsion are precise and uncomplicated. The meats are in the same style: sophisticated, but not overly so, like the Alsatian squab with a rose supreme, its leg slow roasted on a bed of caramelized pear with an unsweetened chocolate reduction, or juicy medallions of lamb with cabbage or vegetable flan, fresh and Provençal. Then there are the desserts, which hit the mark: chocolate cappuccino, an exotic fruit brunoise and the vanilla cream with pears and Chantilly before the real dessert which is an Ethiopian mocha jelly with a soft ganache and frozen mixed spice cream. This is great art.

● Le Bistro des Saveurs

35, rue de Sélestat.
Tel. 03 88 49 90 41. Fax 03 88 49 90 51.
Closed Mon., Tue., 3 weeks Oct.,
24 Jan.–10 Feb., 25 July–11 Aug.
Prix fixe: 32€ (lunch), 44€, 70€.

Anything is possible, even a delicious meal in the eatery run by Thierry Schwartz, a gifted pupil of the Robuchon school! Previously at the Taverne du Mont d'Arbois in Megève, he has now made his nest in a chic mountain bistro setting with whitewashed walls. Our former qualms are forgotten. The hour of simplicity has arrived, bringing some fine, rustic moments: the "simple" carrots from the Truttenhausen farm, cooked four hours and served with a jus made from poultry bouillon and cumin, fresh young Munster cheese, with shallots, in the "Bibelesskäs" style, skate in romaine salad with capers, slow-roasted milk-fed veal confit cannelloni, without

forgetting the amusing Vosges snack (an egg over easy with toast and smoked sausage) featured on the "back from the market" set menu the other day. The cheese plate is an ode to the art of unpasteurized dairy production in the Vosges. The desserts (vanilla éclair, Piedmont-style Tatin and Picon Bière cocktail, a tribute to Yolande Haag) are fine efforts. The young waitstaff is energetic and the wine list has a range of regional libations (not the most famous of vintages). In short, the restaurant now displays a delightful sincerity and enthusiasm.

● La Stub du Parc

169, rte d'Ottrott.
Tel. 03 88 95 50 08. Fax 03 88 95 37 29.
info@hotel-du-parc.com
www.hotel-du-parc.com
Closed dinner, Sun., Mon., 10 Dec.–mid-Jan.
Prix fixe: 14€ (child).
A la carte: 40€.

Marc Wucher has pulled off an ongoing underhanded trick here with this paneled dining room to the right of his celebrated hotel's entrance. Open only at lunchtime, it enchants guests with its woodwork, banquettes, nooks, fine wooden flooring, superb stained glass, engravings, marquetry, Italian lamps and hushed atmosphere beneath a low ceiling. We savor grandmotherly dishes that are often forgotten elsewhere. In fact, the menu is an anthology of traditional Alsatian delights: the smoked herring tartare, oven-crisped tête de veau, Munster cheese grumbeerekiechle (a regional potato cake) with its green salad, spice-seasoned goose foie gras with toast are all splendid. Great cuisine at bistro prices? Yes, you could say that. The Saint-Léonard duckling in cocotte, stuffed and oven-roasted pork trotters and mushroom schniederspättle (the local stuffed dumplings) with veal jus are simply remarkable. They are accompanied by Haute Forêt Noire beer, with a smooth head, and local wines—not the most familiar of vintages—which are quite dazzling. Then there are the tastefully classical desserts: Malabar and Carambar ice creams, a frozen meringue dessert and the strawberry Melba. In short, pure delight distilled with precision and generosity in a rare ambiance.

● La Cour des Tanneurs   SIM

Ruelle du Canal-de-l'Ehn.
Tel. 03 88 95 15 70. Fax 03 88 95 43 84.
Closed Tue., Wed., 20 Dec.–5 Jan.,
2 weeks beg. July.
Prix fixe: 20€ (weekday lunch), 25€, 35€.
A la carte: 45€.

Roland and Martine Vonville are dependable as ever, and give a warm welcome indeed to their "court". Tribute is paid to seasonal and regional produce in the kitchen run by Cour d'Alsace and Parc veteran Roland. Shrimp brochette with curry on a bed of lentils, pike-perch served with seasonal vegetables, veal cutlet with morels and the frozen walnut kouglof are prepared with admirable precision. Each day brings its share of appealing suggestions and the splendid Loew Pinot Gris still features prominently on the excellent wine list.

● Chez Gérard   SIM

46, rue du Général-Gouraud.
Tel. 03 88 95 53 77. Fax 03 88 47 09 37.
gerard.eckert@free.fr
www.chez-gerard.net
Closed Tue. dinner, Wed., Thu. lunch, Jan.,
2 weeks Nov.
Prix fixe: 9,50€ (lunch), 12,50€ (lunch),
16,50€ (lunch), 26€.
A la carte: 40€.

Among the town's best value for money is this good-natured *winstub* with its warm welcome and sincere cuisine. Gérard Eckert, who was chef at the Cour d'Alsace and our Bistro of the Year award winner, is said to have an urge to travel to the Far East. For the moment though, this rosy-cheeked, generous innkeeper is still at work, deftly and inexpensively preparing duck foie gras, choucroute done fisherman's style, oven-crisped head cheese and pork totters and a frozen meringue and nougat dessert in the style of Alsace. The unpretentious wines are in the same vein.

● La Halle aux Blés   SIM

Pl du Marché.
Tel. 03 88 95 56 09. Fax 03 88 95 27 70.
www.halleauxbles.com
Prix fixe: 6,50€ (child). A la carte: 35€.

A congenial brasserie that only closes one day of the year is a useful address to know. Francis Kern's reliable, versatile cuisine is sufficiently well prepared, so guests flock to this former medieval covered market, rejuvenated by Daniel Irion, where they make short work of an onion tart, goose foie gras, choucroute with fish, meat cuts, spare-ribs and the Hans dessert cup with Gewurztraminer.

● L'Agneau d'Or   SIM

99, rue du Général-Gouraud.
Tel. 03 88 95 28 22. Fax 03 88 95 40 66.
alagneaudor@orange.fr
Closed Mon., Tue.
Prix fixe: 24€, 29€, 31€, 8€ (child).

This *winstub* has been taken over by Laurent Wolf, who has maintained its traditional tavern feel and reliable cuisine. A head cheese and wine aspic terrine with vinaigrette, garlic-seasoned frog legs, grilled salmon filet with bacon, pike-perch on sauerkraut cooked with Riesling, Armagnac-seasoned veal kidney and the stuffed rabbit saddle with Pinot Noir sauce are very honest.

▼	SHOPS

BUTCHER & CHARCUTERIE

▼ Pierre Baltzinger

20, rue Sainte-Odile.
Tel. 03 88 95 51 67.
www.baltzinger.fr
As in Barr, Thierry Schweitzer takes great care of his presskopf, country bacon, cervelas, pistachio galantine and chestnut boudin sausage.

CHARCUTERIE

▼ Pierre Cebrowski et fils

1, rue Dietrich.
Tel.-Fax 03 88 95 55 36.
Pierre Cebrowski and his son Patrick maintain the high standards of their sau-

sages made with beer, liver or ham—as well as knacks, presskopf, country bacon and accompaniments for choucroute—with unfailing care.

PASTRIES

▼ Gross
66, rue du Général-Gouraud.
Tel. 03 88 49 98 50.
www.gross.fr
Michel Gross offers his own take on the classics: the iced *"délice d'Alsace"* (fromage blanc ice cream with rhubarb and strawberry coulis), chocolate with Marc de Gewurz, kouglof, mille-feuille, pain de Gênes (moist yellow cake made with almond paste) and Opéra cake are irreproachable in this family confectioner's store established in 1873.

▼ Schaeffer
92, rue du Général-Gouraud.
Tel. 03 88 95 23 53.
For nearly 200 years, this regal institution has been delighting lovers of Black Forest cake, fruit tarts, pastries, *"larme de Sainte-Odile"* (cream flavored with beer and dacquois pastry) and house ice creams.

▼ Urban
82, rue du Général-Gouraud.
Tel. 03 88 95 58 90.
Founded in 1910, this confectioner's store supplies macarons, linzer torte, homemade ice creams and chocolates prepared by Christophe Adrian and Georges Dubois today. A friendly tearoom.

WINE

▼ Cave Barabos
1a, rue des Pèlerins.
Tel. 03 88 95 22 37.
Elsa Barabos runs this cellar with great passion, visiting growers to select her favorite wines. Seven hundred vintages from French producers rub shoulders with rums, Armagnacs dating from 1900 and vintage Calvados.

◆ | RENDEZVOUS

BRASSERIE

◆ La Cloche
90, rue du Général-Gouraud.
Tel. 03 88 49 90 43.
In the beautiful historic dining room, you can catch a bite at any time or enjoy a keg beer. A terrace with a view over the main square.

OBERSTEIGEN

67710 Bas-Rhin. Paris 463 – Molsheim 26 – Strasbourg 66 – Saverne 16.
An airy village in the heart of Alsace's little Switzerland, a step away from the Rocher de Dabo and the Moselle border. The Vosges mountains, hiking trails and pilgrimages.

 | HOTELS-RESTAURANTS

■ Hostellerie Belle-Vue
16, rte de Dabo.
Tel. 03 88 87 32 39. Fax 03 88 87 37 77.
hostellerie.belle-vue@wanadoo.fr
www.hostellerie-belle-vue.com
Closed beg. Jan.–beg. Apr. Rest. closed Sun. (off season), Mon. (off season).
25 rooms: 78€. 3 suites: 108€.
Prix fixe: 25€, 40€, 12€ (child).
A la carte: 60€.

While enjoying your relaxing break, why not pay a visit to Jean-Paul and Cécile Urbaniak? They are attentive in so many little ways and their rooms are as comfortable as you could wish. On the restaurant side, Sébastien Henry, who trained at the Soldat de l'An II in Phalsbourg and with Mathis in Sarrebourg, prepares first-class regional dishes. In the rustic dining room, escargot cassolette, pikeperch with a beurre blanc, saddle of rabbit and a coffee pyramid served with an English tea sauce are faultless.

OBERSTEINBACH

67510 Bas-Rhin. Paris 451 – Bitche 22 – Wissembourg 25 – Strasbourg 66.
A step away from the Palatinate, this one-street village stands at the foot of a line of ruined castles along the border. This is first-rate walking country in the heart of the Vosges nature reserve.

 HOTELS-RESTAURANTS

● Anthon
40, rue Principale.
Tel. 03 88 09 55 01. Fax 03 88 09 50 52.
info@restaurant-anthon.fr
www.restaurant-anthon.fr
Closed Jan. Rest. closed Tue., Wed.
7 rooms: 48–60€. 1 suite: 98€.
Prix fixe: 24€, 45€, 61€.

Barely thirty, but boasting solid experience acquired with great chefs (at the Côte d'Or in Saulieu, the Pinède in Saint-Tropez, the Chabichou in Courchevel and the Buerehiesel in Strasbourg), Georges Flaig has taken up the torch brilliantly in this establishment founded by his great-great-grandfather in 1860. In the heart of the Northern Vosges nature reserve, in the village of Obersteinbach, we are delighted by this former post house converted into a welcoming hostelry. The dishes concocted by the spirited young chef, who focuses on timeless recipes and the region's fine produce, are a model of creativity and precision. Carpaccio of fresh Obersteinbach goat cheese (supplied directly by a neighboring farm) sprinkled with walnuts and grated apples, Schniederspaetle-style ravoli with salmon trout and shallot confit, lamb saddle with ratatouille and cumin-seasoned chickpea curry and the duckling filet with peaches display unfailing integrity of taste. Add a flower sorbet with white chocolate mousse and apricots stuffed with almond cream, served with Amaretto ice cream, along with a wine list based on Alsatian wines (but not exclusively), and you begin to realize that this place is quite a find. Most of the redecorated rooms look out on the romantic ruins. Some even still have their old-fashioned paneled alcoves with fitted beds.

■ Alsace-Village
49, rue Principale.
Tel. 03 88 09 50 59.
www.alsacevillage.com
Closed beg. Jan.–mid-Feb.
Rest. closed Wed., Thu.
12 rooms: 42–52€.
Prix fixe: 25€. A la carte: 30–35€.

A hotel in a natural setting that will smooth away your stress day and night. The renovated, peaceful rooms offer a well-earned rest after a day spent traipsing about the region. However, before you retire, take your time at the dinner table, savoring Christelle Zerafa-Ullmann's suggestions, which are often prepared from organic produce. A taste of the goat cheese with almonds and honey, duck flambéed with Alsatian prune liqueur and the baked apples with caramel sauce and almonds and you will be wishing you could move in.

ORBEY

68370 Haut-Rhin. Paris 427 – Colmar 20 – Munster 25 – Gérardmer 41.
A community covering thirty-eight hamlets in the heart of the Pays du Munster. The scenery is pastoral and countless excursions can be enjoyed on foot or ski.

 HOTELS-RESTAURANTS

■ Au Bois le Sire
20, rue du Général-de-Gaulle.
Tel. 03 89 71 25 25. Fax 03 89 71 30 75.
boislesire@bois-le-sire.fr
www.bois-le-sire.fr
Closed beg. Jan.–beg. Feb. Rest. closed Sun. dinner (off season), Mon. (exc. July–Aug.).
34 rooms: 44,50–68€.
1 suite: 153,50–168,50€.
Prix fixe: 9€ (weekday lunch), 15,50€, 48€, 8€ (child).

With its swimming pool, sauna, Jacuzzi and play area, this modern hotel—half-traditional, half-motel—with renovated, comfortable rooms is a good place to stay. After a hike, all agree that Olivier Ducoudard's cuisine is just the thing. Duck foie gras with potatoes and celery root, escargot brochettes with bacon, Alpine lake trout with potato saffron emulsion and the duck breast with lingonberries are classics that never stale, like the frozen vacherin. Reasonable prices.

■ Wetterer   ❀⌂

206, Basses-Huttes.
Tel. 03 89 71 20 28. Fax 03 89 71 36 50.
info@hotel-wetterer.com
www.hotel-wetterer.com
Closed end Jan.–beg. Feb., 2 weeks Mar., beg. Nov.–beg.Dec. Rest. closed Mon. (Dec., Jan.), Tue. (Dec., Jan.), Wed.
15 rooms: 34–51€.
Prix fixe: 14€, 7,50€ (child).
A la carte: 35€.

Bertrand Wetterer welcomes passing or regular patrons as if they were friends, so they naturally feel at home in the cozy rooms, sauna and rustic dining room, with its reliable regional cuisine (poultry liver terrine, fresh poached trout *au bleu*, classic choucroute and the frozen vacherin).

■ La Croix d'Or   ⌂

13, rue de l'Eglise.
Tel. 03 89 71 20 51. Fax 03 89 71 35 60.
hotel-croixdor@wanadoo.fr
www.hotel-croixdor.com
Closed 10 days Nov., 2 weeks Jan., 2 weeks end June–beg.
July, Mon. Rest. closed Sat. lunch, Mon., Thu. lunch.
16 rooms: 45–49€.
Prix fixe: 11,60€ (weekday lunch), 14,80€, 18,50€, 23€, 32€, 9€ (child), 32€.

Pascal Macé watches over this family guesthouse with care. The neat and tidy rooms, restrained cuisine, terrace and rustic dining room put visitors at their ease. House terrine with crunchy vegetables, local trout with almonds, duck with blueberries and the pain d'épice crème brûlée slip down effortlessly.

 | SHOPS

FARMED FISH
▼ Jean-Paul et François Guidat
Locale known as Pairis. 148, rue Charles-de-Gaulle.
Tel. 03 89 71 21 03 / 03 89 71 28 37.
Specialists in pond-raised fish, Jean-Paul and François Guidat present local char and trout: smoked, in rilettes, in soup and in tart form.

OSTHEIM

68150 Haut-Rhin. Paris 435 – Colmar 11 – Sélestat 13.
What is still here to remind us of Ostheim's fine prewar Grand-Place but a section of wall with a stork nest?

 | HOTELS-RESTAURANTS

■ Au Nid de Cigognes   ⌂

2, rte de Colmar.
Tel. 03 89 47 91 44. Fax 03 89 47 99 88.
hotelauniddecigognes@wanadoo.fr
Closed 15–Feb.–mid-Mar. Rest. closed Sun. dinner (Jan.), Mon. (Jan.), Thu. dinner (Jan.).
50 rooms: 40–64€.
Prix fixe: 13€ (lunch weekdays), 24€, 37€, 9€ (child).
A la carte: 40–50€.

On the Colmar road, we enjoy our stay with Danielle and Martin Utzmann. Aside from the comfortable rooms, we are impressed by the dishes prepared by their daughter, Céline Utzmann-Houx: a delicate panorama of regional produce and recipes. House goose foie gras, crisp layered tart with pike-perch and "flavors of the forest", venison medallion with morels and a frozen meringue and nougat dessert called the *nid de cigognes* (stork's nest) offer a delicious suggestion of the superb surrounding rivers and forests. The fine wine list has been compiled by David Houx. An excellent breakfast.

OSTHOUSE

67150 Bas-Rhin. Paris 501 – Strasbourg 29 – Obernai 18 – Sélestat 23 – Erstein 4.
A simple Ried village and with a fine inn.

HOTELS-RESTAURANTS

■ **A la Ferme**

10, rue du Château.
Tel. 03 90 29 92 50. Fax 03 90 29 92 51.
www.hotelalaferme.com
2 rooms: 83–88€. 5 suites: 114–130€.

In the hands of Jean-Philippe and Brigitte Hellmann, this 18th-century farm has become a modern hostelry. For better, not for worse, the rooms wed tradition to design, particularly in the former tobacco-drying area.

● **L'Aigle d'Or**

14, rue de Gerstheim.
Tel. 03 88 98 06 82. Fax 03 88 98 81 75.
Closed Mon., Tue., 3 weeks Aug.
Prix fixe: 32,50€, 49,50€, 72€.
A la carte: 60€.

The Aigle d'Or is a family business. During his time at the Cerf in Marlenheim, l'Auberge de l'Ill in Illhaeusern and the Tour d'Argent in Paris, the son, Jean-Philippe Hellmann, refined his talent for flavorsome dishes, often of classical inspiration. We enjoy the pan-tossed frog legs on a layer of garlic potato purée, snapper pot-au-feu, pigeon breast and chocolate drops with ripe cherries and admire the woodwork and superb painted lacunar ceiling of the elegant dining room. The wine list offers plenty of choices and the discreet but attentive service does justice to the quality of the dishes. Visitors may prefer to opt for the simplicity of the regional dishes served in the relaxed atmosphere of the *winstub*.

OTTROTT

67530 Bas-Rhin. Paris 489 – Strasbourg 20 – Colmar 45.
A trim village overlooking the vines, a panoramic view of the Vosges mountains, fine hotels and a thriving tourism business: Ottrott is Saint-Paul-de-Vence with added gourmet pleasures and mischievous red wine.

HOTELS-RESTAURANTS

■ **Hostellerie des Châteaux**

11, rue des Châteaux.
Tel. 03 88 48 14 14. Fax 03 88 48 14 18.
leschateaux@wanadoo.fr
www.hostellerie-chateaux.fr
Hotel closed Feb. Rest. closed Sun. lunch (off season), Mon. (off season), Feb., 1 week at end July, 1 week beg. Aug.
61 rooms: 100–265€. 66 suites: 245–265€.
Prix fixe: 36€ (weekdays), 55€, 80€, 16€ (child).
A la carte: 85€.

There are plenty of reasons to visit Sabine and Ernest Schaetzel: the charming, entirely renovated rooms, the swimming pool and the "spa and beauty" facility with its sauna, Jacuzzi and treatments. Added to these pleasures are the delights on offer in the restaurant, run by the master of the house. Layers of sauerkraut, smoked and marinated salmon, rouget with puréed nettles, veal cutlet with roasted chicory jus and the lemon cream soufflé make a delicious spread.

■ **Beau Site**

Pl de l'Eglise.
Tel. 03 88 48 14 30. Fax 03 88 48 14 18.
lebeausiteott@wanadoo.fr
www.hotel-beau-site.fr
Closed Feb. Rest. closed Sun. dinner (off season), Mon. (off season).
18 rooms: 89–162€.
Prix fixe: 19€, 31€, 54€, 10€ (child).
A la carte: 40–45€.

The Schaetzels, who also own the Châteaux, have made this their second establishment. Pascal Heppe's cuisine offers a meticulous take on tradition. The two types of duck foie gras in terrine, salmon with garden savory, oven-crisped tête de veau with baby vegetables and a sweet frozen beer eau-de-vie soufflé with cinnamon are well-conceived. The hotel also boasts attractive rooms and a warm Alsatian décor.

■ A l'Ami Fritz

8, rue des Châteaux.
Tel. 03 88 95 80 81. Fax 03 88 95 84 85.
ami-fritz@wanadoo.fr
www.amifritz.com
Closed 2 weeks Jan. Rest. closed Wed.
19 rooms: 69–90€. 3 suites: 105–140€.
Prix fixe: 23€, 39€, 60€.

The Fritz hostelry offers bright rooms and a quality regional restaurant. In the kitchen, Patrick carefully complies with local culinary tradition, serving up such dishes as an individual pressed rabbit and tarragon terrine with foie gras, pike fish quenelles with crayfish, duck pieces served over sauerkraut ("choucroute" style) and the frozen prune digestif soufflé. Jean-Dominique Gessner recommends wines that provide a flavorsome accompaniment to the dishes. Pleasant service on the terrace in summer and well-chosen set menus.

■ Le Moulin

32, rte de Klingenthal, 1 km nw via D426.
Tel. 03 88 95 87 33. Fax 03 88 95 98 03.
domaine.le.moulin@wanadoo.fr
www.domaine-le-moulin.com
Closed 3 weeks Jan. Rest. closed Sat. lunch, Sun. dinner, Mon. lunch.
20 rooms: 68–76€. 3 suites: 107–150€.
Prix fixe: 27€, 55€.
A la carte: 32–48€.

This former mill presided over by the Schreiber family is a very congenial hostelry. Its yellow and pink tones, cozy rooms, terrace and good-natured welcome all contribute to a refreshing break. At the stove, Olivier concocts regional dishes. The presskopf, trout, choucroute and the house dessert cup are well-prepared and gratifying.

■ Le Clos des Délices

17, rte de Klingenthal, 1 km nw via D426.
Tel. 03 88 95 81 00. Fax 03 88 95 97 71.
contact@leclosdesdelices.com
www.leclosdesdelices.com
Closed Sun. dinner, Bank holidays.
22 rooms: 46–72€. 1 suite: 92–104€.
Prix fixe: 26€, 39€, 49€, 58€, 15,50€ (child). A la carte: 40–45€.

In both winter and summer, Désiré Schaetzel's fine forest hostelry offers a park, swimming pool, sauna, solarium and stylish rooms refurbished in a modern manner. After your walk, the restaurant looks very enticing, with dishes prepared by Ludovic Van Anvers Mael, who plays very tunefully to a regional score. A regional meat and potato casserole called the baeckeoffe with goose foie gras on a Pinot Gris sauce and garnished with a crispy parmesan disk, pie filled with salmon, vegetables and hard boiled eggs, seasoned with green tea and served with a pumpkin potato purée and the dessert of crêpes with orange and milk cream provide a delightful accompaniment to the wines from the family property.

P

LA PETITE-PIERRE

67290 Bas-Rhin. Paris 433 – Haguenau 40 – Saverne 22 – Strasbourg 60.
tourisme.pays-lapetitepierre@wanadoo.fr.
"I showed you La Petite-Pierre, its woodland dowry, the sky born in the branches, the pollen twice living under the blaze of flowers," wrote René Char. The great national forest is still one of the finest in France, while the village on its sandstone pedestal has become a well-known health resort. The renovated château houses the headquarters of the North Vosges Natural Park. Hiking is the queen of leisure activities here.

 HOTELS-RESTAURANTS

■ La Clairière

63, rte d'Ingwiller.
Tel. 03 88 71 75 00. Fax 03 88 70 41 05.
info@laclairière.com
www.laclairiere.com
50 rooms: 120–182€.
Prix fixe: 32€, 49€, 10€ (child).
A la carte: 60€.

On the edge of the forest, this contemporary hotel managed by Lisbeth and Karen Strohmenger offers cozy, comfortable rooms, grounds with a swimming pool and obstacle course, meeting rooms and a fine spa, very Zen in appearance. In the restaurant, Stéphane Schramm (who trained at the Cerf in Marlenheim) serves a gratifying, elaborate, accomplished cuisine, including a tuna carpaccio marinated in avocado oil, roasted pork ribs and cornbread and a soy milk crème-style dessert.

■ Les Trois Roses

19, rue Principale.
Tel. 03 88 89 89 00. Fax 03 88 70 41 28.
www.aux-trois-roses.com
Closed 1 week Jan.
Rest. closed Sun. dinner, Mon.
40 rooms: 46–102€.
Prix fixe: 17€, 45€, 7,50€ (child).

This welcoming 18th-century establishment is overseen with meticulous care by Philippe Geyer. Everything is designed to make the guest comfortable: snug rooms—some with a balcony and a view of the château—cordial lounges, an indoor swimming pool and panoramic dining rooms overlooking the old village and valley, as well as an elaborate, classical cuisine. Foie gras, the "rich" hors-d'oeuvre, almond-crusted trout, wild boar stew with blood sauce, thick-cut boneless rib steak in red wine sauce with bone marrow and the frozen vacherin are a pleasure.

■ Les Vosges

30, rue Principale.
Tel. 03 88 70 45 05. Fax 03 88 70 41 13.
hotel-des-vosges@wanadoo.fr
www.hotel-des-vosges.com
Closed end Feb.–beg. Mar.,
1 week at end July. Rest. closed Tue.
28 rooms: 55–79,50€. 2 suites: 120–170€.
Prix fixe: 23,50€, 54€, 10€ (child).

This mountain inn is run with unquestionable reliability by the Wehrung family. Jean welcomes guests and looks after the cellar, while Eric, the son, has taken over in the office and kitchen. The paneled rooms are in the Vosges style and the dining room has a view of the château, old village and valley. The poached poultry terrine, trout "au bleu", cock in Riesling sauce and the frozen vacherin are classics that never stale. Rich in great Alsatian vintages from the finest years, the house wine list is giddying indeed.

■ Auberge d'Imsthal

On l'étang d'Imsthal, 3,5 km via D178.
Tel. 03 88 01 49 00. Fax 03 88 70 40 26.
reservation@petite-pierre.com
www.petite-pierre.com
Closed end Nov.–beg. Dec.
23 rooms: 49–108€. 1 suite: 154€.
Prix fixe: 10,50€, 25€ (Sat., Sun., lunch), 26€, 7€ (child).
A la carte: 38€.

Nature and relaxation. By a lake in the middle of the forest, this half-timbered hostelry equipped with a fitness center, steam bath and Jacuzzi is a pleasant place to stay. The dishes pay tribute to regional produce, game and fish, with preparations that are often a lost art elsewhere (and very reasonable prices into the bargain). A "Best Value for Money" award this year for the veal in creamy sauce served in puff pastry shells, freshwater fish stew, beef filet in the style of Vieux Strasbourg, a well-presented tête de veau and the real choucroute with its pork cuts and charcuterie. The raspberries served hot with vanilla ice cream deliciously conclude this delightful experience, which we owe to the mayor of the village, Hans Michaely.

■ Le Lion d'Or

15, rue Principale.
Tel. 03 88 01 47 57. Fax 03 88 01 47 50.
contact@liondor.com
www.liondor.com
Closed 10 days beg. July.
42 rooms: 53–98€.
Prix fixe: 19€ (weekday lunch), 29€, 35€, 43€ (wine inc.), 12€ (child).
A la carte: 45–50€.

This family guesthouse with its vast, panoramic dining room, cozier *winstub* area (Loewestuewel), contemporary rooms and care lavished in the name of arbrothérapie is now run by the son, Philippe, chair of the Young Restaurateurs of France. New Wave dishes go side-by-side with preparations based on local produce: grilled scallops with endives and quinoa, hot oysters with parsnips, foie gras maison, Savoie lake trout ravioli with mushrooms. You might try the mixed salad and pan-fried veal cutlets served with Alsatian potato gratin and his kirsch parfait.

In Frohmuhl (67290). On l'étang du Donnenbach, 4 km via forest road.

● Auberge du Donnenbach   SIM

Tel. 03 88 01 57 69. Fax 03 88 01 52 94.
auberge.du.donnenbach@wanadoo.fr
Closed Mon., Tue., Christmas–mid-Jan.
Prix fixe: 7,50€ (weekday lunch), 9€ (weekday lunch), 28€, 7,50€ (child).
A la carte: 35€.

By the lake, Cédric and Myriam Brumm's modern forest inn has the charm of faraway places. Tasting a Beaufort terrine, salmon trout with saffron, poultry breast glazed with honey and the warm quince confit served with vanilla ice cream, we imagine ourselves out there somewhere between Finland and Canada. An extraordinarily refreshing change of air!

In Graufthal (67320). 11 km s via D178 and D122.

■ Au Vieux Moulin

7, rue du Vieux-Moulin.
Tel. 03 88 70 17 28. Fax 03 88 70 11 25.
kavi.moulin@wanadoo.fr
Closed Feb. vac., 1 week at end June–beg. July. Rest. closed Tue. dinner.
14 rooms: 39–70€. 1 suite: 110€.
Prix fixe: 10€ (weekday lunch), 27€ (weekday lunch), 28€, 32€, 8€ (child).
A la carte: 29–41€.

Wood and bright colors—red, yellow and orange—decorate this attractive hotel standing by a lake in the forest. The friendly Kassel family offers a very Alsace-oriented cuisine concocted by new chef Nicolas Loutre. The smoked wild boar ham, trout meunière, beef tenderloin and the foie gras with Pinot Noir sauce are a delight.

In Graufthal.

● Le Cheval Blanc   COM

19, rue Principale.
Tel. 03 88 70 17 11. Fax 03 88 70 12 37.
www.auchevalblanc.net
Closed Mon. dinner, Tue., Wed. dinner, 2 weeks Sept., 3 weeks Jan.
Prix fixe: 9,50€ (lunch), 24,50€, 27€, 32€.

The Stutzmann's inn enchants its guests, who all appreciate Brigitte's warm welcome, as well as Gilles' very fresh, reliable cuisine, mirroring the vagaries of the market. In the smart dining room or on the terrace, we relish the duck foie gras terrine with spiced aspic, monkfish stew in a shellfish bouillon, a cassolette of veal kidneys and the frozen rhubarb parfait. Sensible set menus.

PFAFFENHOFFEN

67350 Bas-Rhin. Paris 458 – Haguenau 15 –
Saverne 26 – Strasbourg 36.
Gateway to the Pays de Hanau, this Northern
Alsace community is worth a visit for its little
museum of painted and popular imagery.

 HOTELS-RESTAURANTS

● **L'Agneau**   COM

3, rue de Saverne.
Tel. 03 88 07 72 38. Fax 03 88 72 20 24.
gisele.ernwein@wanadoo.fr
www.hotel-restaurant-delagneau.com
Closed 2 weeks Sept., 1 week Mar., 1 week
June. Rest. closed Sun. dinner (off season),
Mon. (off season), Tue. dinner (off season).
12 rooms: 50–68€.
Prix fixe: 13€, 25€, 55€, 65€.

What better name for a former 18th-
century sheepcote than "l'Agneau" (the
Lamb)? The three Ernweins—mother
Gisèle welcomes the guests—have refurbished the place fifties style in shades
of ecru and red. The pleasant rooms are
tastefully decorated. At the stove, Anne
(who trained with Loiseau in Saulieu and
Blanc in Vonnas) tinkers with tradition,
offering exuberant, sometimes slightly
bombastic reinterpretations. Her mischievous dishes—foie gras served with
dried fruit chutney, scallop brochettes
with Serrano ham "chips", pink garlic-seasoned lamb with basil, a raspberry macaron or the frozen vacherin—are childhood
treats. To help you choose among the 250
wines from every region of France, ask for
Viviane. Flambéed tarts in the evening
on weekends and a charming, flowered
facade in season.

● **A l'Etoile d'Or**   SIM

14, rue de la Gare.
Tel. 03 88 07 70 64.
Closed Mon. dinner, Tue. dinner, Wed.
Prix fixe: 7,65€ (lunch), 11,22€ (lunch),
32,50€ Sun. lunch, 8€ (child).
A la carte: 35–40€.

Behind the fine, painted facade of this
friendly establishment, we find a warm
welcome and Marie-Reine Steiner's generous cuisine. We feast on good, simple
dishes, such as warmed goat cheese salad,
seafood stew, boneless rib eye with horseradish and the chocolate fondue with fresh
fruits in season. Couscous on the first
Tuesday of the month.

REIPERTSWILLER

67340 Bas-Rhin. Strasbourg 56 – Bitche 21
– Saverne 35 – Haguenau 34.
A town surrounded by forest in the heart of north Vosges, this is a stop for walkers, sportspeople and hunters.

 HOTELS-RESTAURANTS

■ **La Couronne** ❀ 🏠

13, rue de Wimmenau.
Tel. 03 88 89 96 21. Fax 03 88 89 98 22.
sb.kuhm@wanadoo.fr
www.hotel-la-couronne.com
Closed 2 weeks Nov., mid-Feb.–beg. Mar.
Rest. closed Mon., Tue.
16 rooms: 47–60€.
Prix fixe: 18€ (weekday lunch),
28€ (weekday lunch), 37€, 49€.

This modern house on the edge of the forest offers a rural, comfortable setting. The rooms are spic and span, the welcome from Sylvie warm and Bernard Kuhm's cooking gives priority to produce in season without neglecting the regional aspect. House head cheese and wine aspic terrine, foie gras served two ways, pike-perch with morels and celery root purée and veal kidneys served with mustard are accompanied by well-chosen regional wines.

RHINAU

67860 Bas-Rhin. Paris 458 – Obernai 26 – Strasbourg 33.
Overlooking Germany and its dashing Europark, this village on the banks of the Rhine seems to be waiting for an eternal ferryboat. Its stylish auberge creates the link between two borders.

 HOTELS-RESTAURANTS

■ **Aux Bords du Rhin** 🛏

10, rue du Rhin.
Tel. 03 88 74 60 36.
Fax 03 88 74 85 98/03 88 74 65 77.
Rest. closed Mon., Tue.
21 rooms: 34–41€.

Prix fixe: 24€, 30€, 8€ (child).
A la carte: 35–45€.

The ferry that crosses the Rhine leaves from just outside the house of the Bernas. The rooms are sweet, Gabrielle gives a kind welcome and Patrice cooks, with a sure hand, goose foie gras, frog legs with garlic and parsley, pike-perch served cooked in wine with noodles, sirloin steak with béarnaise sauce and a frozen meringue dessert with whipped cream. This is well-prepared classic cooking.

● **Au Vieux Couvent** ⬭ V.COM

6, rue des Chanoines.
Tel. 03 88 74 61 15. Fax 03 88 74 89 19.
Closed Mon. dinner, Tue., Wed., 2 weeks
Feb., 3 weeks July.
Prix fixe: 35€, 82€. A la carte: 80–90€.

A stone's throw from the Rhine, the Albrecht family continues the legend. A family working together in harmony is a joy they share with their guests. Jean the poet—formerly an electrician, even if he doesn't like to be reminded of it—enchants with his roaming and unexpected cuisine, playfully created with his son Alexis and then passing through the hands of the Pourcel brothers; this is an Alsatian synthesis of modernism and tradition. He goes on "herb outings" to discover the wild plants of the region that find expression in the dishes he develops. The startlingly self-taught chef with the brilliance of an old pro offers swordfish carpaccio with balsamic vinegar and herbs, blue lobster with diced root vegetables and saffron sauce, a slice of Rhin river eel caught by Martin Thalgott served with a locally produced stuffed ravioli, veal sweetbreads pan tossed and served with parsley and sorrel risotto. Everything delights. But the best is kept for the end, when the magicians of the ovens reveal their festival of desserts, a cascade of marvels: a flavorful violet or strawberry tiramisu, lemon and Campari panna cotta, a chocolate cookie served hot and arbutus-berry lollipop… time seems to stand still. The wine list offers a superb choice of 500 reputable vintages.

In Diebolsheim (67230). 5,8 km D468 and D203.

● **A la Couronne** `SIM`

4, rue Jean-de-Beaumont.
Tel. 03 88 74 81 07. Fax 03 88 74 63 89.
Closed Tue. dinner, Wed., 2 weeks Christmas–New Year's, 2 weeks beg. Aug.
Prix fixe: 9€ (weekday lunch), 12€, 15€, 18€, 8€ (child). A la carte: 35–42€.

Annabel and Karl Renaut have made their modern house into a restaurant frequented by families on Sundays. One does not grow weary of crayfish ravioli with orange and ginger butter, house duck terrine with poultry livers, pike-perch with chanterelles and chive butter, tête de veau with sauce gribiche and a soft dark chocolate cake with mandarin orange sorbet. Smiling welcome and service; reasonable prices.

RIBEAUVILLE

68150 Haut-Rhin. Paris 427 – Colmar 15 – Mulhouse 59 – Sélestat 15.
info@ribeauvilleriquewihr.com.
The first Sunday in September, during the "Pfifferdaj", the whole vineyard gets together for a joyful, medieval feast. But Ribeauvillé also has a gastronomic celebration every day, with its proud craftsmen, its great vintages, its elite distillers and its distinguished restaurants.

 HOTELS-RESTAURANTS

■ **Le Clos Saint-Vincent**

Rte de Bergheim.
Tel. 03 89 73 67 65. Fax 03 89 73 32 20.
reception.leclos@wanadoo.fr
www.leclossaintvincent.com
Closed mid-Dec.–mid-Mar.
Rest. closed lunch, Tue.
19 rooms: 95–200€. 2 suites: 185–230€.
Prix fixe: 45€.

Surrounded by vineyards on the plain of Alsace, this sixties house breathes tranquility. The Chapotin family cheerfully offers rustic chic with its huge, carefully decorated rooms, the garden and the terrace. Arnaud Chapotin's regional cooking blends Munster cheese in puff pastry with Gerwurtz Marc, venison medallions with red cabbage and a classic tarte Tatin with vanilla ice cream for dessert.

■ **Les Seigneurs de Ribeaupierre**

11, rue du Château.
Tel. 03 89 73 70 31. Fax 03 89 73 71 21.
Closed Christmas–1 Mar.
6 rooms: 120–150€. 4 suites: 150–170€.

Under the direction of Marie-Madeleine and Marie-Cécile Barth, this house near the church has been transformed into a charming establishment with carefully prepared rooms. Tasty breakfasts.

● **Au Valet de Coeur**
  & Hostel de la Pépinière

40, rte de Sainte-Marie-aux-Mines.
Tel. 03 89 73 64 14. Fax 03 89 73 88 78.
reception@valetdecoeur.fr
www.valetdecoeur.fr
Rest. closed Sun. dinner,
Mon. (exc. Bank holidays), Tue. lunch.
17 rooms: 43,50–82€.
Prix fixe: 33,50€ (weekdays), 45€, 62€, 83€. A la carte: 75€.

Trained at the Taillevent and Fer Rouge schools, Jean-Pierre Egert knows how to give guests a wonderful welcome to his large house at the edge of the forest. They are delighted by the covered swimming pool and the calm of the old-style rooms, also appreciating the pretty creations of chef Christophe Cavelier. In the luminous dining room, pigeon in aspic terrine with pistachio oil, monkfish "osso bucco" and lemon-seasoned new potatoes, duck "hamburger" with pan-seared foie gras and the chocolate and raspberry desserts are both precise and creative.

■ **Le Ménestrel**

27, av du Général-de-Gaulle.
Tel. 03 89 73 80 52. Fax 03 89 73 32 39.
menestrel2@wanadoo.fr
www.menestrel.com
29 rooms: 73–99€.

For those following the wine trail, Jacqueline John's establishment is very practical:

the modern rooms are rather well laid out while the sauna, the hammam and the Jacuzzi allow one to recuperate in style; the breakfasts are also superb.

■ **La Tour** ⌂

1, rue de la Mairie.
Tel. 03 89 73 72 73. Fax 03 89 73 38 74.
info@hotel-la-tour.com
www.hotel-la-tour.com
Closed Jan., Feb.
31 rooms: 63–94€.

Françoise Alt-Kientzler, sister of a famous wine-maker, has transformed this former viticultural enterprise in the middle of a town into a guesthouse. The rooms are cozy and quiet, particularly those overlooking the courtyard. The sauna, the hammam and the spa allow pleasant relaxation.

● **Le Relais des Ménétriers** ●COM

10, av du Général-de-Gaulle.
Tel. 03 89 73 64 52. Fax 03 89 73 69 94.
Closed Sun. dinner, Mon., Thu. dinner,
1 week at end July.
Prix fixe: 11€ (lunch), 22€, 24€, 35€.
A la carte: 40€.

Regional tradition and modern cuisine blend harmoniously in the dishes prepared by Patrick Serreau. Comfortably seated, a good bottle on the table—chosen from the 660 referenced wines—one enjoys, without breaking the bank, potato quenelles served with a medallion of foie gras, a stew of pike-perch with ravioli seasoned with Riesling and a filet mignon with Munster. The strawberry gratin with orange flower water concludes a meal that has been impeccably served.

● **Le Zahnacker** ●SIM

8, av du Général-de-Gaulle.
Tel. 03 89 73 60 77. Fax 03 89 73 66 61.
joseph.leiser@wanadoo.fr
Closed Thu., Jan., Feb.
Prix fixe: 22€.
A la carte: 40€.

Seasonal, fresh produce takes pride of place at Joseph Leiser's restaurant. A fine practitioner of his art, this chef formerly with Gaertner contrives to make the mouth water without increased prices. The regional wines easily marry with scallops over salad with an orange vinaigrette, seafood choucroute, veal kidneys with chanterelles and rich chocolate cake napped with an orange sauce. Agreeable atmosphere of a neighborhood *winstub* and local wines from the owner's cellar.

● **Wistub Zum Pfifferhus** ⌂SIM

14, Grand-Rue.
Tel. 03 89 73 62 28.
Closed Wed., Thu. (exc. June–Oct.), Jan.–mid-Mar., 2 weeks July.
Prix fixe: 24€.
A la carte: 38€.

Non-smoking for a very long time, this historic tavern enables one to get a better appreciation of Roland Langer's cooking, served in a fun, neo-medieval setting. One is guided by Jacques Thomann towards charcuterie salad with grilled gizzards and smoked goose breast, head cheese and wine aspic terrine, pike-perch served over sauerkraut, veal in cream sauce over puff pastry shells with house-made spätzle and almond milk ice cream washed down with Alisier is extremely tasty. The cellar is always full of amazing wines to discover.

● **Auberge à l'Etoile** SIM

46, Grand-Rue.
Tel. 03 89 73 36 46. Fax 03 89 73 67 28.
henry38@wanadoo.fr
Closed Mon. dinner, Tue., 2 weeks Nov., Jan.
Prix fixe: 16,50€, 26,50€.
A la carte: 45€.

Jean-Marie Henry has made this old 18th-century building into an up-and-coming inn. He offers very carefully prepared home cooking based on local produce. Duck foie gras, veal sweetbreads in terrine, pike-perch with noodles, veal kidneys with old-style mustard sauce and the Alsatian frozen vanilla raspberry vacherin cheerfully hit the spot.

● Le Cheval Noir   SIM

2, av du Général-de-Gaulle.
Tel. 03 89 73 37 83. Fax 03 89 73 38 73.
frick.p@wanadoo.fr
Closed Mon., Mar.
Prix fixe: 19,70€, 21€, 8€ (child).
A la carte: 30€.

This restaurant annexed to the Zahnacker is imbibed with a good-natured
simplicity. One comes for local flat
savory tarts in various flavors, the vineyard-keeper's salad, trout with almonds,
pike-perch on sauerkraut, pork cheeks in
a stew flavored with Pinot Noir and fresh
fromage blanc with blueberries. The
prices don't hurt and the atmosphere is
equally pleasant.

● S'Rappschwirer Stebala   SIM

6, pl de l'Ancien-Hôpital.
Tel. 03 89 73 64 64. Fax 03 89 73 67 28.
Closed Tue. dinner, Wed., 2 weeks Nov.,
2 weeks Jan., 2 weeks Feb.
Prix fixe: 15,50€, 18€, 23,50€.
A la carte: 35€.

Jean-Marie Henry is also on the other side
of the high street in this restaurant that
bears the name, in Alsatian, of his town.
The cooking is simple and cheery. Onion
tart, pike-perch with noodles, a veal escalope with chanterelles and crème brûlée
go down without a murmur. The paneled
décor is charming and the local flat savory
tarts to be recommended.

▼ | SHOPS

CHARCUTERIE

▼ Jean-Jacques Feltzinger

39, Grand-Rue.
Tel. 03 89 73 60 53.
Just the place to stock up on pork filet,
sausages with kirsch, ham, galantine
(cold, stuffed pork appetizer, molded in
aspic), terrines, cervelas or bacon, and to
enjoy a choucroute or a baeckeofe in the
adjoining dining room.

▼ Hubert Siedel

78, Grand-Rue.
Tel.-Fax 03 89 73 60 23.
Hubert Siedel presents smoked pork
shoulder, country bacon, accompaniments for choucroute, tortes, munster,
terrines and ham.

EAUX DE VIE

▼ Jean-Paul Gisselbrecht

32, Grand-Rue.
Tel. 03 89 73 30 51.
René De Miscault, also present in
Lapoutroie, Fougerolles and Nol, runs
the house label. Pear, peach, Marc de
Gewurz or plum are all of great quality.

▼ Gilbert Holl

Rte de Sainte-Marie-aux-Mines
8, av Jacques-Preiss.
Tel. 03 89 73 70 34.
www.gilbertholl.com
Gilbert Holl produces Alsace's first whiskey, which he sells in his store along
with housemade *alisier* (service berry),
absinthe, pear, kirsch, raspberry, Marc
de Gewurz, gentian and elderflower.

▼ Jean-Paul Metté

9, rue des Tanneurs.
Tel. 03 89 73 65 88.
www.distillerie-mette.com
Philippe Traber has carried on the trusted
methods of his late uncle Jean-Paul and
produces 85 eaux de vie and 21 liqueurs,
including top-notch Marc de Gewurz,
raspberry, kirsch or plum.

▼ Windholtz

31, av du Général-de-Gaulle.
Tel. 03 89 73 66 64.
www.terre-net.fr/windholtz
Michel Windholtz offers fine spirits distilled from the fruits of the region: a
superb mirabelle plum, as well as *alisier*
(service berry), sour cherry, black cherry,
strawberry, quince and kirsch that are
among the best in Alsace.

MINERAL WATER

▼ Carola

48, rte de Bergheim.
Tel. 03 89 73 24 24.
Drawn from a great depth and bottled in this factory, Carola water is a local specialty sold in blue (still), red (carbonated) and green (lightly sparkling) bottles.

PASTRIES

▼ Vilmain

58, Grand-Rue.
Tel. 03 89 73 64 41.
There has been a change of owner at this famous store, but the superb pastries are still the same. The Sacher torte; tarts with sour cherry, rhubarb, or mirabelle plums; soft kouglof; langhopf; famous brie with kirsch; Cointreau dessert; streusel; linzer torte; and Black Forest cake would tempt a saint.

TABLETOP & KITCHENWARE

▼ Beauvillé

19, rte de Sainte-Marie-aux-Mines.
Tel. 03 89 73 74 74.
www.beauville.com
This quality establishment offers colorful, elaborately patterned tablecloths, dish towels and fabrics that are exported worldwide. The factory store presents the perfect opportunity to treat yourself.

RINGENDORF

67350 Bas-Rhin. Paris 463 – Strasbourg 32 – Pfaffenhoffen 6 – Kirrwiller 2.
The country of Hanau, the Alsace of orchards and beautiful half-timbered houses, is to be found right here.

 RESTAURANTS

● La Ferme de Suzel ⛺ SIM

15, rue des Vergers.
Tel. 03 88 03 30 80.
Closed lunch (exc. weekends), Mon., Tue.
2 weeks beg. Sept., 2 weeks Feb. vac.
Prix fixe: 45€.
A la carte: 40€.

Prettily decorated as a typical farmhouse, the house of the Suzels, alias Odette Jung, is an enchanting place. Under the welcoming gaze of a good hostess who has her eye on everything, one hesitates before a menu that changes frequently but which is always tempting. A pork trotter terrine with balsamic vinaigrette, Red Label salmon in an Ile de Ré black potato crust, duck leg confit with two cabbages, sour cherries pan tossed with sugar and the frozen vacherin testify to the real know-how of the wonderful Suzel. The check is small in comparison to the generosity of the food.

RIQUEWIHR

68340 Haut-Rhin. Paris 437 – Ribeauvillé 5 – Sélestat 19 – Colmar 13.
info@ribeauville-riquewihr.com.
The "pearl of the vineyards" has emerged intact, or almost, from the Middle Ages. Its Dolder door has celebrated its 700-year anniversary and its winemakers are proud of their famous hillside vineyards. It has now found a new tourist and gastronomic vocation.

 HOTELS-RESTAURANTS

■ La Couronne 🏠

5, rue de la Couronne.
Tel. 03 89 49 03 03. Fax 03 89 49 01 01.
www.hoteldelacouronne.com
36 rooms: 60–68€. 4 suites: 110
Half board: 70–130€.

The rooms of this establishment, made up of typical 16th-century houses, enjoy modern comforts. In the middle of the old town, it is nonetheless quiet. The welcome is delightful and, in the annex, families happily stay in well-equipped apartments.

■ Hôtel du Schoenenbourg 🏠

Rue du Schoenenbourg.
Tel. 03 89 49 01 11. Fax 03 89 47 95 88.
www.hotel-schoenenbourg.fr
54 rooms: 50–122€.

The rooms of this modern hotel at the foot of vineyards are light and well equipped for a stay of several days. For the comfort of their guests, Jacques and Mayo Kiener have made available a good-sized swimming pool, gym, solarium and sauna.

■ A l'Oriel

3, rue des Ecuries-Seigneuriales.
Tel. 03 89 49 03 13. Fax 03 89 47 92 87.
info@hotel-oriel.com
www.hotel-oriel.com
21 rooms: 67–97€. 1 suite: 155€.

The house is several centuries old but the rooms, with their rustic décor, include every comfort. Located right in the heart of the town, this hotel makes a good stop-off on the wine route.

■ Le Riquewihr

3, rte de Ribeauvillé.
Tel. 03 89 86 03 00. Fax 03 89 47 99 76.
www.hotel-riquewihr.fr
Closed Jan.–mid-Feb.
44 rooms: 60–90€. 6 suites: 90–115€.

This family hotel offers large comfortable rooms but also a fitness suite, heated swimming pool and Internet.

■ Le Sarment d'Or

4, rue du Cerf.
Tel. 03 89 86 02 86. Fax 03 89 47 99 23.
www.riquewihr-sarment-dor.com
Rest. closed Sun. dinner (exc. Dec.), Mon., Tue. lunch, mid-Jan.–beg. Feb.
10 rooms: 60–80€.
Prix fixe: 20€, 25€, 37€, 48€, 9,50€ (child). A la carte: 50€.

Built in the city fortifications, this charming hotel in a regional setting provides modern, comfortable rooms. Mirianne Merckling and her daughter Isabelle give a smiling welcome while the cooking of father Gilbert does the rest, with tuna tartare with herring caviar, whole roasted Atlantic sea bass with olive oil and basil, lamb chops with slow-roasted garlic and cherries in eau-de-vie.

● La Table du Gourmet

5, rue de la 1er-Armée.
Tel. 03 89 49 09 09. Fax 03 89 49 04 56.
latable@jlbrendel.com
www.jlbrendel.com
Closed Tue., Thu. lunch, Wed. lunch, mid-Jan.–mid-Feb.
Prix fixe: 36€, 90€.
A la carte: 100€.

After having converted several charming suites in his 16th-century winemaker's house, as well as adopting a new concept, the D'Brendel Stub, Jean-Luc Bernard, known as JLB, has given himself over to energetically working in the kitchens of his restaurant aimed at gourmets. His cooking is both stamped with orginality and anchored in the region. Our man goes exploring in the fields himself for herbs, flowers, berries and roots to go into his dishes. Regulars to the place vote in numbers for corn bread-coated and fried frog legs with pink garlic purée, fire-roasted Breton lobster with old-style preserved tomatoes, veal sweetbreads, thinly sliced cold artichoke with chanterelle cream and a big white fish roasted with almonds and raspberry candies for gourmets who also have great appetites. The smile of his sister Fabienne, who watches over the house, contributes to the prevailing good humor of the place, which seems to continue indefinitely, long after the last mouthful has been swallowed.

● Auberge du Schoenenbourg

2, rue de la Piscine.
Tel. 03 89 47 92 28. Fax 03 89 47 89 84.
auberge-schoenenbourg@wanadoo.fr
www.auberge-schoenenbourg.com
Closed lunch, beg. Jan.–beg. Feb.
Prix fixe: 35€, 45€, 63€, 78€.
A la carte: 75€.

The architecture of the building, like the interior decoration, is contemporary. The garden of aromatic herbs gives the opportunity for a scented walk and the terrace offers a superb view over the vineyard that stretches into the horizon as well as of the walls surrounding the town. The cooking, also in the spirit of the times, is the work of François Kliener, who trained with Bise in Talloires and at the Auberge de l'Ill. Natural produce has pride of place in a menu that changes according to the rhythm of the seasons. Summer features iced melon soup and crisp ham. The salmon trout with fresh parsley and coriander jus is a real explosion of tastes. Suckling pig tenderloin with old-style mustard sauce is a piece of genius. The raspberry and rhubarb feuilleté with nougatine ice cream makes a light, fruity end to the meal. The service is very attentive, the charm of sommelier Anne Humbrecht equalled by her professionalism and the prices of the special menus are agreeably reasonable.

● D'Brendel Stub

48, rue du Général-de-Gaulle.
Tel. 03 89 86 54 54.
Closed Wed., 3 weeks Jan.
A la carte: 45€.

Jean-Luc Brendel has created a stir with his modern inn in an ancient house. The contemporary setting with its black tones, a visible rotisserie, and a menu with its synthesis of tradition and modern tastes are all offered by the craftsman of La Table du Gourmet. The bottles of local wine (at rather unpleasant prices) accompany clever dishes. A Bargkass-garnished flat savory tart, breaded head cheese and wine aspic terrine, ham, chicken with chanterelles, a caramelized ham shank with sauerkraut, Alsatian brioche and woodfire–smoked cream sauce all make a good impression.

● Au Tire-Bouchon   SIM

29, rue du Général-de-Gaulle.
Tel. 03 89 47 91 61. Fax 03 89 47 99 39.
www.riquewihr-zimmer.com
Closed Christmas.
Prix fixe: 16,50€, 17,50€, 19€, 40€,
9€ (child).
A la carte: 40€.

The Zimmers have created a *winstub* out of this winemaker's house. Régine receives the guests while Thierry Marjorie serves the regional cause in the kitchen. Escargot streudel, rouget and veal trotter in an individual pot, foie gras with potatoes, baeckofe-style, beef with flakes of salt and a chestnut biscuit are well conceived. Local wines are offered, at affordable prices.

ROSENAU

68128 Haut-Rhin. Paris 493 – Colmar 59 – Mulhouse 24 – Altkirch 25 – Bâle 15.
Between Sundgau and little Camargue, a village of Alsace that flirts with the Rhine and the Huningue canal.

●	RESTAURANTS

● Au Lion d'Or   COM

5, rue de Village-Neuf.
Tel. 03 89 68 21 97. Fax 03 89 70 68 05.
Closed Mon., Tue., Feb., 2 weeks Aug.
Prix fixe: 13€ (weekday lunch), 23€,
28€, 41€.

Théo Baumlin offers, on the covered terrace on fine days or otherwise in the attractive restaurant, well-composed menus that change with his moods and the seasons. Foie gras terrine with aspic, arborio risotto with vegetables, chanterelles and parmesan, rabbit leg over noodles, frozen kirsch and a Fougerolle sour cherry kougelhopf make one want to take up residence here. Wonderful welcome.

ROSHEIM

67560 Bas-Rhin. Paris 482 – Strasbourg 31
– Molsheim 7 – Obernai 6.
accueil@rosheim.com.
The long street filled with old monuments, its yellow sandstone church, its pagan house, the oldest in the province, but also Rosenwiller, an almost mountainous neighbor with its country-side vineyards and the Jewish cemetery hidden by the forest, all make it worth the detour.

 HOTELS-RESTAURANTS

● **Hostellerie du Rosenmeer**   ○⌂
45, av de la Gare.
Tel. 03 88 50 43 29. Fax 03 88 49 20 57.
info@le-rosenmeer.com
www.le-rosenmeer.com
Closed Feb. vac., 2 weeks end July–beg. Aug.
Rest. closed Sun. dinner, Mon., Wed.
Winstub closed lunch, Mon.
20 rooms: 40–98€.
Prix fixe: 74€ (wine inc.), 110€ (wine inc.).
A la carte: 60€.

Hubert Maetz was for ten years in succession the second in command to Westermann in Buerehiesel. He is also the efficient, but discreet, partner of our colleague Simone Morgenthaler on the TV channel France 3 who illustrates her "sweet and savory" programs in dialect with recipes from people of the region prepared by this serene maestro. At home, the gentle Hubert runs his *winstub* (known as "D'Rosemer"), looks after the special menus for the regulars (onion soup and pike-perch with käseknäpfle, a local fromage blanc dumpling) and watches over his very comfortable hotel. It is true that, if the whole effect is more functional than charming, his establishment is comfortable, the service smiling and exact, the cellar abundant, without forgetting the good wines produced by papa Maetz. But one comes first and foremost to discover, in a light restaurant with its huge shuttered bay windows opening onto the outside, the ideas of the moment: truffle-seasoned quick-seared minced scallops presented

with a layer of raw scallops on top, pan-seared scallops with walnuts and an herb salad, Atlantic sea bass cooked on pine bark with mugwort jus and the duck foie gras carpaccio with Vin Jaune and a foie bonbon. The roasted capon with its firm and delicious meat, deboned and served with the stuffed and rolled drumstick and his delicious buewespaetzle fall in the same vein, with a wink to the region. Add to this superb desserts: orange and saffron salad with mousse and sorbet of the same flavors and roasted and cara-melized Victoria pineapple with coconut Chantilly and a meltingly delicious milk sorbet, and you will say to yourself that here is a truly fine place.

■ **La Petite Auberge**   ⌂
41, rue du Général-de-Gaulle.
Tel. 03 88 50 40 60. Fax 03 88 48 00 90.
christophe-vasconi@wanadoo.fr
Closed vac. Mar., end June–beg. July.
Rest. closed Wed., Thu.
5 studios: 45-86€.Prix fixe: 20€,
9,50€ (child). A la carte: 45€.

Neat rooms in a paneled hotel and a classic cuisine in a pleasant inn: this is the domain of the modest Richard Vasconi. Scallop salad with lobster butter, spicy roasted sea bream, beef tenderloin with escargots and the frozen kouglof are dishes of which one never tires.

● **Auberge du Cerf**   COM
120, rue du Général-de-Gaulle.
Tel.-Fax 03 88 50 40 14.
Closed Sun. dinner, Mon., 2 weeks Jan.
Prix fixe: 12€ (lunch), 15€, 20€.
A la carte: 35–45€.

Pierre Eber keeps a wise and watchful eye on this 16th-century house that pays homage to Alsace in all its forms. Escargots in puff pastry with Munster cheese, pike-perch in fish broth, choucroute and a frozen vacherin all slip down without a second thought. The cheerfulness of the establishment is contagious and the checks not too inflated.

SHOPS

BREAD & BAKED GOODS

▼ Kapfer

54, rue du Général-de-Gaulle.
Tel.-Fax 03 88 50 41 79.
Old-fashioned loaves ("*papilou*") with chestnuts, beer, rye, or poppyseeds are made with an Alsépi flour. The kouglof and Black Forest cake are appealing.

▼ Rohmer

104, rue du Général-de-Gaulle.
Tel. 03 88 50 41 73.
This establishment has been producing good bread for four centuries. Country-style, flavored or baked in a dish; seasonal tarts; and ropfkuche make a fine impression.

CHARCUTERIE

▼ Muller

130, rue du Général-de-Gaulle.
Tel. 03 88 50 22 55.
Rémy Muller deftly prepares cervelas, ham, galantine, smoked ham, knacks, country bacon, beer sausage, presskopf and choucroute garnie.

CHEESE

▼ Siffert Frères

35, rte de Rosenwiller.
Tel. 03 88 50 20 13.
www.fromagerie-siffert.com
The Sifferts offer only the best munster produced in the Vosges. Blocks of Langmuhl, Hansi made with poire Williams and farm-made munster are irresistible.

ROUFFACH

68250 Haut-Rhin. Paris 458 – Colmar 15 – Mulhouse 28 – Bâle 60.
General Lefebvre's old native stomping grounds hides several treasures, including a dramatic square containing beautiful houses with oriels and redans and a large church that played host to the birth of the legendary women's revolt. Vineyards all around.

 HOTELS-RESTAURANTS

■ Château d'Isenbourg ❀🏚

Tel. 03 89 78 58 50. Fax 03 89 78 53 70.
isenbourg@grandesetapes.fr
www.isenbourg.com
40 rooms: 57–410€. 1 suite: 530€.
Prix fixe: 45€, 62€. A la carte: 75€.

Overlooking vineyards, this 18th-century château offers many pleasures. Large, comfortable rooms with stylish furnishings, two swimming pools (one covered), a fitness suite, hammam and Jacuzzi contribute to the joy of being there. The cuisine is not to be outdone. Didier Lefeuvre serves his adopted region skillfully with jumbo shrimp fried in angelhair pasta, scallops in an endive tarte Tatin, farm-raised poultry breast simmered in Riesling and a chocolate soufflé. Large cellar in which Alsace plays the main role and excellent service.

■ La Ville de Lyon 🏚

1, rue Poincaré.
Tel. 03 89 49 65 51. Fax 03 89 49 76 67.
www.villes-et-vignobles.com
Closed 10 days Christmas–New Year's.
50 rooms: 48–82€. 7 suites: 110€.

This inn makes an ideal base for visiting the region. The rooms furnished in Louis XV, Louis XVI or contemporary styles, the outdoor heated swimming pool, the hammam, the Jacuzzi and the health center immediately make one want to return. (See Restaurants: Philippe Bohrer.)

● **Philippe Bohrer** ○ V.COM

1, rue Poincaré.
Tel. 03 89 49 62 49. Fax 03 89 49 76 67.
villedelyon@villes-et-vignoble.com
www.villes-et-vignoble.com
Closed Sun., Mon. lunch, Wed. lunch,
3 weeks Mar., 1 week at end July,
1 week beg. Aug.
Prix fixe: 27€, 38€, 61€, 80€.

Philippe Bohrer has had a dream career: Loiseau, Lameloise, Gaertner, Bocuse, l'Elysée.... Which allows one to forecast the best future for this native of Upper Rhine who has decided to come back to settle in his home of Rouffach. Three dining rooms with a warm décor of welcoming pale wood where one can eat dishes that swing between regional tradition and innovation. One makes quick work of beet ravioli with their caramel, Atlantic sea bass filet with aromatic herbs and black morels, breast of guinea hen with slow-cooked shallots and a hoseradish-seasoned pigeon, poached then oven browned. We finish on a note both sweet and rather acidic with variations on the theme of rhubarb and strawberries served with ice cream. The welcome is wonderful, the service very attentive and the wines selected with discernment.

● **Winstub de la Poterne** SIM

7, rue de la Poterne.
Tel. 03 89 78 53 29. Fax 03 89 78 50 28.
www.flaneurvert.com
Closed Sun. dinner, Mon., Wed. dinner, Feb. vac.
Prix fixe: 8,25€ (weekday lunch), 22€, 28€, 7,50€ (child). A la carte: 30–35€.

Jacques Wipff has made this lively tavern into the gastronomic center of his town. Oxtail and foie gras terrine in wine aspic, pike-perch simmered in Riesling with buttered noodles, a liver quenelle and the apple streudel meet with universal acclaim. Friendly service, serious wine list and reasonable prices.

In Bollenberg (68250). 6 km via N83, exit for D15.

● **Au Vieux Pressoir** COM
  & Hôtel du Bollenberg

Domaine du Bollenberg.
Tel. 03 89 49 60 04 (rest.)
03 89 49 62 47 (hotel). Fax 03 89 49 76 16.
info@bollenberg.com www.bollenberg.com
Hotel closed Christmas.
Rest. closed Sun. dinner (off season).
45 rooms: 45–61€. 1 suite: 105€.
Prix fixe: 25€ (weekday lunch), 26€ (wine inc.), 33€ (Sat., Sun., lunch) 10€ (child).
A la carte: 45–50€.

In the Meyer family, love of hospitality and the culinary arts have been passed down from generation to generation. In the guesthouse, Michel Runner prepares classics such as foie gras, pike-perch cooked in wine, pork trotter medallions accompanied with local Saint Appoline wine and a frozen kouglof with Marc de Gewurz, created by Blaise Meyer. There is a choice of thirty or so *eaux-de-vie*. One can sleep in one of the comfortable rooms of the hotel where Marie-Madeleine Holtzheyer gives a warm welcome. Hammam, sauna, fitness suite.

▼	SHOPS

PASTRIES

▼ **Urweiller**

2, rue du Marché.
Tel.-Fax 03 89 49 61 04.
Claude Urweiller delights us with "*cailloux de Rouffach*" (cinnamon and chocolate), berawecke, bredele, kouglof, gingerbread and orange parfait (known as "Lefebvre", in honor of the Field Marshal).

REGIONAL PRODUCTS

▼ **A l'Eléphant**

4, rue de la Poterne.
Tel. 03 89 78 50 20.
Marylène Michel-Muller selects the finest products of Alsace: pottery, fabrics, gingerbread, wines from Clos Saint-Landelin, eaux de vie from Isenbourg and Christine Ferber jams.

SAINT-HIPPOLYTE

68590 Haut-Rhin. Paris 434 – Colmar 20 –
Ribeauvillé 7 – Saint-Dié 42 – Sélestat 10.
Across from the Haut-Koenigsbourg and its massive silhouette, this village, crowded in season, is well placed on the wine route.

 HOTELS-RESTAURANTS

■ Hostellerie Munsch
& Aux Ducs de Lorraine

16, rte du Vin.
Tel. 03 89 73 00 09. Fax 03 89 73 05 46.
www.hotel-munsch.com
Closed 2 weeks Nov., 10 days at end Jan.,
beg. Feb.–beg. Mar.
Rest. closed Tue. dinner, Wed.
36 rooms: 50–120€. 4 suites: 120–175€.
Prix fixe: 22€, 55€.

The hotel, with its flowery balconies and sculptured wood exterior, has large rooms that are prettily decorated and which give a bird's eye view of the vineyard and the Haut-Koenigsbourg. Christophe Meyer, who has worked at Lameloise's and Loiseau's, defends his region passionately but also goes beyond it. As demonstrated by the duck foie gras escalope with seasonal fruits, the monkfish medallion with saffron, the veal medallion croustillant with herbs and a generous chocolate dessert plate that gives unabating pleasure. Wines of Alsace have pride of place, skillfully promoted by enthusiastic sommelier Mike Eschbach.

■ Le Parc

6, rue du Parc.
Tel. 03 89 73 00 06. Fax 03 89 73 04 30.
hotel-le-parc@wanadoo.fr
www.le-parc.com
Closed beg. Jan.–beg. Feb., 10 days end
June–beg. July.
Rest. closed Mon. lunch, Tue. lunch.
30 rooms: 72–140€. 1 suite: 155€.
Prix fixe: 20€, 31€, 50€, 10€ (child).

Here is an Alsace of heart and friendship, in both the welcome and at the table, in the *winstub* or in the restaurant where Joseph Kientzel successfully revisits regional classics. Rabbit sausage with pumpkin and foie gras, a cream and black radish palate cleanser, goose foie gras three ways (house special with Gewurz, another spicy, and the third oven-crisped "crumble" style), locally fished salmon trout, open ravioli with coq au vin and pistachios and the aniseed crème brûlée served with an exotic fruit crumble are carefully worked and accompanied by an impressive wine list. Spacious, calm rooms, swimming pool and sauna—an ideal stopover on the wine route.

SAINT-LOUIS

68300 Haut-Rhin. Paris 549 – Ferrette 24 –
Mulhouse 31 – Colmar 66.
This is both the doorway to Switzerland to the winding Sundgau, a border town in neutral colors that plays host to a book festival. Gastronomy is on the scene.

 HOTELS-RESTAURANTS

■ La Cour du Roy

1, rue de Lectoure.
Tel. 03 89 70 33 33.
www.hotelfp-saintlouis.com
Rest. closed Sat. lunch, Sun. dinner, Mon.,
end Dec.
30 rooms: 54–200€.
Prix fixe: 28–52€.

This former beer warehouse in a Renaissance style, dated 1906, has been converted into a contemporary hotel with very well-prepared rooms. Luxurious restaurant, timbered bar decorated on the theme of medieval beasts: a great overall effect!

■ L'Europe

2, rue de Huningue.
Tel. 03 89 69 73 55. Fax 03 89 67 92 06.
www.hotel-deleurope.com
27 rooms: 55–102€. 1 suite: 90€.

Behind the brick exterior of this 19th-century house with a neo-gothic tower are hidden comfortable, old-style rooms and a much-appreciated French and American billiard room.

■ Berlioz

rue Henner.
Tel. 03 89 69 74 44. Fax 03 89 70 19 17.
info@hotelberlioz.com
www.hotelberlioz.com
Closed 10 days Christmas–New Year's.
21 rooms: 55–70€.

One has the choice between "Louis XVI" or "boat" rooms in this thirties hotel near the station. The welcome of Patrick Valin and the breakfasts make it a pleasant stopover.

In Hégenheim (68220). 7 km sw via D469.

● Auberge du Boeuf Rouge   SIM

9, rue de Hésingue.
Tel. 03 89 69 40 00. Fax 03 89 67 78 69.
boeuf.rouge@libertysurf.fr
Closed Sat. lunch, Sun. (exc. groups).
Prix fixe: 11€ (lunch), 22€ (lunch),
10€ (child). A la carte: 38€.

Alsace is totally present in the establishment of Martin Dirrig. The setting is rural, the place warm and the cuisine of Didier Risacher follows suit. Griled marbled duck and goose foie gras, the local flat garnished pies, pork cuts and charcuterie over sauerkraut and slow-cooked quetche plums with little pain perdu croutons and cinnamon ice cream meet with universal acclaim. Rapid service and low prices.

In Hésingue (68220). 4 km w via D419.

● Au Boeuf Noir   V.COM

2, rue de Folgenburg.
Tel. 03 89 69 76 40. Fax 03 89 67 77 29.
j.giuggiola@tiscali.fr
Closed Sat. lunch, Sun. dinner, Mon.,
2 weeks Mar., 2 weeks Aug.
Prix fixe: 28€ (lunch), 36€ (lunch, wine inc.), 45€, 69€. A la carte: 68€.

Jean-Pierre Giuggiola is an artist of multiple facets. He paints, and exhibits his colorful works on the light walls of his restaurant, but it is in the kitchen that he really shows what he's capable of, giving free rein to his imagination to create new combinations of successful flavors. One makes very short work of lobster and truffle salad, oven-browned pike-perch filet with seasonal vegetables, deboned pigeon cut into slices and the berry mille-feuille wih vanilla ice cream. Josiane "Giugiu" is a charming mistress of the house who gives good advice when it comes to selecting wines. The check is not excessive, encouraging one to go back to taste the things one couldn't try the first time.

In Huningue (68330). 2 km e via D469.

■ Tivoli

15, rue de Bâle.
Tel. 03 89 69 73 05. Fax 03 89 67 82 44.
info@tivoli.fr
www.tivoli.fr
Rest. closed Sat., Sun., Christmas–New Year's vac., 1 week at end July,
2 weeks beg. Aug.
41 rooms: 62–150€.
Prix fixe: 13€ (lunch), 24€, 45€.
A la carte: 50€.

Philippe Schneider, student of Jung and of the Hæberlins, excels in reinterpreting traditional dishes with finesse and a light touch. We like his venison terrine with foie gras, salmon trout roasted skin-side down, black tiger shrimp, venison medallion and the classically prepared torche au marron (a chestnut and meringue dessert). Eric Gollentz, a connoisseur of wines from the region and elsewhere, always gives good advice while the service is high quality and the checks remain reasonable. In the brasserie, the fast dishes of the day are executed with care and are very good value. The rooms, decorated in contemporary style, are functional.

In Village-Neuf (68128). 3 km ne via N66 and D21.

● Le Cheval Blanc   N SIM

6, rue de Rosenau.
Tel. 03 89 69 79 15. Fax 03 89 69 86 63.
www.lechevalblanc.fr
Closed Christmas–beg. Jan.,
3 weeks in summer.
12 rooms: 45–48€.
Prix fixe: 17€, 21€, 39€ (wine inc.), 48€.

Massimo Cataldi, who worked at the Rendez-Vous de Chasse in Colmar, is trying to do a good job in his roadside restaurant. He works seriously with regional products and treats game with solemnity, offering wild boar in various forms: ham, head cheese, sausage, chops, civet, venison saddle or medallions, pheasant, pigeon, wild duck, young partridge and breasts of game hen. Everything is reasonably priced. In the bar corner, where the dish of the day is served (as in the rather kitsch restaurant), the special menus are also dispensed with seriousness. There is nothing to change in the goose foie gras, pike-perch on a bed of slow-cooked leeks and horseradish, nor the desserts (crème brûlée and an apple and walnut oven-crisped dessert).

In Village-Neuf.

● **La Nouvelle Brasserie Runser** SIM

2, rue de Saint-Louis.
Tel. 03 89 67 11 15. Fax 03 89 69 45 08.
Closed Christmas.
Prix fixe: 12€ (lunch), 21€, 29€, 32€.
A la carte: 45€.

Eric Runser has successfully kept this very contemporary brasserie going. One comes here, right on the border, to talk but also to enjoy a slice of foie gras with Port wine jelly, jumbo shrimp brochettes, sole meunière, beef sirloin steak and a frozen kouglof, created by good disciple Denis Beck. Professional service and moderate prices.

▼	SHOPS

BUTCHER

▼ **Hassler**

8, rue de Village-Neuf.
Tel. 03 89 89 79 69.
www.hassler1898.com
Since 1898, the Hassler family have been preparing quality Alsatian-style pork haunch, choucroute garnie, smoked pork shoulder, gendarmes, knacks, presskopf or pistachio galantine.

BUTCHER-CHARCUTERIE

▼ **Eckert**

14, rue de Hésingue.
Tel. 03 89 69 18 51.
The Eckerts are champions of hiriwurst, a sort of local Montbéliard sausage. Their presskopf, pork knuckle, country bacon, Sundgauvien ham and foie gras are also mouthwateringly good.

CHARCUTERIE

▼ **Hertzog**

5, rue de Huningue.
Tel. 03 89 69 73 33.
boucherie-hertzog.com
Véronique Ott boasts quality cervelas, knacks, fleischwurst or smoked hiriwurst, pâté and liver sausage, filet mignon in pastry and stuffed veal breast.

CHOCOLATE & PASTRIES

▼ **Christian Bauer**

74, rue de Mulhouse.
Tel. 03 89 67 29 94.
Christian Bauer's vosgiens (blueberry mousse, raspberry, cassis), linzer torte, and "*Exotic*" (hazelnut biscuit, mango-passion fruit mousse) are superb. His chocolates score a resounding success with his Swiss neighbors.

TABLETOP & KITCHENWARE

▼ **La Boutique**

1, av du Général-de-Gaulle.
Tel. 03 89 69 19 13.
Silverware, crystal, china (Christofle, Bernardaud, Haviland) and jewelry (Baccarat, Bernardaud): Catia Courteix's taste is faultless.

SARRE-UNION

67260 Bas-Rhin. Paris 409 – Strasbourg 84 – Metz 82 – Sarreguemines 23.
The capital of the "hump" of Alsace is unfortunately poor in terms of restaurants, but the surrounding areas contain nice surprises.

● | RESTAURANTS

In Altwiller (67260). 6 km nw via Harskirchen.

● **L'Ecluse 16**   SIM

Locale known as Bonne-Fontaine.
Tel. 03 88 00 90 42. Fax 03 88 00 91 94.
Closed Mon. lunch, Tue., 2 weeks beg. Mar.,
2 weeks beg. Sept.
Prix fixe: 17€ (weekday lunch), 28€, 42€.

Again this year, we have fallen in love with Jean-Yves Leroux's pretty brick inn, bordering the haulage route. This typical 1900s house offers a tasteful modern interior where one has the pleasant experience of eating well. Lime-seasoned trout with chanterelles, grilled swordfish steak with spicy bibelekäs (fresh fromage blanc with herbs), braised veal sweetbreads with meat jus and frozen pistachio cannelloni, it is a gastronomic sin. The touch of chef Jean-Yves Roux, added to these classic dishes, hits the bull's-eye every time.

In Berg (67320). 12 km se via N61 and D15.

● **Bellevue**   SIM

Tel. 03 88 00 62 26.
Closed Tue. dinner, Wed.,
10 days Christmas–New Year's.
Prix fixe: 8,50€ (lunch), 21,50€, 25€, 32€.

Sonia Gilger, who works in the kitchen with her sister, while her daughter Carmen gives a smiling reception, cultivates her huge kitchen garden. This blonde and cheerful fairy godmother has made this panoramic establishment in the heart of the hump of Alsace into her little gastronomic domain. There is the café corner, the tables for the dish of the day (salad with sausage and Gruyère, roasted pork tenderloin with pan-tossed potatoes and zucchini) and the *winstub* room with its collection of engravings, plates and souvenirs. Salad with sausage and Gruyère, and a pork tenderloin with pan-tossed potatoes and zucchini gratin, Head cheese and wine aspic terrine, pâté in pastry crust, escargots, Alsace-style meat dumplings (fleischschnackas), old-style ravioli and tête de veau are like grandma made them.

In Burbach (67260). 10 km se, N 61.

● **Le Windhof**   V.COM

3, Windhof.
Tel. 03 88 01 72 35. Fax 03 88 01 72 71.
bernard.kehne@wanadoo.fr
www.windhof.fr
Closed Sun. dinner, Mon., Tue. dinner,
2 weeks Jan., 3 weeks Aug.
Prix fixe: 19€, 27,50€, 42€, 46€, 53€,
61€.
A la carte: 50–65€.

On the plateau of Lorraine, this large, exposed farm is deceptive. The wooden interior is luxurious and charming with its vast, double dining room and its well-spaced and well-placed tables. The Kehné family run the establishment with professionalism but it is the son, Laurent, back from his classes with the greats (Crocodile, Auberge de l'Ill, Cerf at Marlenheim, Cygne at Gundershofen), who has bowled the house style over, balancing it with his sense of finesse and lightness: swordfish carpaccio with fennel (served as an amuse-gueule), flat savory mini-tart, surf and turf, niçoise-style tomato and pepper tart with pan-tossed sardines, scallop carpaccio with pan-tossed little squids, pan-cooked sturgeon with truffle oil-seasoned risotto, classic pan-tossed veal kidney with mustard sauce and the strawberry mille-feuille with basil sauce. The wine list is full of wonderful discoveries, nicely charged.

In Siewiller (67320). 12 km se via N61.

● **Restaurant de la Gare**   SIM

9, rte Nationale.
Tel. 03 88 00 99 46. Fax 03 88 01 20 28.
Closed Mon., Tue. dinner, Sept., 2 weeks Jan.
Prix fixe: 23€, 25€, 8,80€ (child).
A la carte: 32€.

The Benedick's café-restaurant is a joy. Céline on reception is all smiles and in the kitchen, Frédéric, trained by Albrecht in Rhinau, creates delicious tartes flambées at the weekend and serious dishes during the week. Duck breast and foie gras salad, fish stew with horseradish sauce, sirloin steak with ceps and the chocolate profiteroles are eaten in a relaxed atmosphere.

▼ SHOPS

CHARCUTERIE
In Diemeringen. 9 km w.
▼ Gangloff
57, Grand-Rue.
Tel. 03 88 00 41 84.
Patrick prepares the produce and Pascal, Annick and Alain handle sales and service: the Gangloffs have been dedicated to supplying mouthwatering terrine, ham, presskopf and sausages since 1932. The true pork butcher's art in Alsace Bossue! (Another store: 79b, rue Principale, 67430 Mackwiller, tel. +33 (0)3 88 00 40 94).

SAULXURES

67420 Bas-Rhin. Paris 408 – Strasbourg 62 – Saint-Dié 32.
The road climbs towards the peaks, drifts off towards Hautes-Vosges, leaving the Bruche valley on its right and nodding towards the fir trees. You come to the village and its dome bell, the inn tucked away in a corner.

HOTELS-RESTAURANTS

La Belle Vue
36, rue Principale.
Tel. 03 88 97 60 23. Fax 03 88 47 23 71.
labellevue@wanadoo.fr
www.la-belle-vue.com
Closed 1 week at end Mar., 10 days end July–beg. Aug., 2 weeks Nov. Rest. closed Tue., Wed.
4 rooms: 84€. 2 suites: 122–163€.
Prix fixe: 19,50€, 23€ (weekdays), 30€, 33€, 36€, 72€.

We like the enthusiasm of Valérie Boulanger, who is at the helm of this happy house. The very smiling reception, the cozy rooms, the wood décor and the generous breakfasts all give pleasure. The cuisine of Marc Koeniguer follows trends with spicy duck tartare with arugula salad, vanilla-seasoned sea bream, slow-cooked venison with blood sauce served with cabbage and the caramel-glazed macaron, even if it isn't always easy to forget that imaginative creator, Denis Boulanger, who departed too soon. On the cellar side, a Zotzenberg Grand Cru Tokay labelled Albert Seltz and a Pinot Noir labelled Trimbach make astounding companions to the meal.

SAVERNE

67700 Bas-Rhin. Paris 447 – Strasbourg 39 – Haguenau 37 – Molsheim 28.
info@otsaverne.fr.
It was from the *col* of Saverne that Louis XIV made his famous comment: "What a beautiful garden!" Also in Saverne are the *Tres Tabernae* ("three taverns") of the Romans that affirmed and began Alsace's ancestral vocation of hospitality extended with good humor and modesty.

HOTELS-RESTAURANTS

■ Hôtel de l'Europe
7, rue de la Gare.
Tel. 03 88 71 12 07. Fax 03 88 71 11 43.
info@hotel-europe-fr.com
www.hotel-europe-fr.com
Closed 2 weeks Christmas–New Year's.
27 rooms: 60,50–89,50€. 1 suite: 83–123€.

Each room honors a country of the European Union, conferring an original atmosphere on this hotel. Located near the station, its convenience is also an asset.

■ Chez Jean

"Rosestiebel"

3, rue de la Gare.
Tel. 03 88 91 10 19. Fax 03 88 91 27 45.
chez.jean@wanadoo.fr
www.chez-jean.com
Hotel closed 2 weeks end Dec.–mid-Jan.
Rest. closed Sun. dinner, Mon.,
2 weeks mid-Dec.–beg. Jan.
25 rooms: 61–83€.
Prix fixe: 27€, 47€.

It was a convent and has become a very good town center hotel. There is the kindness of the Harters, the rooms decorated in Alsatian style, warm and practical, Jean-Pierre's reliable cuisine, the S'Rosestiebel *winstub* as well as Chez Jean, which delights connoisseurs with poultry in aspic, soufflé with lobster sauce, the famous tête de veau, classic and the frozen Grand Marnier soufflé. The terrace is welcoming in summer and the wines of Alsace that are on offer don't make the check rocket.

■ Le Clos de la Garenne

88, route du Haut-Barr.
Tel. 03 88 71 20 41. Fax 03 88 02 08 86.
clos.garenne@wanadoo.fr
www.closgarenne.com
Rest. closed Sat. lunch, Tue. dinner,
Wed. dinner, Feb. vac.
14 rooms: 32–86€.
Prix fixe: 16€ (weekday lunch), 36€ (wine inc.), 45€, 55€, 12€ (child).
A la carte: 75€.

In the middle of a pretty wooded park, this very recent family house has been tastefully decorated by Virgine and Sébastien Schmitt. The modern, Savoie-style rooms, as pretty as a picture, are an invitation to spend some wonderful moments, particularly at breakfast time. In the restaurant, Sébastien, past master in the art of making tartes flambées, ventures towards a more modern cuisine. Here one enjoys slow-cooked pears with pan-seared foie gras, big langoustines with pumpkin cream, marbled rabbit terrine with beet purée, game in season and the chocolate and mirabelle plum dessert. The wines offered by Manu Minck are outstanding.

■ Villa Katz

42, rue du Général-Leclerc.
Tel. 03 88 71 02 02. Fax 03 88 71 80 30.
tavernekatz@wanadoo.fr
www.tavernekatz.com
6 rooms: 54–100€. 4 suites: 75–100€.
Prix fixe: 16€ (lunch), 24€, 38€, 42€, 55€, 12€ (child).

Suzy Schmitt, who also has the Taverne Katz, watches lovingly over her Jugendstil "folly", loved in the past by a descendant of emperor William II, the baron of Holland. The rooms are sweet and comfortable and the good traditional dishes of Franck Pellegrino are worth the detour. A slice of foie gras, fish stew, farm-raised duck and a woodruff-seasoned beignet with compote are irresistible.

● Zuem Staeffele

1, rue R.-Poincaré.
Tel.-Fax 03 88 91 63 94.
michel.jaeckel@wanadoo.fr
www.strasnet.com/staessele.htl
Closed Sun. dinner, Wed., Thu. dinner, Christmas–New Year's, 10 days at end July,
2 weeks beg. Aug.
Prix fixe: 21,50€ (weekday lunch), 29,50€ (weekday lunch), 37€, 52€.
A la carte: 55€.

Opposite the Rohan château, the Jaeckels house is one of the lasting kind. Michel is modest and industrious and is not content just to deliver local recipes: he is continually reinventing them, using market produce, and is never short of ideas. Langoustine ravioli served over sweet-and-sour sauce and a melon and pan-seared foie gras salad set the tone. There is a pan tossed monkfish and smoked bacon, duck breast with rhubarb and a curry-seasoned lamb medallion with beans, peaches and almonds. An apricot dacquoise with almond milk ice cream and a simmered peach with green tea sauce make gentle endings to the meal. The wines are a passionate celebration of Alsace, without overlooking other regions. Fabienne who welcomes her guests as if they were old friends, has a communicative smile and there is a general atmosphere of good humor that isn't undermined by the discreet check.

● **Château du Haut-Barr** 🏠COM

Tel. 03 88 91 17 61. Fax 03 88 91 86 26.
hautbarr@free.fr
www.notrealsace.com/chateau-du-haut-barr
Closed Mon., Thu. dinner, 1 Nov.,
3 weeks Feb.
Prix fixe: 19€, 28,50€, 30,50€,
7€ (child). A la carte: 38€.

Bernard Baudendiestel is the king of the fortified castle from where one can admire the town and the plain of Alsace. His cuisine is like he is—provocative—but the regional products are treated in a personal way and with heart, as demonstrated by his superb goose foie gras, salmon tagliatelli with trout roe, veal kidneys with whole grain mustard and Armagnac-flavored plum ice cream. The fisherman's catch and tartes flambées in the evening in the brasserie section are another reason for making the stop. Pretty summer terrace.

● **Taverne Katz** 🏠🏠🏠 SIM

80, Grand-Rue.
Tel. 03 88 71 16 56. Fax 03 88 71 85 85.
tavernekatz@wanadoo.fr
www.tavernekatz.com
Closed Christmas.
Prix fixe: 16€ (lunch), 24€, 38€.

This tavern shines out like a Renaissance pearl, with its wood decoration, beamed ceiling, engravings by Hansi and Untereiner, kelsch tableclothes and dishes that pay reverence to the history of Alsace. The menu even enacts a kind of festival: an escargot, white cabbage, goose gizzards and slow-cooked chestnut salad, horseradish-seasoned pork trotter, grumbeerekiechle (potato cakes), nudelstrudel (rolled stuffed noodles) or the marvelous poultry timbale. It all moves and delights with a childlike feel of playfulness. The establishment is run by Suzy Schmitt, with her son Pierre in the restaurant. The des-

serts, simple and good (a mirabelle plum chaud-froid or streudel), the wines chosen with "nose", the well-pulled Saverne beer: in short, one sees that the place has kept a spirited role as a retro institution. Pleasant summer terrace.

● **Le Carpaccio** SIM

22, Grand-Rue.
Tel. 03 88 02 07 74. Fax 03 88 91 26 43.
Closed Sun. lunch, Thu.
Prix fixe: 16€ (lunch), 40€ (lunch),
8€ (child). A la carte: 35€.

Mimmo de Calabre has made his crimson and oriel establishment into a nice little advertisement for transalpine cuisine. Carpaccio, pizzas, cheese tortelloni, spaghetti carbonara, saltimbocca and frozen chocolate truffle are simply astounding, served in an amusing Neo-Pompeiian décor. Several fine Pouilles or Abruzzes wines do not increase the check (too much). Slow service.

In Ernolsheim-les-Saverne (67330). 6 km route de Bouxwiller.

● **Le Daubenschlag** SIM

87, rue Principale.
Tel. 03 88 70 30 16.
Closed Sat. lunch, Mon., Tue.
A la carte: 28€.

Pierre Sansig, installed in a former barn, delights his guests with his sweet and savory tartes flambées. They also come for the cured ham plate with raw vegetables, fish brochette and the meats (beef sirloin or veal filet). The wines served in pitchers are good value and the prices not brutal.

In Monswiller (67700). 3 km n via D425.

● **Kasbür** ○COM

8, rue de Dettwiller.
Tel. 03 88 02 14 20. Fax 03 88 02 14 21.
www.restaurant-kasbur.fr
Closed Sun. dinner, Mon., 2 weeks Jan,
2 weeks Aug.
Prix fixe: 19€ (lunch), 38€, 46€, 55€.

A "kasbür" is a farmer-cheesemaker, an ancestor of the Kieffer family whose profession is depicted in the fresco decorating the outside of this thirties building with updated décor. Yves Kieffer in the kitchen pays homage to the grand cuisine learned in Paris at the Tour d'Argent and at Vézelay with Meneau. He makes the most of the good regional produce by serving it in original, carefully prepared dishes, in rock bottom-priced formula menus. We enjoy the view of the forest and fields of Haut-Barr while tasting escargots served in parsley soup, Atlantic sea bass filet, pike-perch streudel, rack of lamb and the suckling pig. When it is time for dessert, we hesitate between a strawberry and rhubarb dessert with fresh cheese ice cream, cherry confit on old-fashioned shortbread and the caramel ice cream. The considerate welcome and attentive service of Béatrice persuade us that this was the right choice.

In Saint-Jean-Saverne (67700). 4 km n via D115.

■ **Kleiber**

37, Grand-Rue.
Tel. 03 88 91 11 82. Fax 03 88 71 09 64.
info@kleiber-fr.com
www.kleiber-fr.com
Closed 23 Dec.–mid-Jan.
Rest. closed Sat. lunch, Sun. dinner.
16 rooms: 46–70€.
Prix fixe: 10€ (lunch), 20€, 45€, 10€ (child).

Because of its location next to the regional nature park of Vosges, this family hotel is the headquarters of hikers as well as ATB lovers. In the village, it offers well-equipped rooms in the style of Louis-Philippe and a good, unpretentious cuisine under the management of Stéphane Lorentz, who watches father Georges out of the corner of his eye. Beef stew served pressed into the form of a cake, organic salmon on a bed of vegetables with mushroom risotto, apple and pear regional desserts and the tartes flambées at the end of the week are also right on the mark.

▼ | SHOPS

BREAD & BAKED GOODS

▼ **Reutenauer**

79, Grand-Rue.
Tel. 03 88 91 36 72.
Country-style loaf, mixed grain bread, rye and kouglof make a delicious impression at this traditional bakery.

BUTCHER & CHARCUTERIE

▼ **Schlotter**

86 Grand-Rue.
Tel. 03 88 01 80 90.
Didier Schlotter prepares quality artisan charcuterie—cervelas, knackwurst, bacon, smoked ham, beer sausage—along with nice meats.

CHARCUTERIE

In Saint-Jean-Saverne. 4 km n via D115.

▼ **Denis Wollbrett**

6, Grand-Rue.
Tel. 03 88 91 19 05.
Kings of fine smoked produce in Alsace, Denis Wollbrett and his son Hervé work enthusiastically on ham, country bacon, pistachio galantines, foie gras, torte made with Riesling, knacks and choucroute. We adore their potato sausage for grilling, and the liver sausage, a mix of veal and pork, perfect on a fresh baguette.

CHOCOLATE

▼ **Bockel**

12, rue des Sources / 77, Grand-Rue.
Tel. 03 88 91 29 49 / 03 88 02 06 78.
www.planet-chocolate.com
Jacques Bockel's one concern is quality. He supplies irresistible "kamasutra", chocolate praline roses, truffles, chocolate bars, various ganaches and chocolate "sausage".

PASTRIES

▼ **Jung**

3, rue Poincaré.
Tel. 03 88 91 15 85.
Philippe Jung painstakingly bakes traditional cakes. Chocolate and vanilla éclairs, religieuses (a dessert made o iced éclairs, said to resemble a nun)

kouglof, mille-feuille and fruit tarts will have you melting.

 Boistelle

92, Grand-Rue.
Tel.-Fax 03 88 91 10 55.
www.boistelle.com
Christian Boistelle deftly prepares bouton de rose, chocolate Saverne, streusel, Black Forest cake, kouglof or langhopf. Chocolates, ice creams and fine desserts.

TABLETOP & KITCHENWARE

▼ **Cristallerie Carabin**

52, Grand-Rue.
Tel. 03 88 91 11 93.
Finely worked carafes and ewers, and cut and hand-worked glasses. Open to visitors, the workshop restores antique crystalware.

◆ | RENDEZVOUS

TEA SALON

◆ **Haushalter**

66-68, Grand-Rue.
Tel. 03 88 91 13 30.
Eric Haushalter's pastries reflect the sweet-toothed traditions of Alsace. In the hushed tearoom or on the terrace in summer, we delight in his desserts: pineapple-rum, "Havane" (vanilla and chocolate biscuits with a rum mousseline), mille-feuille or fruit tarts.

SCHARRACHBERGHEIM

67310 Bas-Rhin. Paris 470 – Strasbourg 25 – Marlenheim 5 – Molsheim 8 – Saverne 22.
The start of the wine trail: don't miss villages like Traenheim and Le Dompeter or the baptistry of Dalenheim.

 HOTELS-RESTAURANTS

● **Lauth et fils**   SIM

63, rue Principale.
Tel. 03 88 50 66 05. Fax 03 88 50 60 76.
www.brasserie-restaurant-lauth.com
Closed 2 weeks Christmas–New Year's,
2 weeks beg. Aug.

Rest. closed lunch, Mon., Tue.
8 rooms: 35–46€.
A la carte: 35€.

This country brasserie, as huge as a concert hall, offers regional specialities astutely reworked by the master of the house, Daniel Lauth. Smoked herring in cream, artisanal head cheese terrine and wine aspic, grilled pork shank basted with beer eau-de-vie and frozen soufflé seasoned with Marc de Gewurztraminer exude authenticity. The beer is brewed on site and the wines are from neighboring producers. It is all good, and not expensive. The nine rooms are simple and tranquil. In addition, in the evening there are exquisite tartes flambées made in a wood-burning oven.

SCHIRMECK

67130 Bas-Rhin. Paris 410 – Strasbourg 53 – Sélestat 59 – Saint-Dié 39.
cc.hautebruche@wanadoo.fr.
This crossroads town of the Bruche valley opens out onto a secret, thicketed and wooded Vosges. Here are a string of very rural hamlets with smart inns that make clean little stopovers.

 HOTELS-RESTAURANTS

In Natzwiller (67130). 6 km sw via N420 and D130.

■ **Auberge Metzger**   🍴❀🏠

55, rue Principale.
Tel. 03 88 97 02 42. Fax 03 88 97 93 59.
auberge.metzger@wanadoo.fr
www.hotel-aubergemetzger.com
Closed Sun. dinner, Mon., 3 weeks Jan.,
2 weeks end June–10 July.
16 rooms: 54–75€.
Prix fixe: 13€ (weekday lunch), 19€,
24€ (lunch), 37€ (dinner), 55€ (dinner).

The Metzgers give a passionate account of Alsace, and the cuisine of Yves, who honors local produce, follows suit. Here one enjoys house charcuterie, a half-dozen escargots prepared Alsatian style (stuffed with spiced butter and herbs and cooked in local wine), stuffed pike-perch simmered in Riesling, suckling pig loin in a spicy sauce with morels and crêpes flavored with Kirsch. It is billed at a fair price and it all makes one want to spend several nights in the cozy rooms of this Vosges inn with flower-filled balconies. A very charming reception from Corinne and prompt service.

In Les Quelles (67130). 7 km sw via D420, D261, and forest road.

■ **Neuhauser**   ❀ 🏠
La Broque, Schirmeck.
Tel. 03 88 97 06 81. Fax 03 88 97 14 29.
hotelneuhauser@wanadoo.fr
www.hotel-neuhauser.com
Closed 2 weeks Nov., Feb. vac.
10 rooms: 62–79€. 2 suites: 119–152€.
Prix fixe: 20€, 25€, 34€, 45€, 10€ (child).
A la carte: 36–45€.

In this family hotel in open countryside, nestled at the top of a hill in the Bruche valley, one can choose between one of the pretty modern rooms or an apartment in one of the three wooden chalets. Pierre and Michel Neuhauser look after their guests with good local produce: duck foie gras with prunes, salmon trout, stuffed rabbit and wild forest berry dessert. Exquisite *eaux-de-vie* that are distilled in-house.

SELESTAT

67600 Bas-Rhin. Paris 440 – Colmar 22 – Strasbourg 51 – Mulhouse 63.
accueil@selesta-tourisme.com.
At the crossroads of the rapid Colmar-Strasbourg route, Sélestat is famous for its humanist library, devotional bells and beautiful Renaissance houses as well as for the wine routes of Vosges and the Rhine.

| | HOTELS-RESTAURANTS |

● **Abbaye de la Pommeraie**   ◑🏠
8, bd du Maréchal-Foch.
Tel. 03 88 92 07 84. Fax 03 88 92 08 71.
pommeraie@relaischateaux.com
www.relaischateau.com/pommeraie.
www.pommeraie.fr

Rest. closed Sun. dinner, Mon. lunch.
12 rooms: 141–246€. 2 suites: 291–316€.
Prix fixe: 51€, 90,50€. A la carte: 90€.

Christiane and Pascal Funaro run a good-natured Relais & Châteaux. The relaxed atmosphere, smiling service, rooms of sure taste and the pleasant garden are all a joy while the cuisine of Daniel Stein is not to be outdone. In the restaurant, Le Prieuré, beautiful woodwork and perfectly straight tables match the noble, clean food. Crab mille-feuille with slow-cooked vegetables, lobster with market vegetables, venison filet with apricot chutney and eggplant semolina and an Isaphan-themed ice cream sandwich with mascarpone, basil and raspberry make delicious feasts. Sensible checks and attractive Alsace wines complete the picture (see also the *winstub* S'Apfelstuebel).

■ **Auberge des Alliés**   🏠
39, rue des Chevaliers.
Tel. 03 88 92 09 34 / 03 88 92 28 00.
Fax 03 88 92 12 88.
auberge.allies@wanadoo.fr
www.auberge-des-allies.com
Hotel closed 24 Dec.–2 Jan.
Rest. closed Sun. dinner, Mon., Christmas–beg. Jan., end June–mid-July.
18 rooms: 48–65€.
Prix fixe: 21€, 26€, 8€ (child).

This old town center inn offers rooms with every comfort in a tasteful Alsatian atmosphere. The reception is courteous and the cuisine of Roland Roesch simple and good. Escargots, goose foie gras, roasted pike-perch with Alsatian red wine sauce and prunes, served in an old-style *winstub* setting, are generous and not excessively charged.

■ **Vaillant**   🏠
Pl de la République.
Tel. 03 88 92 09 46. Fax 03 88 82 95 01.
hotel-vaillant@wanadoo.fr
www.hotel-vaillant.com
47 rooms: 65–95€.
Prix fixe: 15€, 24€, 29€, 34€,
7,50€ (child).

Claire Faller has gradually redone this modern building, with its tastefully laid out rooms. In the restaurant, creamed chestnuts with morels, paupiette of pike-perch with green vegetables, beef sirloin steak with slow-cooked shallots and a Pinot Gris sauce and an iced Kirsch parfait are eaten with pleasure. This year, a brasserie has been created in the bar.

● S'Apfelstuebel   SIM

At the Abbaye de la Pommeraie, 8, bd du Maréchal-Foch.
Tel. 03 88 92 07 84. Fax 03 88 92 08 71.
pommeraie@relaischateaux.com
www.relaischateaux.com/pommeraie
Prix fixe: 26€ (weekday lunch), 35€ (lunch, wine inc.), 51€ (wine inc.).

This library-style "*stub*", decorated on a theme of apples, is as pretty as a picture. Audrey Meyer chooses the wine to accompany in fine manner the dishes concocted by Daniel Stein: slow-cooked vegetable terrine with smoked salmon, ginger-seasoned emperor fish served on a bed of fresh spinach, veal medallion with eggplant, tomato and basil mille-feuille and a strawberry Melba with Tagada strawberry bonbons.

● Au Bon Pichet   SIM

10, pl du Marché-aux-Choux.
Tel.-Fax 03 88 82 96 65.
Closed Sun. dinner, Mon. dinner,
2 weeks end Aug.–Sept.
Prix fixe: 15,80€ (lunch), 25€ (dinner).
A la carte: 35–55€.

The old hospital of the town, situated on the edge of the Ill, houses a traditional restaurant equipped with a recently renovated rotisserie room. Without making the check rocket, one can enjoy house terrine, red tuna tartare, a solid boneless rib steak, magnificent veal kidney roasted in its fat and the seasonal fruit tart cooked with heart by the ruddy-faced Roland Barthel, a former butcher who knows his meat like a true expert.

● La Vieille Tour   SIM

8, rue de la Jauge.
Tel. 03 88 92 15 02. Fax 03 88 92 19 42.
vieille.tour@wanadoo.fr
www.vieille-tour.com
Closed Mon.
Prix fixe: 11€ (weekday lunch), 19€, 33€, 44€, 55€.

Samy and Nicolas Rhulmann are giving an uncomplicated new life to this typical house flanked by an old tower. They have redone the restaurant, conserving the traditional style and cooking side by side, interpreting regional dishes with charm. House half-duck, half-goose foie gras terrine with Black Sureau sirop, pike-perch poached in red wine with frog legs, lamb medallions in pastilla with diced mushrooms simmered in cream and the roasted Victoria pineapple with caramel sauce and a house financier with honey ice cream make a good impression. Diligent service and prices that are not excessive.

In Rathsamhausen (67600). 5 km e via D21 and D209.

■ Les Prés d'Ondine

5, route de Baldenheim.
Tel. 03 88 58 04 60. Fax 03 88 58 04 61.
message@presdondine.com
www.presdondine.com
Closed mid-Jan.–mid-Feb.
Rest. closed Sun. dinner, Wed.
8 rooms: 65–105€. 4 suites: 105–135€.
Prix fixe: 32€ (wine inc.).

A stay in this pretty inn beside the Ill is stamped "relaxation". Stéphane Dalibert has decked it out with all the attractions: sweet, cozy rooms, sitting room/library, fitness center, hammam, Jacuzzi. You need to take the time to taste the good food concocted by the master of the house. Alsatian-style salad, trout or pike-perch filet, traditional choucroute and the kouglof pain perdu are extremely well conceived.

In Schnellenbuhl (67600). 8 km via D159 and D424.

■ Auberge de l'Illwald

Locale known as de Schnellenbuhl.
Tel. 03 88 85 35 40. Fax 03 88 85 39 18.
contact@illwald.fr
www.illwald.fr
Closed 24 Dec.–10 Jan.,
1 week at end June–mid-July.
Rest. closed Tue., Wed.
9 rooms: 65–110€.
Prix fixe: 10€ (weekday lunch), 30€ (Sat., Sun.), 8,50€ (child). A la carte: 36€.

Brigitte and Christian Schwartz have very quickly taken the measure of their smart hotel with its Alsatian charm. Eight additional rooms have been created in the two local houses made of pink sandstone. As for the *winstub*, it has become a landmark in the region. In the packed restaurant with its fresco by Edgar Mahler, one makes quick work of head cheese and wine aspic terrine, pike-perch simmered in red wine, rabbit leg with star anise seasoning and licorice-flavored strawberries. The slate menu board changes every day but the classics of Alsace are faithful to their post.

▼ SHOPS

BREAD & BAKED GOODS

▼ Bernard Reibel
19, rue de la Grande-Boucherie.
Tel. 03 88 92 80 40.
Bernard lightly bakes pretzels, onion tart, leckerli (chewy nut cookies with spices and candied lemon rind), gingerbread, pâté baked in pastry and kouglof. A large variety of special breads: anise, muesli, black rye, chestnut, spelt.

▼ Martin Sittler
3, rue de la Grande-Boucherie.
Tel. 03 88 92 24 93.
Loaves with rye, whole grains, beer or sourdough, and Alsépi bread, all mouth-wateringly delicious, are served with a smile here.

BUTCHER

▼ Richard Jaegli
3, pl de la Victoire.
Tel.-Fax 03 88 92 32 52.
Exquisite choucroute, Charolais beef, lamb from Limousin and wild game in season, carefully selected by Richard Jaegli.

BUTCHER & CHARCUTERIE

▼ Haubensack Frères
13, rue R.-Poincaré.
Tel.-Fax 03 88 92 11 84.
Charles and Pierre Haubensack prepare blood sausage, cervelas, foie gras, liver sausage, pâté in a pastry crust, torte or knacks, and sells Limousin beef, salmon and house-smoked ham.

CHEESE

▼ La Petite Ferme Riedwasen
2, pl d'Armes.
Tel. 03 88 58 48 22.
Caroline and Jean-François Bauer select mature goat cheese from all over France, fine delicatessen products (vinegar, oils, mustard) and a wide range of growers' wines.

EAUX DE VIE

In Châtenois. Route de Villé.

▼ Legoll
Tel. 03 88 85 66 90.
www.legoll.com
René Legoll is a quiet virtuoso of eaux de vie (raspberry, kirsch, mirabelle plum, quetsche plum, sloe) and artisanal jams (apple with nuts and cinnamon, sour cherry with kirsch).

PASTRIES

▼ Gross
1, pl de la Victoire.
Tel. 03 88 92 00 42.
www.gross.fr
Well-known in Obernai, Michel Gross presents traditional and modern confectionery: mille-feuille with chocolate and sour cherries, chocolate "festival" dessert, "Piccadilly", "Valparaiso" and éclairs.

▼ Kamm

15, rue des Clefs.
Tel. 03 88 92 11 04.
In the tearoom or on the terrace of this pedestrian-zone store, customers enjoy light dishes, desserts, tarts or mousses with fruit and chocolates, all prepared by Jean-Paul Kamm.

▼ Sontag-Koffel

2 et 10, rue du 17-Novembre.
Tel. 03 88 92 02 53.
The streusel, kouglof, "exotica", chocolate cake, Belle Hélène, caramel ganaches, chocolate bars, pistachio-almond dessert or praline feuilleté are wondrous indeed at Philippe and Antoine Koffel's place.

▼ Wach

7, rue des Chevaliers.
Tel.-Fax 03 88 92 12 80.
Benoît Wach's local fame is founded on his éclairs, Black Forest cake, mille-feuille, génoise pastry, Paris-Brest, kouglof, "*chevalier*" cake and gourmet pastry goblets in many flavors: fruits in summer, chocolates in winter.

WINE

▼ La Bonne Bouteille

8, rue du 4e-Zouave.
Tel. 03 88 92 31 30.
A mine of excellent advice, Philippe Sporer provides rare Burgundies and fine Alsatian vintages, along with foreign wines of excellent extraction. His Calvados, Armagnacs and aged cognacs are commendable.

▼ Vino Strada

Galerie marchande, Intermarché.
Tel.-Fax 03 88 92 90 44.
www.vinostrada.fr
Decorated with old barrels and grape pickers' baskets, Isabelle Kraemer's modern cellar is filled with her special favorites from every winegrowing region. A fine collection of old whiskeys.

SESSENHEIM

67770 Bas-Rhin. Paris 504 – Strasbourg 32 – Haguenau 17 – Wissembourg 44.
The memory of Goethe's love for Frédérique Brion, the daughter of a local pastor, lights up the history of the village. People come here from the other side of the Rhine in a romantic pilgrimage.

●	RESTAURANTS

● Au boeuf   🏠 COM

1, rue de l'Eglise.
Tel. 03 88 86 97 14. Fax 03 88 86 04 62.
contact@auberge-au-boeuf.com
www.auberge-au-boeuf.com
Closed Mon., Tue.
Prix fixe: 28€ (lunch, weekdays), 43€, 56€, 12€ (child).

This is a picture postcard inn, right out of a drawing by Hansi, and the atmosphere is very friendly. The cuisine of Yannick Germain dusts off classics of the region. Stewed scallop and jumbo shrimp with lobster jus, Kochersberg escargots in mushroom shells, Atlantic sea bass in puff pastry with tomatoes and fennel, Doriath farm duck cooked three times in fine sour cherry sauce and strawberry and lavender dessert with Bourbon vanilla ice cream are top-quality. There is also the visit to the Goethe museum which is part of the house. The cellar is rich in local wines. Adorable reception from Christiane and Claudine.

In Dengolsheim (67770).

● A l'Agneau   COM

11, route de Strasbourg.
Tel. 03 88 86 95 55. Fax 03 88 86 04 43.
Closed Mon., Tue., 2 weeks Feb.
Prix fixe: 26€ (lunch). A la carte: 40–50€.

The Wendlings have based their establishment on friendship. Gérard, in the kitchen, delights his customers with his asparagus and morel mushroom in puff pastry, John Dory filet roasted with sour cherries and the veal escalope with Madeira- and truffle-seasoned foie gras sauce. For dessert, one has a party with the brown sugar-caramelized cherry blinis with acacia milk. Carine gives an extremely kind welcome although the prices are unfortunately less attractive. Lovely summer terrace.

SEWEN

68290 Haut-Rhin. Paris 452 – Epinal 79 – Mulhouse 39 – Belfort 32 – Colmar 66.
This area of south Vosges is where the Upper Rhine joins the Territory of Belfort. In the hollow of valleys, this is the green massif.

 HOTELS-RESTAURANTS

■ Les Vosges

38, Grand-Rue.
Tel. 03 89 82 00 43. Fax 03 89 82 08 33.
info@hoteldesvosges.com
www.hoteldesvosges.com
Closed Sun. dinner, Wed., mid-Dec.–end Dec., 1 week Jan.
16 rooms: 51–60€.
Prix fixe: 16€ (weekday lunch), 21€, 25€, 33€, 9€ (child).

The advantage with Jean-Michel Kieffer is that one knows exactly what one is going to find: a warm welcome, cozy rooms, a pleasant environment with the river running through the garden and the terrace to idle on. And then there is the cuisine of a chef trained in the school of Bocuse and Crocodile: simmered cabbage with foie gras, pan-tossed langoustines and wild mushrooms, chanterelle-stuffed quail and a frozen kouglof are extremely well made and reasonably priced.

SIERENTZ

68510 Haut-Rhin. Paris 483 – Mulhouse 16 – Altkirch 19 – Bâle 17 – Colmar 52.
Bordering Sundgau, this southern area of Alsace is near Switzerland and the Rhine and is a crossroads town of likable proportions.

HOTELS-RESTAURANTS

● Auberge Saint-Laurent

1, rue de la Fontaine.
Tel. 03 89 81 52 81. Fax 03 89 81 67 08.
www.auberge-saintlaurent.fr
Closed 2 weeks Mar., 2 weeks Aug.
Rest. closed Mon., Tue.
10 rooms: 80–100€.
Prix fixe: 39€, 48€, 50€, 70€, 18€ (child). A la carte: 90€.

The whole Arbeit family works for the well-being of their guests in this former coaching inn. The charming receptionist, Anne, who is also the sommelier, is helped by her daughter Marie, while father Marco takes up his position in the kitchen. This technician, who is both joyful and rigorous in his methods, cooks up lively, fresh, light and even inventive dishes that emerge out of local tradition: duck foie gras with cabbage confiture, pike-perch roasted skinside down with slow-cooked and fried leeks, frog legs tossed in parsley, garlic and butter, served with parmesan risotto, pigeon with a smoked bacon cabbage fricassée and a frozen sour cherry soufflé. It all feeds the wonderful dreams that one has in the rustic-modern rooms decorated on countryside themes. Very fine cellar and cared-for surroundings.

SOUFFLENHEIM

67620 Bas-Rhin. Paris 494 – Strasbourg 48 – Haguenau 14 – Baden-Baden 29.
Bordering the large forest of Haguenau, this is the capital of colored pottery.

●	RESTAURANTS

● Au Boeuf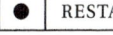
48, Grand-Rue.
Tel. 03 88 86 72 79.
Closed Christmas, New Year's.
Prix fixe: 11€ (weekday lunch), 19€, 25€.

This is a welcoming 17th-century inn converted into a modern, comfortable hotel with terrace and smart dining room. One comes for the gentle atmosphere, well-pulled beers, local vintages and traditional local food.

In Auenheim (67480). 4 km e via N63.
● Au Tisonnier   SIM
8, rte de Soufflenheim.
Tel. 03 88 86 32 25. Fax 03 88 53 05 83.
Closed Wed., Thu., mid-Jan.–beg. Feb.
Prix fixe: 8€ (weekday lunch).
A la carte: 40€.

Julien Schmitt-Andt learned his craft at Buerehiesel then worked in the great establishments of Paris and the Basque coast before returning to the kitchens of this family *winstub* with a modern feel. Head cheese and wine aspic terrine, scallop risotto, cod filet in a pastry crust with mussel sauce, boneless rib steak with coarse-ground black pepper and a quince parfait keep their promises. The service is professional and the prices friendly.

▼	SHOPS

TABLETOP & KITCHENWARE
▼ Vincent Pirard
10, rue de Bischwiller.
Tel. 03 88 86 60 07.
Pitchers, floral vases, bed warmers (traditional hot water bottles), heart-shaped cake molds, crinoline pots, tinted terrine dishes, ceramic dishes and kache-lofes make fine, typically Alsatian gifts, as does the local Süffloum pottery.

SOULTZMATT

68750 Haut-Rhin. Paris 471 – Colmar 21 – Mulhouse 34 – Guebwiller 11.
With wine, water, forest and roads climbing up to the roads of Hautes-Vosges, Soultzmatt has it all.

	HOTELS-RESTAURANTS

■ Vallée Noble
Id Finkwaeldélé.
Tel. 03 89 47 65 65. Fax 03 89 47 65 04.
www.valleenoble.com
Rest. closed Sat. lunch (off season), Sun. dinner (off season).
50 rooms: 59–170€.
Prix fixe: 16€ (vegetarian), 26€ (*terroir* menu), 32€, 40€, 10€ (child).

The Betters run this beautiful establishment with courtesy and efficiency. The rooms are comfortable and the grounds and swimming pool add to the stay. The classic menu is attractively priced.

STRASBOURG

67000 Bas-Rhin. Paris 490 – Bâle 147 – Karlsruhe 81 – Luxembourg 219.
otsr@strasbourg.com.
The European beauty who has refurbished her parliament, rebuilt her hotels, cosseted her university site (may Goethe watch over his statue) and stood her ground on the banks of the Rhine while continually looking after her green spaces, pedestrian streets, the flowing Ill and beautiful houses. French and German, playing with its dual culture and playing the cosmopolitan with charm, offering up its old districts to be visited, from the cathedral to Petite France but also the very "Prussian" Place de la République, Strasbourg is obviously nothing like other French towns. This exotic charm is reflected in its varied restaurants, its *winstubs* and its star eating places. Several pages in a guide is not enough to exhaust its secrets.

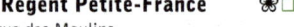

■ HOTELS

■ Régent Petite-France

5, rue des Moulins.
Tel. 03 88 76 43 43. Fax 03 88 76 43 76.
rpf@regent-hotels.com
www.regent-hotel.com
Rest. closed Mon.
56 rooms: 235–305€. 16 suites: 465–485€.
Prix fixe: 32€, 37€. A la carte: 60€.

Behind its 300-year-old facade, this hotel situated in former ice houses at the heart of Petite France houses extremely well-equipped rooms and suites in a contemporary décor. The view onto the rushing flow of the Ill is superb and calm guaranteed in this pedestrian zone. Champagne bar and Le Pont Tournant restaurant (see Restaurants). Excellent service and valet parking.

■ Régent Contades

8, av de la Liberté.
Tel. 03 88 15 05 05. Fax 03 88 15 05 15.
rc@regent-hotels.com
www.regent-hotels.com
45 rooms: 175–225€. 2 suites: 295–420€.
Half board: 293–261€.

Near the Ill, in the old imperial quarter, this 19th-century building is a hotel of charm. The spacious rooms are intelligently set out, the Belle Epoque breakfast room superb and it is a pleasure to drink in the Regency bar. Sauna and Jacuzzi for relaxation.

■ Hilton International

Av Herrenschmidt.
Tel. 03 88 37 10 10. Fax 03 88 36 83 27.
contact@hilton-strasbourg.com
www.hilton-strasbourg.com/
238 rooms: 150–325€.
5 suites: 330–1100€.
Prix fixe: 27–32€ (le jardin du Tivoli),
28–34€ (la Table du Chef).

This modern caravanserai offers spacious rooms that have been carefully equipped. Two bars, the Churchill and the Bugatti, and two restaurants, the Jardin du Tivoli

and the Table du Chef, make it one of the most popular places in town.

■ Holiday Inn

20, pl de Bordeaux.
Tel. 03 88 37 80 00. Fax 03 88 37 07 04.
histrasbourg@alliance-hospitality.com
www.holidayinn-strasbourg.com
Rest. closed Sat. lunch, Sun. lunch.
170 rooms: 100–250€. 1 suite: 560–660€.
Prix fixe: 22€ (weekday lunch),
26€ (weekday lunch) 9€ (child).

A stone's throw from the Parliament and the Palais de la Musique, this great modern "thing" offers huge, well-equipped rooms. Guests have free access to the health club (swimming pool, sauna, hammam) and the business center. Laid-back and jazzy atmosphere in the lounge bar. In the La Louisiane restaurant there is a choice between local dishes and food with a more Mediterranean accent (red sea bream on a bed of oven-crisped Provençal vegetables, lamb chops with a southern-style vegetable flan and tiramisu).

■ Sofitel

Pl Saint-Pierre-le-Jeune.
Tel. 03 88 15 49 10. Fax 03 88 15 49 99.
h0568@accor-hotels.com
100 rooms: 195–225€. 24 suites: 305–350€.

In the middle of the town, this "historic" Sofitel—it was the first link in the chain—offers cozy rooms, some with a view of the St. Pierre-le-Jeune church. Le Thomann is a desirable meeting place and the house restaurant is supervised by Antoine Westermann (see Restaurants: Inside).

■ Beaucour

5, rue des Bouchers.
Tel. 03 88 76 72 00. Fax 03 88 76 72 60.
info@hotel-beaucour.com
www.hotel-beaucour.com
42 rooms: 66–135€. 7 suites: 163–281€.

This hotel composed of five small old houses gives a home-away-from-home welcome. The wonderful service, the carefully prepared rooms, the delicious breakfasts and the reasonable prices instantly touch the hearts of Guy-Pierre Baumann's guests.

■ L'Europe ⌂

38, rue du Fossé-des-Tanneurs.
Tel. 03 88 32 17 88. Fax 03 88 75 65 45.
info@hotel-europe.com
www.hotel-europe.com
Closed 1 week at end Dec.
51 rooms: 62–135€. 9 suites: 140–185€.

It is best to book to secure a room in this hotel next to the cathedral in the pedestrian area. It combines calm and comfort. Attended parking in the basement.

■ Hôtel de France ⌂

20, rue du Jeu-des-Enfants.
Tel. 03 88 32 37 12. Fax 03 88 22 48 08.
www.hotel-de-france.com
66 rooms: 95€. 10 suites: 130€.

Good value rooms in the center of town is the secret of this hotel's success, in addition to the charming reception and the attention given to comfort.

■ Grand-Hôtel Concorde ⌂

12, pl de la Gare.
Tel. 03 88 52 84 84. Fax 03 88 52 84 00.
le.grand.hotel@wanadoo.fr
www.le-grand-hotel.com
83 rooms: 98€. 2 suites: 149€.

An elegant glass lift serves the rooms of this sixties hotel which has old-fashioned charm but every modern comfort. Varied breakfasts.

■ Maison Rouge ⌂

4, rue des Francs-Bourgeois.
Tel. 03 88 32 08 60. Fax 03 88 22 43 73.
info@maison-rouge.com
www.maison-rouge.com
140 rooms: 83–175€. 2 suites: 275–320€.

Every detail of this hotel has been chosen to create an original, harmonious whole: the red facade, the coordinated furniture and paintings and the high-tech facilities are in confident good taste. Both reception and service are perfect.

■ Mercure-Centre ⌂

25, rue Thomann.
Tel. 03 90 22 70 70. Fax 03 90 22 70 71.
h1106@accor-hotels.com
www.mercure.com
98 rooms: 99–145€.

In the very center of town, this practical chain hotel combines comfort, professionalism and reasonable prices. Parking.

■ Monopole-Métropole ⌂

16, rue Kuhn.
Tel. 03 88 14 39 14. Fax 03 88 32 82 55.
infos@bw-monopole.com
www.bestwestern-monopole.com
90 rooms: 85–134€. 5 suites: 150€.

This hotel near the station is hidden away in a quiet street. More than 100 years old, it offers rooms with old-style or contemporary décor, some decorated by local artists. The sitting rooms house works of the cultural heritage of Alsace. Wonderful reception.

■ Novotel-Centre Halles ⌂

4, quai Kléber.
Tel. 03 88 21 50 50. Fax 03 88 21 50 51.
h0439@accor.com
www.novotel.com
98 rooms: 109–159€.
Prix fixe: 22,50€, 31€ (wine inc.), 8€ (child).

This Novotel could serve as a model for its professional welcome, its efficient rooms in white and beige and its Côté Jardin restaurant which serves a well-made traditional cuisine (salads, grilled meats and daily specials).

■ Le Dragon ⌂

2, rue de l'Ecarlate.
Tel. 03 88 35 79 80. Fax 03 88 25 78 95.
hotel@dragon.fr
www.dragon.fr
30 rooms: 69–116€. 2 suites: 149€.

In this 17th-century building near the banks of the Ill, Jean Zimmer watches over his designer rooms in shades of gray. Fine view over the roofs of the Jean Sturm school and the top of St. Thomas church.

Pretty paved courtyard. The lobby and sitting room hold various exhibitions.

■ Cardinal de Rohan

17-19, rue du Maroquin.
Tel. 03 88 32 85 11. Fax 03 88 75 65 37.
info@hotel-rohan.com
www.hotel-rohan.com
36 rooms: 70–135€.

This charming hotel at the center of the town in the pedestrian zone is the epitome of elegance. Furnished with antiques, the comfortable rooms each have their own personality.

■ Cathédrale

12, pl de la Cathédrale.
Tel. 03 88 22 12 12 / 08 00 00 00 84.
Fax 03 88 23 28 00.
reserv@hotel-cathedrale.fr
www.hotel-cathedrale.fr
47 rooms: 75–160€.

Opposite the cathedral and the Kammerzell house, this building from the Renaissance period is a charming hotel run by Alain Cézard. The reception is pleasant, the rooms attractively set out and in the building next-door five luxuriously equipped apartments allow one to stay the week.

■ Diana-Dauphine

30, rue de la Première-Armée.
Tel. 03 88 36 26 61. Fax 03 88 35 50 07.
www.hotel-diana-dauphine.com
Closed Christmas–New Year's.
45 rooms: 70–135€.

This hotel of discreet charm is well situated. The historical town is a few minutes walk or tram ride away. Cozy rooms and an elegant sitting room have been redecorated in contemporary style. Private parking.

■ Gutenberg

31, rue des Serruriers.
Tel. 03 88 32 17 15. Fax 03 88 75 76 67.
hotel.gutenberg@wanadoo.fr
www.hotel-gutenberg.com
42 rooms: 65–98€.

This house in the center of the old district is worth seeing for its walls dating from 1745 and its elegant flowered facade with crafted balcony. The rooms, some of which look onto the cathedral and the statue of Gutenberg, are furnished in the old style. Sensible prices.

■ Hannong

15, rue du 22-Novembre.
Tel. 03 88 32 16 22. Fax 03 88 22 63 87.
info@hotel-hannong.com
www.hotel-hannong.com
Closed 1 week Jan.
72 rooms: 76–182€.

In the very heart of the town center, on the site of the Hannong pottery works, this charming establishment marries tradition and modernity. It is decorated like a town house, from the lobby, with its elegant wooden staircase, to its contemporary rooms, with original parquet floors and wall fabrics. The sweetest have a sloping ceiling.

■ Hôtel des Princes

33, rue Geiler.
Tel. 03 88 61 55 19. Fax 03 88 41 10 92.
hoteldesprinces@aol.com
www.hotel-princes.com
Closed 10 days beg. Jan., 3 weeks Aug.
43 rooms: 98–125€.

The European Parliament and the Orangerie park are very close to this hotel which, in the heart of the business area, offers large, quiet rooms.

■ Villa d'Est

12, rue Jacques-Kablé.
Tel. 03 88 15 06 06. Fax 03 88 15 06 16.
res.villa@cieldenuit.com
www.hotel-villa-est.com
48 rooms: 105–125€.

This hotel with direct access from the motorway is nonetheless situated in a quiet area. The Palais des Congrès and European Parliament are close by. Some rooms are classic, others more contemporary but all offer modern comforts. Fitness center with hammam, sauna, balneotherapy and exercise bikes.

■ Relais Mercure Saint-Jean

3, rue du Maire-Kuss.
Tel. 03 88 32 80 80. Fax 03 88 23 05 39.
h1813@accor-hotels.com
www.mercure.com
52 rooms: 59–119€.

This hotel is close to the most popular tourist spots of the town. The rooms equipped in functional style and well sound proofed are equipped with high-speed soundproofed WiFi.

■ Villa Novarina

11, rue Westercamp.
Tel. 03 90 41 18 28. Fax 03 90 41 49 91.
www.villanovarina.com
5 rooms: 75–150€.

Christine and Jacques Claus have opened this charming guesthouse not far from the Orangerie park. Swimming pool, garden, relaxation, Internet and delicious breakfasts figure on the agenda.

■ Couvent du Franciscain

18, rue du Faubourg-de-Pierre.
Tel. 03 88 32 93 93. Fax 03 88 75 68 46.
info@hotel-franciscain.com
www.hotel-franciscain.com
Closed Christmas–New Year's.
43 rooms: 39–70€.

In the 14th century, the town of Strasbourg gave the Franciscans the management of this hotel-hospice where poor travelers could find bed and board. Since 1525, private individuals have been owners of the place. Clean rooms and breakfasts eaten under the gaze of gourmet Franciscans in the fresco by André Wenger. Sensible prices and private parking.

■ L'Elégant

Rue du Général-Conrad.
Tel. 03 88 60 02 85. Fax 03 88 61 50 81.
bateaulelegant@free.fr
www.bateau-lelegant.com
Closed Sun., Mon.
39 rooms: 45–60€.

Prix fixe: 12€ (weekday lunch), 27€, 35€, 6€ (child). A la carte: 40€.

This thirties boat with its upper and lower deck cabins is another way of spending a good night in the town. It is moored in the ramparts dock which it sometimes leaves to make river crossings. It serves a good market cuisine (escargot lasagne, monkfish in seafood broth and pain d'épice crème brûlée).

■ Hôtel Suisse

2-4, rue de la Râpe.
Tel. 03 88 35 22 11. Fax 03 88 25 74 23.
info@hotel-suisse.com
www.hotel-suisse.com
25 rooms: 45–99€.

Next to the cathedral and the banks of the Ill, this old hotel offers wood-trimmed rooms equipped with Internet connection. Beautiful terrace and delicious breakfasts.

■ Les Trois Roses

7, rue de Zurich.
Tel. 03 88 36 56 95. Fax 03 88 35 06 14.
www.hotel3roses-strasbourg.com
32 rooms: 47–86€.

An Austrian atmosphere in the rooms, warm wood and soft duvets make a cozy ensemble. The breakfast buffet is copious, the sauna relaxing and the river banks nearby.

In Entzheim (67960). 12 km via A35 (exit 8), D400 and D392.

■ Père Benoît
"Steinkeller"

34, rte de Strasbourg.
Tel. 03 88 68 98 00. Fax 03 88 68 64 56.
hotel.perebenoit@wanadoo.fr
Closed Christmas–New Year's, 3 weeks Aug.
Rest. closed Sat. lunch, Sun., Mon. lunch.
60 rooms: 54–72€.
Prix fixe: 19€, 24€, 6,50€ (child).

Three kilometers from the airport, this 17th-century farm makes a friendly stopover. Welcomed by Denis Massé, one sits down to revive energies with duck foie gras, pork cheeks with mustard, pear gratin with almond milk ice cream and wood fire-flambéed tarts, all washed down with beers or local wines. The prices are sensible and the rooms comfortable.

In Ostwald (67540). 7 km via A35 (exit 7) and route de Schirmeck.

■ Château de l'Ile

4, quai Heydt.
Tel. 03 88 66 85 00. Fax 03 88 66 85 49.
ile@grandesetapes.fr
www.chateau-ile.com
60 rooms: 190€. 2 suites: 715€.
Prix fixe: 30€ (lunch), 35€ (lunch, wine inc.), 49€, 67€, 16€ (child).
A la carte: 35–40€.

This neo-Gothic house hidden away in the middle of wooded grounds bordering the Ill makes a beautiful stopover. The rooms are decorated in an antique style and are well equipped. Spa, sauna, hammam, Jacuzzi, swimming pool and terrace allow moments of relaxation. Yannick Mattern, the new chef, brings finesse to a carefully crafted rustic cuisine in the *winstub* and more sophisticated fare in the refined restaurant (wild boar terrine with foie gras and chestnuts, roasted pikeperch and variations on the fig).

In Plobsheim (67115). 12 km s via route d'Offenburg.

■ Le Kempferhof

351, rte du Moulin.
Tel. 03 88 98 72 72 / 03 88 98 71 82.
Fax 03 88 98 74 76.
info@golf-kempferhof.com
www.golfkempferhof.com
Closed 22 Dec.–9 Jan. Rest. closed Sun. dinner.
29 rooms: 150–200€. 4 suites: 200–230€.
Prix fixe: 15€, 32€, 38€, 42€.
A la carte: 45€.

Legendary cinematic scenes serve as décor in the designer, contemporary rooms of this very beautiful 19th-century manor house surrounded by an eighteen-hole golf course. The cuisine of Sébastien Hahn, the new chef, also deserves to be filmed. Crab mille-feuille, roasted monkfish served on a bed of slow-cooked leeks,

poultry breast with Vin Jaune sauce and a fresh fromage blanc tiramisu are supervised by boss Guillaume Robuchon, who worked at Au Crocodile.

●   **RESTAURANTS**

● Au Crocodile

10, rue de l'Outre.
Tel. 03 88 32 13 02. Fax 03 88 75 72 01.
info@au-crocodile.com
www.au-crocodile.com
Closed Sun., Mon., Christmas–New Year's, 1 week beg. Jan., beg. July–beg. Aug.
Prix fixe: 56€ (lunch), 85€ (dinner), 113€ (dinner), 127€ (dinner).
A la carte: 120–130€.

Every year, Emile and Monique Jung dedicate themselves to a historic and gourmet celebration. In 2006, it was Mozart, on the occasion of the 250th anniversary of his birth, with a menu that paid him homage. Oxtail soup with bone marrow flan, duck liver schnitzel with raspberry vinaigrette, horseradish and sherry sauce, swordfish in anchovy spread with olive oil and preserved lemons, grilled young toro steak with artichokes and beans with a smoked butter emulsion interpret, in concrete manner, *The Magic Flute* or *Don Juan*. For dessert, a cloud of whipped mascarpone on a disk of white cake soaked in mocha and rum and a summer fruit dessert with spice sorbet and a lemon cumin elixir are reminders that the composer of *Cosi Fan Tutte* was a great lover of sweet things. An exercise in style? Yes, of course, proving that Emile Jung can do everything, mastering every trick with expertise and awareness. As, for example, in that starter inspired by Heston Blumenthal, the young genius of Bray-on-Thames: a nitrogen-frozen flake of mint that cleans the palate in the blink of an eye. But one can also come here to taste the dishes drawn from the region, which make splendid creations. There is, for example, the sublime cold sweet pea soup with a poached egg, grilled duck liver seasoned with rhubarb and served with a citrus ginger jus, pike-perch and carp in Pinot Noir sauce and carrot purée with julienned leeks and a slab of pork trotters with suckling pig chops and Tarbais beans, served in the style of Luxembourg. Add to this a choice of desserts, which have made a huge leap over the past few years, such as a crispy coffee-flavored confection with a Tahitian vanilla cream and coffee ice cream. The wines, suggested by the expert Gilbert Mestrallet, are the perfect accompaniment. The service, orchestrated by the baton of the indispensable Monique Jung, is really one of the best in France. This is a great establishment.

● Le Buerehiesel ⊙V.COM

4, parc de l'Orangerie.
Tel. 03 88 45 56 65. Fax 03 88 61 32 00.
westermann@buerehiesel.fr
www.buerehiesel.com
Closed Sun., Mon., 1–20 Jan., 3 weeks Aug.
Prix fixe: 35€ (lunch), 65€, 108€.
A la carte: 90€.

Antoine Westermann has abandoned Strasbourg for Paris (where he runs Drouant and Mon Vieil Ami), leaving his restaurant and the kitchens under the direction of his son Eric, charging him with giving back soul and meaning to the great establishment in the Orangerie park. At the time of publication, it is is too early to predict the future. Eric has changed the style of the house, lowering the prices, selling off the silver, getting rid of some of the grandeur as well as some of the staff. The new Buerehiesel is here. One still has the vinicultural advice of the wise Jean-Marc Zimmermann, the charm of the place—an old Molsheim farm—with its modern, loft-style room and a cuisine that, through lightened versions of classics, highlights quality produce. There is no reason not to savor veal sweetbreads with parsley and garlic served with chanterelles, pâté wrapped in veal and farm-raised pork with white poultry livers, schniederspaetle (local stuffed dumplings) with frog legs and chervil, a whole Quiberon whiting cooked in butter, garlic and parsley, served with sautéed baby vegetables and the roasted Pyrénées lamb chops and roast with simmered artichokes and peppers

and Tarbais beans. And then the desserts, which have always been a strong suit of the establishment: crispy coffee and salted-butter caramel dessert served with coffee ice cream, caramelized beer brioche with roasted pear ice cream. It is too soon to judge or evaluate the establishment. Let us give one plate to begin—and wait to see what gives.

● Maison Kammerzell 🏠V.COM

16, pl de la Cathédrale.
Tel. 03 88 32 42 14. Fax 03 88 23 03 92.
info@maison-kammerzell.com
www.maison-kammerzell.com
Hotel closed Feb. vac. Rest. closed Christmas.
9 rooms: 69–117€.
Prix fixe: 29,50€, 37€, 45€, 8€ (child).
A la carte: 42–52€.

La Maison Kammerzell dates from 1427 (although the present flamboyant architecture is from 1589) and is one of the most beautiful buildings in Strasbourg. Each of its rooms has its history and it is thanks to Guy-Pierre Baumann that it has become a gourmet hotel. He has entrusted the kitchens to faithful Hubert Lépine. Duck foie gras with Gewurztraminer aspic, borsch with tiny diced beets, roasted monkfish filet with summer savory-seasoned young fava beans, wild boar belly stuffed with foie gras and truffles, slow-cooked potatoes and pumpkin purée and a honey milk chocolate mousse with a brownie and chocolate ice cream renew the house repertoire—choucroute remaining the signature of the place. The cellar is full of good intentions, essentially local ones. The almost-secret nine rooms of the Baumann hotel, which are reached by a 16th-century spiral staircase, give a privileged view of the cathedral bells.

● Maison des Tanneurs 🏠V.COM

42, rue du Bain-aux-Plantes.
Tel. 03 88 32 79 70. Fax 03 88 22 17 26.
maison.des.tanneurs@wanadoo.fr
www.maison-des-tanneurs.com
Closed Sun., Mon., 3 weeks Jan.
Prix fixe: 24€ (lunch), 28€ (lunch).
A la carte: 55€.

François Leenhardt attentively looks after this beautiful 16th-century building. The chefs René Breitel and Roland Laemmer always follow tradition with escargots, onion tart, trout with almonds, guinea hen with a green peppercorn stuffing, classic choucroute, roasted ham and a quince tart. One isn't bowled over, true, but there are also no unpleasant surprises.

● L'Estaminet Schloegel 🏠◎V.COM

19, rue de la Krutenau.
Tel.-Fax 03 88 36 21 98.
Closed Sat. lunch, Sun., Mon. lunch, Christ-mas–New Year's, 3 weeks Aug.
Prix fixe: 25€ (lunch). A la carte: 60€.

Himber & Humbert are the new duo heading this former faux café that has become a truly good restaurant. Philippe Himber, formerly at the Western Grill, is the boss. Zealous Stéphane Humbert until recently worked at Pralong 2000 in Courchevel. Their partnership gives rise to professionalism incarnate in a fresh, intimate little restaurant. This is a fine, precise cuisine without embellishments but closer to the truth of the produce. For example, crab salad with fines herbes and grated celery root in mayonnaise with an audacious mango sauce, roasted pike-perch filet with bone marrow on toast and pan-tossed slices of polenta, slow-cooked wild duck stew with hot foie gras, served with baby vegetables in a ginger bouillon and red wine–braised beef cheek and potato casserole with fried parsley. No pretension or pointless frills in the dishes. In short, everything one loves, served with diligence by smiling and motivated wait-resses. Add to this wines from Alsace sought out with "nose" (like the pinot noir of Maurice Schoech) and fine, fresh desserts (quince and pear Tatin-style tart with caramel ice cream and a vanilla-sea-soned fresh fromage blanc mousse and warm blueberry compote, served with a cookie). Enough to talk, just opposite the Pont au Chat, of "another" event in the Krutenau.

● Le Penjab ◎V.COM

12, rue des Tonneliers.
Tel. 03 88 32 36 37. Fax 03 88 32 18 55.
lepenjab@wanadoo.fr
Closed Sun., Mon. lunch, Thu. lunch.
Prix fixe: 21€, 42€, 47€, 9,30€.
A la carte: 55€.

Eric Jenny charges the Paris-Bombay gastronomic ticket at a heavenly price. Quality produce, freshness and proper handling are the ingredients that make up a celebratory meal. Eric, whose mother Harco runs the famous Vietnamese res-taurant the Tour de Jade in the avenue des Vosges, offers in a cared-for setting, with its Indian wood decorations, chicken or shrimp samosas, eggplant or onion beig-nets, shrimp korma with coconut milk, savory cheese nan, mashli masala (spicy fish curry), lamb tandoori and the Kash-mir-style chicken with spicy yogurt and saffron rice. Clean flavors and exquisite mild or spicy sauces: everything unfolds with ceremonial grace in these elegant and refined surroundings. The desserts (pistachio ice cream, gulab jamun and a cinnamon beignet) give a smiling end to the meal.

● La Cambuse ◎COM

1, rue des Dentelles.
Tel. 03 88 22 10 22. Fax 03 88 23 24 99.
cambuse@wanadoo.fr
Closed Sun., Mon., 3 Aug., Christmas.
A la carte: 52€.

Everything in Babeth Lefebvre's restau-rant evokes the sea. The décor created by her husband Philippe transports us as if by magic into the inside of a boat cabin—and off we go, cruising down the Ill, the sole captain on board, ready to take on every-thing to sail around the world's oceans. Babeth proudly flies the colors of a cui-sine that resembles her: generous, bold and inventive. Nothing of regional cui-sine, then. Our destination is the open sea and flavors of elsewhere, far from the little France where she has nonetheless set up home. Pleasure is guaranteed with shrimp with mango and green papaya, matjes mille-feuille with wasabi and apples, never meat, but extremely fresh fish like the pineapple turbot and sea bream with basil-infused olive oil. On the dessert side, one can choose to follow the trip towards the islands with the chocolate tart with coconut cream or to return and anchor nearer to French shores, reminded of its vineyards and orchards with Cognac-flavored peach gratin. The wine list is replete with fine Chilean and American wines rubbing shoulders with the best Alsatian vintages. Philippe has just the right words to persuade and reel in the indecisive. Last surprise—and not the least—is that the check turns out to be reasonable for such an offering.

● Le Pont aux Chats

42, rue de la Krutenau.
Tel.-Fax 03 88 24 08 77.
Closed Sat. lunch, Wed., 2 weeks Feb.,
2 weeks Aug.
Prix fixe: 19€ (weekday lunch).
A la carte: 50€.

Valère and Véronique Diochet, who have been at this former Krutenau *winstub* for two years, very quickly managed to win over the whole of Strasbourg with a formula that combines tradition and modernity in both its décor and its food. The old windows and contemporary décor in the entirely renovated restaurant are a mirror-like reflection of the local produce that is subjected to unusual but clever interpretations of our friend Valère. His apprenticeship with Westermann, to whom he was second in command, doubtless plays its part, giving him knowledge of all the local producers and farmers from whom he gets high quality products. All that remains is the skillful treatment that produces salad with marinated sardines and artichokes, Label Rouge salmon pan tossed with fresh almonds, a slice of plaice and little pan-fried squids with preserved lemons, oven-crisped lamb shoulder with rosemary jus and poached white and yellow peaches served with blackcurrant jus and lemony thyme-seasoned shaved ice. On fine days, all this is appreciated much more on the terrace installed on the small internal courtyard and it is a year-round plea-

sure to eat here, punctuated by a glass of wine chosen à la carte on the advice of Véronique. The service leaves nothing to chance and the prices, despite so many good results, continue to be gentle.

● La Casserole

24, rue des Juifs.
Tel. 03 88 36 49 68. Fax 03 88 24 25 12.
Closed Sat. lunch, Sun., Mon., Aug.
Prix fixe: 15€ (lunch, weekdays), 27€, 50€.

Eric Girardin was a sommelier at Le Bateau Ivre in Courchevel and at Mischler's in Lembach. Today he is at the helm in the kitchen and no one would criticize him in his new function. Bubbling over with ideas, he changes the menu in its sweet, colorful little frame every few weeks. It is an opportunity for the regulars or passing customers to regularly experience the latest creations of this amateur chef who is mad about good wine and good cuisine. Foie gras with fruit chutney, sea bream with pepper oil, roasted pork tenderloin with slow-cooked cumin-seasoned carrots and a freshly sliced pear carpaccio with vanilla and chocolate truffle ice cream make a very good impression. In the restaurant, the sweet Marylin provides a pleasant, energetic service that adds pleasure to the food. Attractive special menus.

● Le Festin de Lucullus

18, rue Sainte-Hélène.
Tel.-Fax 03 88 22 40 78.
caroline.thiercelin@tiscalli.fr
Closed Sun., Mon., end Feb.–beg. Mar.,
3 weeks Aug.
Prix fixe: 14€ (lunch), 27€ (dinner).
A la carte: 40–45€.

The red of the completely renovated restaurant echoes the cuisine of Eric Thiercelin: colorful, energetic and fashionable. The influence of the South is definitely present. Crab seasoned with garden herbs, olive oil and lemon, the grilled tuna steak with summer vegetables, kouglof with slow-cooked wild duck pan-seared foie gras—one doesn't tire of either the scents or the flavors. This good, inexpensive special menu ends wonderfully with the raspberry crème brûlée shortbread with flecks of vanilla.

● **Le Panier du Marché**

15, rue Sainte-Barbe.
Tel. 03 88 32 04 07. Fax 03 88 23 64 52.
lepanierdumarche@hotmail.fr
Closed Sun.
Prix fixe: 19,50€ (lunch), 27€.

Fresh and well-handled is how one could describe the cuisine of Christophe Couvent. Here, only special menus are offered, but always at a tiny price. Pan-seared duck foie gras with spicy chocolate, grilled tuna steak, rack of lamb with artichokes and a small coconut tart with caramelized banana will win over lovers of southern-inspired cooking.

● **Le Thomasien**

12, rue des Dentelles.
Tel. 03 88 32 76 67.
Closed Sat. lunch, Sun., Mon. lunch (exc. Christmas market days).
Prix fixe: 23€, 29€. A la carte: 35–40€.

Henri Velty doesn't posture. There is nothing more sincere than the food of his stone house in Petite France situated not far from the church of St. Thomas. We have good memories of the duck foie gras prepared two ways, served with fig chutney, seafood brochette (tuna, cod, large shrimp) and the grilled rack of lamb with tandoori spices polished by this native of Bugnéville in Vosges. The wild blueberry and sparkling wine sabayon accompanied by a pink grapefruit sorbet makes a fresh ending to the meal. Efficient service and really nice prices.

● **La Tour de Jade**

57, av des Vosges.
Tel. 03 88 35 14 37.
Closed Sat. lunch, Sun., Mon. lunch, 3 weeks Aug.
Prix fixe: 15€ (lunch), 28€, 35€.
A la carte: 35€.

Harco Jenny is an old-fashioned Vietnamese mother who scolds you if you don't finish her generous portions. But as everything she serves is delicious, no one complains. On the first floor of a smart building dating from 1900, in a room laid out like a private dining room, one enjoys fine, fresh food: pho (like it's served in Hanoi), ban cuon (steamed ravioli), fish of the day cooked with coconut milk, caramelized pork and the ginger ice cream slip down as effortlessly as can be. The great chefs of Alsace have understood the situation and come here to celebrate after their kitchens close.

● **La Cruche d'Or**

6, rue des Tonneliers.
Tel. 03 88 32 11 23.
Rest. closed Sun.,
2 weeks end Feb.–beg. Mar.
14 rooms: 55–60€.
Prix fixe: 24€, 28€. A la carte: 40€.

In the middle of a gastronomic street, Carine and Serge Jung have taken over, with spirit, an old tavern. The wooden, polished surroundings are shiny bright, the service obliging, the restaurant cheerful and there are also hotel accommodations. Serge, who worked at Buerehiesel, looks after both regional specialities and dishes that reflect the times. Slow-cooked onion tart, fine pâté in pastry crust, foie gras with Port aspic and slow-cooked apricots, pike-perch served on noodles, veal escalope Viennoise, fleischschnacka (Alsatian-style meat dumplings) and jumbo shrimp and chanterelle penne make one want to take up residence. Traditional desserts and selected wines.

● **Inside**

At Sofitel, 4, pl Saint-Pierre-le-Jeune.
Tel. 03 88 15 49 05. Fax 03 88 15 49 99.
h0568fb@accor-hotels.com
www.sofitel.com
Prix fixe: 29€ (weekday lunch).
A la carte: 55€.

Antoine Westermann, who supervises the kitchens of the Sofitel gourmet brasserie, has redone the décor in a contemporary style and offers a modern cuisine. A thin tart with marinated tuna, pâté in a pastry crust with foie gras, grilled mackerel filet with chop suey-style vegetables and the roasted pike-perch with potato purée with ceps and onion jus are well conceived. The venison parmentier with Pinot Noir sauce and foie gras makes a fine, modernized version of traditional cooking and, on the dessert side, Breton shortbread with spiced figs and yogurt sorbet takes one straight back to childhood.

● Le Pont Tournant   N COM

At the Régent Petite France,
5, rue des Moulins.
Tel. 03 88 76 43 00.
www.hotelsregent.com
Closed Sun., Mon., lunch weekdays (winter, exc. groups).
Prix fixe: 30€, 35€.

In the most beautiful hotel in town, this designer restaurant (with its minimalist makeover) and its bare black tables, red and carmine walls and armchairs and gray-beige banquettes is chic. The menu does good business by offering, under the lead of young Cédric Kallenbach, creamed Jerusalem artichokes seasoned with truffles, pan-crisped tête de veau with mustard, grouper seasoned with garam masala and the rack of lamb in a salt crust. The desserts (chocolate and coffee cream) slip down effortlessly.

● L'Alsace à Table   COM

8, rue des Francs-Bourgeois.
Tel. 03 88 32 50 62. Fax 03 88 22 44 11.
info@alsace-a-table.fr
www.alsace-a-table.fr
Closed 24 Dec. dinner, 1 Jan. dinner
Prix fixe: 22€, 27€, 12€ (child).
A la carte: 50€.

Here is a misleading name for a restaurant! With such a title, one expects to find onion tart and toasted goose choucroute. In fact, Guy-Pierre Baumann has made it into a seafood restaurant. In a 1980 art nouveau setting, one enjoys a well-prepared seafood cuisine. The seafood platter, fish served with sauerkraut, monkfish medallions with seasoned eggplant purée, monkfish soufflé with squid ink tagliatelli

and the orange sorbet topped with sangria, created by Patrice Loisse, is eaten simply and without fuss.

● L'Atable 77   COM

77, Grand'Rue.
Tel. 03 88 32 23 37. Fax 03 88 32 50 24.
latable77@free.fr
www.latable77.com
Closed Sun., Mon., 2 weeks Dec., 2 weeks July.
Prix fixe: 24€ (lunch), 30€ (lunch), 50€.
A la carte: 60€.

In purified surroundings of gray and orange, Stéphane Kaiser, who was the student of Emile Jung before proving himself at Ledoyen in Paris, has chosen to return to his roots by settling in the Alsatian capital. With him, nothing is left to chance—from the refined presentation to the carefully executed preparation and including the choice of natural produce stuffed with flavors. One is seduced by a fashionable, light cuisine that does not always satisfy one's hunger. But frozen sweet pea cream with whole grain mustard sauce, breaded and fried fish with typical minestrone vegetables in aspic, pan-tossed cod with thinly sliced radishes, tandoori-spiced suckling pig, oven-crisped pain d'épice dessert and an orange cream dessert with anise ice cream are well conceived. The wine list, explained by Guillaume Buecher, is not limited to just this region. The service, like Delphine's attentive welcome, is friendly while the special menus, particularly those for lunch, make one want to become a regular here.

● Brasserie Kirn   COM

6-8, rue de l'Outre.
Tel. 03 88 52 03 03. Fax 03 88 52 01 00.
www.brasseriekirn.fr
Closed Sun. dinner, Christmas, 1 May.
Prix fixe: 17,50€ (lunch), 19,90€ (lunch), 23,50€ (lunch), 29,50€ (weekday dinner) 9,50€ (child). A la carte: 55€.

Jean-Paul Kirn's neo–Belle Epoque brasserie is the meeting place for those who love grilled monkfish medallions with peanut sauce, bone marrow with Guérande salt, milk-fed veal hanger steak, half-pound boneless rib steak, a sweet take on the regional casserole with apples, pears and grapes and the seasonal seafood buffet. Nice service and prices.

● Fleur de Sel   COM
22, quai des Bateliers.
Tel. 03 88 36 01 54.
Closed Sun., Mon. lunch, 1 week beg. Jan.,
1 week at end Mar., 3 weeks Aug.
Prix fixe: 12€ (weekday lunch), 15€ (week-
day lunch), 16€ (weekday lunch).
A la carte: 45€.

Françoise and Jean-Paul Schaller, who used to run Julien, a neo-art nouveau gourmet and upmarket boudoir, have recreated it in greater simplicity. The decoration of off-white stucco produces a contemporary look. And, on the kitchen side, Steve Meschberger cooks a fashionable bistro-type cuisine. Slow-cooked vegetables in a flat puff pastry, smoked ham, steamed in papillote, oven-crisped swordfish with basil and tempura-style vegetables, browned cheese-topped lamb medallions with Espelette peppers served with a carrot mousseline and polenta and the rich chocolate cake served with orange sorbet hold their own.

● Le Mandarin   COM
7, rue du Vieux-Marché-aux-Poissons.
Tel. 03 88 75 52 08. Fax 03 88 65 16 23.
www.restaurantlemandarin.com
Closed Sun. dinner, Mon.
Prix fixe: 44€, 52€, 70€. A la carte: 45€.

This modest Chinese restaurant uses quality produce and produces carefully prepared dishes. Herbert Sin gives a cheerful welcome and steamed dim sum, ginger-seasoned sole, Canton-style beef sirloin steak cooked at the table, half a Peking duck for two and a coconut dessert are invitations to an amazing journey.

● La Mauresse   COM
7, rue du Vieux-Marché-aux-Poissons.
Tel. 03 88 75 55 27. Fax 03 90 29 43 85.
www.mangerenalsace.com
Closed Sun. dinner, Mon.

Prix fixe: 8,50€ (weekday lunch), 29€, 54€.
A la carte: 50€.

Jacky Mercier has made discretion and consistency his bywords. Lovers of seafood know that his fish and crustacea are completely fresh. Fish soup, salmon tartare with fresh mint, whole Atlantic sea bass flambéed in Pastis, fish served with sauerkraut and a champagne sauce and the Catalane-style crème brûlée are delicious and the wine selection isn't bad.

● Le Pont des Vosges   COM
15, quai Koch.
Tel. 03 88 36 47 75. Fax 03 88 25 16 85.
pontdesvosges@noos.fr
Closed Sun.
A la carte: 50€.

The chic atmosphere, the fifties armchairs and the setting of a lively brasserie on the first floor of a building in the imperial quarter; this Lipp of Strasbourg is run by Annie Leclerc—but it is a gourmet Lipp. Annie, who has piercing blue eyes and who notices everything, is not satisfied with having the most popular establishment in town. She also feeds her guests with refinement and the cuisine of the young Jean-Philippe Schubnel gets everyone on board, with thinly sliced ceps served carpaccio style, monkfish and salmon in individual aspic terrine, smoked herring terrine, veal kidney with mustard sauce (also prepared English style) and the frozen nougat with honey sauce, which give simple pleasure.

● Le R   COM
53-55, Grand-Rue.
Tel. 03 88 22 09 25.
Closed lunch, Sun., Mon.
Prix fixe: 15€, 30€, 45€.

This is the "happening" restaurant of Strasbourg, which has taken over. No sign on the outside street—it has all happened by word of mouth. Richard Meier, formerly of La Rivière, has opened a Starckian place on two floors where a serious team works behind a clear screen to produce "intuitive cuisine". On offer, the tapas menu, vegetable spring rolls with spicy foam, scallop sashimi and grilled rouget. The orange flower water-seasoned mousse with a lacy vanilla cookie will surprise you.

● Villa Casella `COM`

5, rue du Paon.
Tel. 03 88 32 50 50 / 03 88 66 37 96.
Fax 03 88 22 36 47.
info@villacasella.com
www.villacasella.com
Closed Sat. lunch, Sun., 2 weeks Christmas–New Year's, 1 week at Easter,
3 weeks Aug.
Prix fixe: 22€ (lunch, wine inc.), 40€, 50€.
A la carte: 55€.

Antonio Casella has made this good-natured trattoria into the star Italian restaurant of the town center. There are sometimes too many covers and a service that finds it hard to keep up, but the overall effect is effortlessly seductive. A mixed vegetable antipasto, pear and Gorgonzola risotto, monkfish medallion with artichokes, grilled beef tagliata with a balsamic reduction and parmesan and a pistachio panna cotta are well conceived. The transalpine wine list is a fund of good things.

● Le Village d'Asie `COM`

1, av du Général-de-Gaulle.
Tel. 03 88 61 05 79. Fax 03 88 61 06 19.
Closed Mon., 2 weeks Aug.
Prix fixe: 21€, 26€, 30€. A la carte: 45€.

As its name indicates, this restaurant takes us to the Far East in a little gustatory journey starting in the heart of the Esplanade area. Hong Kong, Peking, Shanghai and Canton are among the destinations to which Alain Li invites us with steamed shrimp, chicken and meat spring rolls, steamed turbot, fish and shellfish stew, Peking-style glazed duck, honey-seasoned pork roast and flambéed crêpes with mango compote. Friendliness is freely available, as is discretion. In terms of prices, one comes back down to earth very gently.

● Gavroche ⌂○`SIM`

4, rue Klein.
Tel.-Fax 03 88 36 82 89.
restaurant.gavroche@free.fr
www.restaurant-gavroche.com
Closed Sat., Sun., Christmas–New Year's,
1 week at end Aug.
Prix fixe: 33€. A la carte: 60€.

He was the shy and retiring one, the student of the greats who remained in the shadows. Having learned the craft at Le Buerehiesel, Le Cerf and La Cheneaudière, Benoît Fuchs is now firmly asserting himself. His inn, formerly of unnattractive rough-cast stone, has been redecorated in soft shades, with yellow walls in the tadelakt style and the atmosphere of a private club. There are several tables and twenty or so covers that are taken by storm, as if gourmets have spread the word. Tradition is helped out by creativity and ideas from elsewhere renew the tried and true recipes. Nathalie Fuchs, lively and smiling, explains the menu with spirit, also giving advice on wine. In short, this laboratory of future cooking is devilishly seductive. The other evening, big scallops served in a foamy bouillon, quail brochettes glazed with foie gras sauce, grilled tuna steak medallions with whole grain barley risotto, the wonderful "lamb lollipops" with a side of yogurt seasoned with Indian spices and red bean mousseline were the work of an artist. Work that the desserts live up to: vanilla and passion fruit panna cotta and a shortbread tartlette with pineapple and a mascarpone and lime mousse. It seems that this enthusiastic restaurant is worth the applause (if one overlooks the courtyard toilets). This little Gavroche is undoubtedly a great one.

● L'Atelier du Goût ◐🍴`SIM`

17, rue des Tonneliers.
Tel. 03 88 21 01 01.
Closed Sat., Sun., Christmas–New Year's,
1 week Feb., 2 weeks Aug.
Prix fixe: 20,50€ (lunch). A la carte: 35€.

Esther and François Morabito, who ran Le Panier du Marché, have created an event with this refined snack bar in a green and orange design. The black radish and squid tempura, the cep paté in the style of Vosges and the pan-tossed gnocchi and arugula make nifty and fashionable offerings. One feels at ease in this bar/*table d'hôte* to enjoy grilled scallops with a polenta cake, creamy risotto with a summer savory-seasoned suckling pig fricassée and the rare-cooked calf's liver with a carrot mikado and fresh grapes. The desserts are a divine surprise (mango cheesecake, pear and quince sorbet and the local dessert called the quechtartle, with ice cream or fresh fromage blanc and cinnamon). The wines are a fund of good things and the natural beer St. Pierre is drunk with great gusto.

● L'Assiette du Vin   SIM
5, rue de la Chaîne.
Tel. 03 88 32 00 92. Fax 03 88 23 54 71.
Closed Sat. lunch, Sun., Mon. lunch,
3 weeks Aug.
Prix fixe: 15€ (lunch) 23€, 27€, 50€.

Philippe Roth, a former student of the Lyon chefs Orsi, Lacombe and Chavent, doesn't like monotony. He creates his modern and spirited cuisine with products gleaned from the market. His menu board sets out food that is well thought out and precisely executed. Eggplant and goat cheese mille-feuille, grilled squid with marinated summer vegetables, grilled beef and peanut cookies with pan-simmered peaches are all attractive. One washes down this feast with a vintage selected from 650 choices—the name of this restaurant is no accident.

● Lohkäs   N SIM
25, rue du Bain-aux-Plantes.
Tel.-Fax 03 88 32 05 26.
Closed Thu., Fri. lunch, 3 weeks Jan.,
2 weeks July.
Prix fixe: 22€, 27€. A la carte: 38€.

This beautiful 1676 inn has kept its distinctive character and its semi-basement setting, with traditional stove upstairs and old-fashioned organ. Hot Munster salad, onion tart, pike-perch simmered in sparkling wine, goose liver simmered with apples and veal kidneys with mustard sauce are, without pretending to be great cuisine, carefully prepared and welcome dishes.

● Alambar   N SIM
15, rue du Vieux-Marché-aux-Vins.
Tel. 03 88 75 16 00.
Closed Sat. lunch, Sun.
A la carte: 25–35€.

Albert Schmitt, the head of P'tit Max, Place de l'Homme de Fer, has created a fresh, Italian-style garden setting and a dynamic restaurant team in this cool brasserie. Caramelized fennel salad with an orange foam, salmon steak with beurre blanc, preserved lemons and risotto, seafood linguini, foie gras tagliatelli and pancetta easily hold their own. Pasta (lasagne, penne and fusili) and focaccia and sunny wines all give pleasure.

● Le Bouquet Garni   N SIM
41, rte de l'Hôpital.
Tel. 03 88 34 66 86.
www.lebouquetgarni.fr
Closed Sat. lunch, Sun., Mon. dinner,
1 week Christmas–New Year's, 1 week Feb.,
3 weeks Aug.
Prix fixe: 9€ (lunch), 20€.
A la carte: 35€.

Gaëtan Serge, formerly of Le Munstertuewel, took over a rather anonymous Neudorf house and has transformed both interior and exterior. The cuisine of Frédéric Olivier, formerly of Le Buerehiesel, is not lacking in character. Goose foie gras terrine with a dried fruit compote, sea bream with fennel sauce, poultry breast with celery cream and a frozen kouglof with local Marc de Gewurz are all attractive offerings on the 20€ special menu.

● Canas y Tapas   N SIM
12, quai St-Nicolas.
Tel. 03 88 35 05 60.
A la carte: 20-30€.

Jean-Luc Desombre has, with a motivated team, created an Iberian experience on a bank of the Ill. Bar, tiles, tapas and cogollos like those of the Basque country, ham and Catalan-style tomato-rubbed bread with ham make one want to dance the flamenco. The produce is of high quality; the "a Feria" octopus plate and the Andalousian squid strike a marine note that goes down very well. Add to this the rosé Gran Feudo Chivite de Navarre and one has the impression that the cost of the ticket from Alsace to Spain is not expensive.

● Chan Chira   Ⓝ SIM
2, rue des Moulins.
Tel. 03 88 32 68 34.
Closed Sat. lunch, Sun. lunch, Mon. lunch,
3 weeks in winter
A la carte: 45€.

Replacing a charming tearoom, this establishment in Petite France houses a high-quality Thai restaurant on two floors. The house has a quiet atmosphere, with red lamps, beams, exotic furniture and incense. Shrimp spring rolls, papaya salad, beef "lap" and lemon-sautéed chicken are flawlessly professional.

● Le Cornichon Masqué   Ⓝ SIM
17, pl du Marché Gayot.
Tel. 03 88 25 11 34.
Closed Sun., Mon., 1 week at end Dec.,
3 weeks Jan.
A la carte: 35€.

Gilles Moercker knows how to welcome people to this charming building situated on one of the prettiest little squares of the town. The bar as you go in, the daily slateboard menu, the wide-awake waitress, the sensible prices, the dessert selection and the fruity wines: it all seduces. Stuffed goose neck, herring with cream, tuna carpaccio, tongue salad with lentils and cod filet with mashed potatoes go down well with everyone.

● Gölbasi   Ⓝ SIM
35, Grand-Rue.
Tel. 03 88 75 68 54.
Closed Mon., 4 days Christmas–New Year's.
Prix fixe: 8€ (dish of the day).
A la carte: 25€.

Deniz and Hasan Cihangir, originally from Gölbasi in southeastern Turkey, have opened a modest embassy to their country in the heart of the Grand-Rue. One comes to this relaxed atmosphere to taste the house grilled meats, the doner kebab, with its spit-caramelized meat, the chopped meat kofte and Tavuk Sis (chicken brochettes). The Yakut Kavaklidere is a pleasure to drink.

● Pierre, Bois, Feu   Ⓝ SIM
6, rue du Bain-aux-Roses.
Tel. 03 88 36 25 59.
Closed Sat. lunch, Sun. lunch, Tue.,
Wed. lunch.
A la carte: 40€.

Renaud Schneider, who has already roamed around the world a fair bit (in Frankfurt at Bistro 77, at Edel's in Sélestat, in Porto-Vecchio at the Tropicana), has chosen the means of a friendly, smart bistro next to the river and the cathedral, in a wooded, rustic setting, to make his fortune. One enjoys, according to the changing menu, breaded and fried vegetables, coddled egg with foie gras, blood sausage with onions and the boneless rib steak. Everything looks good.

● Le Pub 38   Ⓝ SIM
38, rue Wimpheling.
Tel. 03 88 60 58 80.
lepub38@free.fr
Closed Sat., Sun., 2 weeks beg. Aug.
Prix fixe: 13,50€ (lunch).
A la carte: 40–55€.

Exit the Villa Médicis. This faux pub has rediscovered its first identity under the management of Hubert Dormann, a tall, attractive man (if a little stiff) who has gathered a serious team around him. The house has been renovated with a contemporary look and offers the fine cuisine of a young former chef of the Villa Casella. Marinated raw tuna, eggplant mille-feuille, San Daniele ham fougasse and spaghetti with clam sauce do not fail to seduce.

● L'Ami Schutz   SIM
1, rue des Ponts-Couverts.
Tel. 03 88 32 76 98. Fax 03 88 32 38 40.
info@ami-schutz.com
www.ami-schutz.com
Closed Christmas–New Year's vac., 1 May.
Prix fixe: 11,85€ (lunch), 20€ (lunch),
22,80€, 24,30€ (lunch), 32,80€, 38,30€.
A la carte: 55€.

Cathy Maisch runs, with brilliance, this *bierstub* that typifies Petite France. The two wooden rooms, one noisy and the other private, have charm. The summer terrace overlooking the Ill is a joy. On the cuisine side, one enjoys escargots and garlic butter in puff pastry, salmon trout with almonds, pork shank seasoned with beer eau-de-vie and the frozen local Marc-flavored kouglof with wild rose sauce.

● L'Ancienne Douane   SIM
6, rue de la Douane.
Tel. 03 88 15 78 78. Fax 03 88 22 45 64.
anciennedouane.rv@elior.com
www.anciennedouane.fr
Closed Christmas.
Prix fixe: 18€, 19,50€.
A la carte: 30–40€.

Touristy but practical, open every day and bordering the Ill, this large, rather factory-like but friendly brasserie, with its waiters in traditional costume, serves typical dishes at low prices. Head cheese and wine aspic terrine, salmon brochette, a generous choucroute with seven types of pork cut and charcuterie, tête de veau with sauce ravigote and pan-simmered quince with cinnamon ice cream fulfil their function perfectly.

● Le Beijing   SIM
8, quai des Pêcheurs.
Tel.-Fax 03 88 35 39 57.
Closed Sat. lunch, Sun. lunch.
Prix fixe: 15€. A la carte: 30–35€.

Contrary to the impression given by the name, Chan Oi Wang originates from Shanghai and his cooking covers the immensity of China. Nothing to criticize in the steamed ravioli, stuffed crab, oven-crisped duck and the flambéed banana beignet, charged at reasonable prices.

● La Bourse   SIM
1, pl de Lattre-de-Tassigny.
Tel. 03 88 36 40 53. Fax 03 88 36 35 46.
nathalie@restaurant-de-la-bourse.fr
www.restaurant-de-la-bourse.fr
Closed Christmas, New Year's.
Prix fixe: 8,50€ (weekday lunch), 20€.
A la carte: 35€.

This huge brasserie with its high ceiling does not pretend to do anything other than to feed agreeably and quickly easily-satisfied crowds with cold beef salad with horseradish, salmon grilled skin-side down with basil, lewerknepfle (local liver dumplings), tartes flambées and streusel accompanied by local wine. Friendly atmosphere and reasonable prices.

● Au Coq Blanc   SIM
9, rue Mélanie.
Tel. 03 88 41 87 77. Fax 03 88 31 61 82.
au.coq.blanc@wanadoo.fr
www.au-coq-blanc.fr
Closed Sun. dinner, 2 weeks Jan.,
mid-Aug.–12 Sept.
Prix fixe: 25€, 31,50€.
A la carte: 40€.

This good establishment in Robertsau is warm and the cooking of François Baur, working under the management of owner Lucien Ennesser, equally so. The clientele orders and the ovens get fired. Roasted quail and foie gras in salad, slow-simmered beef stew served with crispy vegetables, four fishes stew poached in wine with noodles, veal kidney with mustard sauce and a frozen meringue with whipped cream respect tradition. Beautiful summer terrace.

● La Grappa   SIM
5, rue du Vieux-Marché-aux-Vins.
Tel. 03 88 75 98 60.
landosina@wanadoo.fr
Closed Sun., Mon.
Prix fixe: 18€, 25€.
A la carte: 55€.

Franck Riegel has made this local Italian restaurant, in the very center of the town, opposite the tram line, an agreeable stopping-off place. The place is friendly and the cooking follows suit. We like the carpaccio, the oven-crisped parmesan dish, penne seasoned with peppers, Roman-style saltimbocca and the tiramisu. The service is pleasing and the restaurant fills quickly, despite the menu prices, which tend to soar.

● **La Patrie** SIM

1, rue des Balayeurs.
Tel. 03 88 35 16 92. Fax 03 88 36 81 92.
Closed Sun., Mon., Christmas–New Year's,
1 week Feb., 3 weeks Aug.
Prix fixe: 21–28€, 32€.
A la carte: 33€.

The country referred to is Portugal. Pedro Botijo and his chef Jorge de Almeida offer fried cod cakes, shrimp beignets, fisherman's cod, Portuguese mixed meat platter with seafood and the Molotoff pudding sprinkled with red or white wine. Everything breathes the country between Setubal and Faro. Friendly atmosphere and tight prices.

● **Le Rocher du Sapin** SIM

6, rue du Noyer.
Tel. 03 88 32 39 65. Fax 03 88 75 60 99.
Closed Sun.
Prix fixe: 15,50€, 18€, 22€, 8€ (child).
A la carte: 30€.

This good old "comfort food" brasserie has kept the look and menu of former times. One first goes shopping in the nearby shops and then comes to put down one's bags and taste the terrine of wild boar head cheese and wine aspic with vinaigrette, salmon poached in sparkling wine, pike-perch poached in red wine, cheese-stuffed and breaded escalope and a Black Forest cake. The service is assiduous and the check not inflated.

● **Salambo-Amilkar** SIM

2, rue de la Croix.
Tel. 03 88 35 40 50.
Closed Sun., mid-July–mid-Aug.

Prix fixe: 19€, 20€.
A la carte: 30€.

In this exotic, softened setting, one has the impression of having been transported to Megara, as in Salambo, and the gardens of Amilkar. Chadia Ganame looks after the egg or tuna in filo pastry, the fine couscous and tagines. The *pâtisseries* are as sweet as the country and the mint tea, with pine nuts, is served as it should be. It does not cost much to go on the journey here.

● **Secrets de Table** SIM

39, rue du 22-Novembre.
Tel. 03 88 21 09 10. Fax 03 88 21 08 18.
secretsdeable@wanadoo.fr
Closed dinner, Sun.
Prix fixe: 8,70€, 9,90€. A la carte: 15€.

Jean Westermann, brother of Eric at Buerehiesel, runs this chic and tasty fast food restaurant which cuts a dash with its modern, designer canteen setting. One munches Caésar salad, tuna cocktail, salmon marinated in sea salt, ham on toast, chicken and pineapple salad with Middle Eastern spices, without hesitation.

● **Trattoria Da Giovanni** SIM

1, pl Saint-Thomas.
Tel. 03 88 22 20 99.
Closed Sun., Mon., end July–end Aug.
A la carte: 40€.

This pocket-sized trattoria offers the whole of Italy on a plate. Giovanni Lava watches carefully over the antipasti misti, eggplant gratin, grappa-seasoned salad, saltimbocca and tiramisu. Booking is essential.

● **La Vieille Tour** SIM

1, rue Adolphe-Seyboth.
Tel. 03 88 32 54 30.
lercher@hotmail.com
Closed Sun., Mon., 1 week Jan.,
2 weeks July.
Prix fixe: 35€. A la carte: 65€.

Trained by Antoine Westermann, Véronique and Emmanuel Lercher have made this corner house bordering Petite France

131

into a friendly eatery. In a sunny setting of orange walls and blue curtains, one makes short work of house country pâté, mild peppers stuffed with crab, pork trotter cake with ceps, the pistachio crème brûlée and the quetsche plums sautéed with cinnamon. It is well done, even if the à la carte prices give themselves airs.

● **La Vignette**   SIM

29, rue Mélanie.
Tel. 03 88 31 38 10. Fax 03 88 45 48 66.
lavignetterobertsau@cegetel.net
Closed Sat., Sun., 2 weeks Christmas–New Year's, 3 weeks Aug.
Prix fixe: 8,50€ (lunch).
A la carte: 45€.

The fashionable set of Strasbourg congregate in this rural tavern in the heart of Robertsau, where beautiful hostess Danie Douanic and hard-working chef Serge Knapp practice the high art of conviviality and of pleasing the customers. The summer terrace is popular and one enjoys, without holding back, slow-cooked beef terrine with trumpet mushrooms and foie gras, head cheese and wine aspic terrine, grouper roasted with thyme and bay, niçoise-style tripe and the dried fruit dessert with apples and quince. It's lively, relaxed and not too dear.

● **Zuem Ysehuet**   SIM

21, quai Mullenheim.
Tel. 03 88 35 68 62. Fax 03 88 36 50 67.
www.zuem-ysehuet.com
Closed Sat. lunch, Sun., Oct.–end Apr.
Prix fixe: 18€ (lunch), 26€.
A la carte: 45€.

The place, right on the bank of the Ill, skillfully defies fashion. Guido Scheidhauer looks after reception, Sacha Bender after the kitchen and the service on the covered patio at the back is prompt. One eats, without regret, duck foie gras terrine with pears and pistachios, grilled sea bream with fennel and slow-cooked tomatoes, quail stew with shallot confit and the frozen kouglof with Kirsch.

In Fegersheim (67640). 13 km s via N83.

● **La Table Gourmande**

43, rue de Lyon.
Tel. 03 88 68 53 54. Fax 03 88 64 94 95.
Closed Sun. dinner, Mon. dinner, 1 week Jan., 2 weeks July.
Prix fixe: 21€ (lunch), 26€ (dinner), 49€ (dinner). A la carte: 60€.

The Grassers are still energetically looking after this discreet good restaurant. Trained in Austria, from where Anita comes, Philippe serves up light, fresh dishes. The seafood carpaccio, roasted Atlantic sea bass filet, breast of farm-raised young duck with a slice of foie gras and the "all chocolate" dessert are of beautiful quality. The cellar is rich in the finest production of the region. The menus are well conceived.

In Fegersheim.

● **Auberge du Bruchrhein**   SIM

24, rte de Lyon.
Tel.-Fax 03 88 64 17 77.
Closed Sun. dinner, Mon.
Prix fixe: 17€ (weekday lunch), 23€, 28€.
A la carte: 38€.

This fine village inn allows you to have a gourmet meal without breaking the bank. A pressed beef cheek terrine in aspic, seafood choucroute, Atlantic sea bass simmered in dark beer, veal kidney served with red shallots and local noodles and the mirabelle plums flambéed with Schnapps and served with vanilla ice cream are eaten effortlessly. Gilles Salomon cooks with care, while Mandy looks after her customers tenderly.

In Illkirch-Graffenstaden (67400). 5 km via route de Colmar.

● **A l'Agneau**

185, rte de Lyon.
Tel. 03 88 66 06 58. Fax 03 88 67 05 84.
Closed Sun. dinner, Mon., Tue., 1 week beg. Feb., Aug.
Prix fixe: 32€, 15€ (child).
A la carte: 55€.

The Kerns work as a family. Guillaume takes over from his mother Martine in the kitchen while his father Claude gives a lively welcome. There is no need to change a successful menu. Transparent ravioli stuffed with smoked duck foie gras, pike-perch in a thin layer of potatoes, slow-cooked venison stew with blood sauce infused with cocoa served with a layered mashed potato casserole and the extra-dark chocolate fondant with white chocolate mousse hit the target.

In Ittenheim (67370). 12,5 km sw via A35 then N4.

● **Au Boeuf** 🍴SIM

17, rte de Paris.
Tel. 03 88 69 01 42.
info@au-boeuf.com
www.au-boeuf.com
Closed Mon., Tue., 2 weeks June.
Prix fixe: 21,50€.
A la carte: 35€.

This roadside inn, pioneer of the tarte flambée, always scores a bull's-eye. The setting is friendly, the restaurant rustic and the welcome charming. Jean-Jacques and Christian Colin look after the house food, not only the famous flat tarts, but the head cheese in wine aspic terrine, salmon filet and the frozen kouglof. Family atmosphere and gentle checks.

In Mittelhausbergen (67200). 6 km nw via D41.

● **Au Tilleul** SIM

5, rte de Strasbourg.
Tel. 03 88 56 18 31. Fax 03 88 56 07 23.
autilleul@wanadoo.fr
www.autilleul.fr
Rest. closed Tue. dinner, Wed., Feb. vac.,
2 weeks beg. Aug.
12 rooms: 52–60€.
Prix fixe: 16€ (lunch), 21€, 36€ (dinner),
7€ (child).
A la carte: 55–60€.

Lorentzes have run this smart inn since 1888. The rooms are neat and tidy but it is the cuisine of Jacques, the current Lorentz, assisted by Eric Moebs, that makes one want to stay. Pan-seared foie gras with balsamic vinegar, crayfish and frog legs in a puff pastry shell with sauce and a venison medallion with vineyard peaches are

full of inspiration. The Black Forest leaves a good memory and the cellar is full of discoveries from here and elsewhere.

In Pfulgriesheim (67370). 10 km via D31.

● **Bürestuebel** 🍴SIM

8, rue de Lampertheim.
Tel. 03 88 20 01 92. Fax 03 88 20 48 97.
restaurant.burestubel@wanadoo.fr
www.burestubel.com
Closed Sun. (Nov.–Jan.), Mon. (Nov.–Jan.),
Tue., Feb. vac., mid-Aug.–end Aug.
Prix fixe: 17€, 26€.
A la carte: 35€.

The wise Pierre Meyer swears by Alsace and the richness of its local cuisine. He has retained the lesson learned at Mischler's in Lembach and he zealously sets out his region's tastes, returning to simplicity but in the most superlative way. He looks after the tartes flambées, breaded pork trotters, local liver dumplings and the beer-roasted pork shank. The bread is made in house, like the ice creams, and choosing between the "Gretel cup" (sweet and sour cherry sorbet with eau-de-vie) and Bürestuebel (vanilla ice cream, cinnamon-seasoned fruits simmered in red wine) involves a hard decision. Nothing is left to chance in this former farm with its painted wooden fittings, its flowered courtyard and its timbered facade repainted in yellow. Despite the high number of covers, the service is exemplary and the check moderate.

In Pfulgriesheim.

● **L'Aigle** SIM

22, rue Principale.
Tel. 03 88 20 17 80. Fax 03 88 20 76 76.
Closed Sun., Mon., 2 weeks Christmas–New Year's, 3 weeks July
A la carte: 28€.

In their pleasant roadside inn, Marthe and Lydia Roth look after their customers with the tartes flambées baked in the wood-fired oven, wild rabbit in aspic terrine, grilled sirloin with potatoes and the frozen meringue and Chantilly dessert, all washed down with regional wines. Delightful welcome and very gentle checks.

In Plobsheim (67115). 12 km s via route
d'Offenburg.

● **Au Boeuf**   SIM

25, rue du Général-Leclerc.
Tel. 03 88 98 58 25. Fax 03 88 98 73 02.
Closed Sat. lunch, Mon., 1 week Jan.,
3 weeks Aug.
Prix fixe: 19€ (lunch), 26€, 32€.
A la carte: 30€.

It would be a mistake to stay outside admiring the beautiful timbered exterior. You have to come in and sit down in the red, wooden décor of the warm dining room. With the educated advice of Marie-Paule Sutter, you hesitate to choose among stuffed pike-perch simmered in red wine, pork cheeks, tête de veau and a seasonal fruit crumble. The portions are generous and the prices moderate and Vincent Sutter, who formerly worked at the Auberge de l'Ill and at La Poste in La Wantzenau, is a skillful craftsman.

In 67300 Schiltigheim. 3 km via D468.

● **Serge & Co**   COM

14, rue des Pompiers.
Tel. 03 88 18 96 19. Fax 03 88 83 41 99.
serge.burckel@wanadoo.fr
www.serge-and-co.com
Closed Sat. lunch, Sun. dinner, Mon.,
2 weeks July.
Prix fixe: 48€, 58€, 88€.

After having labored in all four corners of the globe, from St. Louis, Missouri to Hong Kong, via Los Angeles and Orlando, Serge Burckel has finally hung up his hat in an inner suburb of Strasbourg. He has made his mark with distinctive fusion cooking that skillfully reinterprets regional classics in a sure-fire winning formula. His good humor spreads through the restaurant as well as the dishes. With his bandana glued to his head, this wonder boy who is always on duty gives the impression that he is just playing around—yet his creations are hard to forget. With him, the frog legs wink at the escargots and the sweet pea purée is classically prepared and served with a warm smoked bacon aspic. He also makes a fun "soft spring roll" with crabmeat served with a shellfish cream. Regional produce is honored with John Dory with morels and asparagus (also with creamed asparagus), hand-rolled noodles with venison, veal kidney ravioli and the head and tongue served cold, carpaccio style, a carnivorous feast. The desserts are playful, with names that raise a smile but an end result that requires respect. Chocolate cigar and pineapple fritters amuse. On the financial side, the clever special menus put his creations within reach of all budgets.

● **La Table Chaude**   COM

43, rte du Général-de-Gaulle.
Tel. 03 88 81 22 24. Fax 03 88 81 47 95.
www.latablechaude.com
Closed Sat. lunch, Sun., Mon. dinner,
3 weeks Aug.
Prix fixe: 20€, 17€, 32€. A la carte: 48€.

Emilio de Matteis, who opened the pizzeria Riva Destra (12, quai Saint-Nicolas. Strasbourg. Tel. 03 88 35 05 60), has left the kitchens of this *tavola calda* to Dominique Roth. The classics are still on the menu, such as parmesan and basil carpaccio, fritto misto, saltimbocca with basil cream and the tiramisu. Warm welcome but checks a little too high.

● **La Taverne de Saint-Malo**   SIM

12, rue Contades.
Tel. 03 88 18 98 00.
Closed Sat. lunch, Sun. dinner, Mon.
Prix fixe: 14€ (lunch), 18€ (lunch), 20,50€ (lunch), 27€ (lunch). A la carte: 45€.

Brigitte and Kaine Palleau—she from Alsace, he from St. Malo—have made this Breton tavern into a high-quality establishment. One forgets the external appearance of a concrete bunker to concentrate on the warm kitsch setting with its knick-knacks on a maritime theme. Marinated smoked herring, seafood tapas, lemon-seasoned sardines with steamed potatoes, fish stew served St. Malo–style, roasted fresh pineapple with caramel and rum raisin ice cream slip down effortlessly.

● WINSTUBS

These wine cafés are the guardians of regional tradition. Warm atmosphere, cozy, wooded décor and simple little dishes, manager (or manageress) of character, wines in jugs and friendly company. To experience a *winstub* is to get a glimpse of the soul of Alsace.

● **Chez Yvonne**   🟢SIM
   "S'Burjerstuewel"
10, rue du Sanglier.
Tel. 03 88 32 84 15. Fax 03 88 23 00 18.
info@chez-yvonne.net
www.chez-yvonne.net
Closed Christmas, New Year's.
A la carte: 35–40€.

Jean-Louis de Valmigère has energetically taken over this celebrated *winstub* where Helmut Kohl, Jacques Chirac and Gerhard Schröder, among others, used to junket. The wood setting with its benches and small corners is cute. In the kitchens, Dominique Radmacher offers both regional recipes and produce and contemporary food on the menu slate: goat cheese terrine with peppers, sauerkraut and pork tart, Munster cheese in puff pastry, roasted pike-perch seasoned with orange peel, pork shank braised in beer and Gewurz-flavored ice are very attractive. The wine list elegantly exceeds the orbit of a *winstub*.

● **Le Clou**   SIM
3, rue du Chaudron.
Tel. 03 88 32 11 67. Fax 03 88 21 06 43.
Closed Sun., Wed. lunch, Christmas,
New Year's.
A la carte: 38€.

Marie Sengel is a prominent figure in Strasbourg. With her husband, she delights her world—politicians and theatrical people—in a very charming wood setting, with onion tart, head cheese and wine aspic terrine, pike-perch served over sauerkraut, ham braised in Pinot Noir and the frozen meringue with whipped cream. The wines in jugs contribute to the convivial atmosphere and the prices won't make you climb the wall. All the same, beware of

overcooking at the end of the week, particularly when the masters of the house are not there (overcooked shriveled sausage and calf's liver).

● **Kobus**   Ⓝ🟢SIM
7, rue des Tonneliers.
Tel. 03 88 32 59 71.
erkohn@wanadoo.fr
Closed Sun., Mon., 1 week Nov.,
3 weeks mid-Jan.–beg. Feb.
Prix fixe: 14,90€. A la carte: 25–35€.

Eric Kuhn has just moved and has changed the name of his establishment, which he runs in the tradition of L'Ami Fritz. But he still gives a very authentic, simple welcome to the specialities of this town-center establishment. Foie gras terrine, duck leg confit, choucroute and strawberry soup with Pinot Noir served with cinnamon ice cream have the good taste of tradition.

● **Fink'stuebel**   🟢SIM
26, rue Finkwiller.
Tel. 03 88 25 07 57. Fax 03 88 36 48 82.
finkstuebel@noos.fr
http://finkstuebel.free.fr
Closed Sun. (exc. marché de Christmas),
Mon., 1 week beg.
Jan., 1 week Feb., 3 weeks Aug.
A la carte: 40€.

Sophie and Thierry Schwaller have successfully taken over the reins of this *winstub* with respect for the traditions of Alsace. First, in terms of food, with kouglof with pork cheeks and foie gras, crispy pike-perch with sauerkraut, beef served with sea salt and horseradish cream and the frozen kouglof with Kirsch, and then in terms of hospitality, with a friendly atmosphere in which beer and local wines flow freely.

● Muensterstuewel `SIM`

8, pl du Marché-aux-Cochons-de-Lait.
Tel. 03 88 32 17 63. Fax 03 88 21 96 02.
munsterstuewel@wanadoo.fr
www.strasnet.com/munsterstub.htm
Closed Sun. (exc. Christmas market days),
Mon., 1 week beg. Jan., 2 weeks beg. July.
Prix fixe: 30€ (lunch, wine inc.), 45€ (wine
inc. dinner).
A la carte: 40€.

This *winstub* with an unpronounceable
name (meaning "wine shop of the cathedral") is run with a masterly hand by
Patrick Klipfel, who is constantly inno-
vating, offering entertainment and good
little dishes. This semi-finalist for the
best sommelier of France, a trainee with
Bocuse and Girardet, is backed up by Jean-
Louis Ohl in the kitchen. The fish comes
from Quiberon and the meat is of perfect quality. Shrimp tails on caramelized
sauerkraut, pork trotter with potatoes in
casserole accompanied by a quick-seared
goose liver, stuffed and slow-cooked oxtail
and the pistachio parfait with quetsche
plum sorbet are astonishing.

● Au Pont-Corbeau `SIM`

21, quai Saint-Nicolas.
Tel. 03 88 35 60 68. Fax 03 88 25 72 45.
corbeau@reperes.com
www.pontcorbeau.com
Closed Sat. (exc. Christmas market days),
Sun. dinner, 1 week Feb., end July–end Aug.
Prix fixe: 11€ (weekday lunch).
A la carte: 35€.

Adorable and one hundred per cent Alsatian, Christophe Andt is a flag carrier for
local traditions. His warm *winstub* is decorated in an old style with frescoes by
Edgar Mahler and woodwork by Raymon
Emile Waydelich. On the plate, an onion
tart, grilled ham, chilled pot au feu salad
with sautéed potatoes, tête de veau and
the dark chocolate and sour cherry terrine seasoned with Kirsch are delicious
and very gently priced. Attractive wines
in pitchers.

● Au Coin des Pucelles `SIM`

12, rue des Pucelles.
Tel.-Fax 03 88 35 35 14.
Closed Sun., Sun. dinner, Bank holidays,
mid-July–mid-Aug.
A la carte: 36€.

The house is historic, the banquettes have
style and the cuisine of Roland Rohfritsch
skillfully signs up with tradition. Head
cheese and wine aspic terrine, duck foie
gras, choucroute, ham and the frozen
vacherin are very honest. Friendly welcome and prices that do not shock.

● Zum Strissel `SIM`

5, pl de la Grande-Boucherie.
Tel. 03 88 32 14 73. Fax 03 88 32 70 24.
zuem.strissel@orange.fr
Closed Christmas, New Year's.
Prix fixe: 13,70€, 22€, 8€ (child).
A la carte: 32€.

Jean-Louis de Valmigère has taken over
this historic house with its colored windows, wine-press room, scupltured casks,
wooden benches and old paintings. He has
polished up the place and left the old team,
who are quietly good and solid, undis-
turbed. Head cheese and wine aspic terrine with vinaigrette, pike-perch on a bed
of sauerkraut, pork shank braised in beer
and the apple tart are all nice.

● Au Cruchon `SIM`

11, rue des Pucelles.
Tel. 03 88 35 78 82.
Closed Sat. lunch (exc. fêtes), Sun. (exc.
fêtes), Mon. lunch, 2 weeks Aug.
Prix fixe: 9€ (lunch).
A la carte: 35€.

This was an establishment famous for the
musical atmosphere led by Fernand Wohl,
whose accordion now features as a wall
decoration. The young Gilles Spannagel
has taken over the house with discretion,
dreaming up finely crafted dishes (pumpkin soup with "the spirit" of foie gras and
pike-perch on a bed of sauerkraut with
Avruga sauce), which does not mean that
the presskopf (transformed into a carrot terrine), boudin noir (with parsnip

purée) are not on the menu. The evening menu (frog leg tartlet) and the desserts (a quetsche plum gratin with cinnamon ice cream) are worthy of praise.

● Zehnerglock · N SIM

4, rue du Vieil-Hôpital.
Tel. 03 88 23 17 42.
Closed Mon.
Prix fixe: 22,50€ (lunch).
A la carte: 35€.

We knew the Zehnerglock for its rustic atmosphere and its fresco of the historic "ten o'clock bell." Yves and Karine Lutz, plus Rachel Schmitt, Yves' sister, are in charge of the establishment which has kept its antiquated character. Yves, formerly of Zimmer-Sengel and Valentin-Sorg, carefully creates goose foie gras with Gewurz aspic and dried fruit compote, escargots and little puff pastry shells with meat and white sauce. A place to watch.

● Au Bon Vivant · SIM

7, rue du Maroquin.
Tel. 03 88 32 77 81. Fax 03 88 32 95 12.
Closed Thu. (exc. lunch season), Fri.
Prix fixe: 15,90€, 18,90€, 30€,
7,50€ (child). A la carte: 36€.

Cédric Moulot and Michel Reuche of the neighboring Tire-Bouchon have just taken over this old tavern. It is too soon to assess the change, but onion tart, pâté in a pastry crust, spit-roasted chicken, goose breast with sour cherries and a chocolate cream dessert seasoned with Kirsch leave fine memories.

● D'Choucrouterie · SIM

20, rue Saint-Louis.
Tel. 03 88 36 52 87 / 03 88 36 07 28.
Fax 03 88 24 16 49.
info@choucrouterie.com
www.choucrouterie.com
Closed Sat. lunch, Sun., 2 weeks Aug.
Prix fixe: 9€ (weekday lunch).
A la carte: 30–35€.

Man of theatre and singer Roger Siffer leaves Théo, conductor of the restaurant, to manage this affable establishment with discernment. Until late into the night, one can eat smoked trout and salmon salad, pike-perch breaded with pain d'épice, local liver dumplings, choucroute served seven different ways and the tarte Tatin, which make a good impression, washed down with edel in pitchers and Météor beer.

● La Petite Mairie · SIM

8, rue Brûlée.
Tel.-Fax 03 88 32 83 06.
Closed Sat., Sun.,
Christmas–New Year's vac.
A la carte: 38€.

A stone's throw from the town hall, Maryse Wenger's tavern is always full. The house duck and goose foie gras combination, head cheese and wine aspic terrine, Mediterranean sea bass filet, ham breaded with pain d'épice and the house-made three-chocolate mousse are fantastic, just like the reception.

● Sel & Poivre · SIM

18, rue du Neufeld.
Tel.-Fax 03 88 34 51 40.
selpoivre@club-internet.fr
Closed Sat. lunch, Sun., 2 weeks Christmas–New Year's, 1 week Aug.
Prix fixe: 8,50€ (lunch), 9,50€ (lunch),
12,50€ (dinner), 18,50€ (dinner).
A la carte: 38€.

Laurent Man has energetically taken over this small, cozy restaurant. Thierry Knobloch creates with profesionnal seriousness the "salt and pepper" hors-d'oeuvre, pike-perch and salmon served over a bed of sauerkraut, a two-pound beef steak and the berry charlotte. Small summer terrace and local wines in a pitcher.

● S'Thomas Stuebel · SIM

5, rue du Bouclier.
Tel. 03 88 22 34 82.
Closed Sun., Mon., Christmas–New Year's,
3 weeks Aug.
A la carte: 29€.

Next to St. Thomas, Thierry Deylot guards another secret. Onion tart, head cheese and wine aspic terrine, pike-perch poached in Riesling, veal kidneys with local noodles and the quetsche plum sorbet are nicely washed down with selected wines.

● S'Wacke-Hiesel

Pl de la Foire-Exposition.
Tel. 03 88 36 64 75. Fax 03 90 41 68 09.
swacke-hiesel.fr
Closed Sat. lunch, Sun., Christmas–New Year's, 2 weeks beg. Aug.
A la carte: 35€.

A stone's throw from Wacken, this faux-wooden hut is passionately run by two sisters, Anne and Michèle Leppert. One comes here to enjoy presskopf, onion tart, oven crisped pike-perch and hanger steak with shallots taken directly from traditional cuisine. The prices are reasonable and the crème brûlée flambée fun.

● La Taverne du Sommelier [SIM]

3, ruelle de la Bruche.
Tel. 03 88 24 14 10.
www.chefstudio.fr
Closed Sat. (exc. Bank holidays), Sun. (exc. Bank holidays), 2 weeks Aug.
A la carte: 38€.

Martin Schreiber, wine expert, shares his encyclopedic knowledge with his customers, who are often passionate wine lovers themselves. His cellar develops along with his discoveries. Game terrine, braised monkfish cheeks, duck breast roasted with quince and spicy pears simmered in red wine accompany the finds of the day.

● Le Tire-Bouchon [SIM]

5, rue des Tailleurs-de-Pierre.
Tel. 03 88 22 16 32. Fax 03 88 22 60 88.
contact@letirebouchon.fr
www.letirebouchon.fr
Prix fixe: 23€, 32€, 8€ (child).
A la carte: 32€.

With its typical exterior, this *winstub* is an institution. Cédric Moulot in the restaurant and Michel Reuche in the kitchen have given it its former dynamism. Pan-seared foie gras with simmered apples, whole pike-perch served on sauerkraut

with a Riesling sauce, hand-cut steak tartare prepared at the table, roasted ham with Munster sauce and an apple streudel with vanilla ice cream are fantastic. Nice welcome, diligent service and moderate prices.

● Zum Wynhaenel [SIM]

24, rue Sleidan.
Tel.-Fax 03 88 61 84 22.
Closed Sun., 1 week beg. Mar., mid-July–mid-Aug.
Prix fixe: 12€ (weekday lunch) 10€ (child).
A la carte: 34€.

Raymond Mainberger is the protective father watching over his rustic tavern tucked away in an art nouveau building. One eats escargots, grilled ham, veal kidney with mustard sauce and chocolate cake without any difficulty. Nice wines in pitchers, summer terrace.

▼ | SHOPS

BREAD & BAKED GOODS

BAKER OF THE YEAR

Au Pain de mon Grand-Père

58, rue de la Krutenau.
Tel. 03 88 36 59 66.

Patrick Dinel, a native of Nancy, intellectual and keen convert to the cause of authentic baking, is very much at home with his dough. Assisted by his son Bruno, he tends to the leaven in his kneading trough and plies his trade in full view of the customers in his rustic store with its wood-burning oven. What he produces has a delightfully old-fashioned flavor. Charentes-Poitou butter, Breton shortbread, whole grain breads, ciabatta, olive fougasse, spelt wheat Coronne, Pogne de Romans, rye Chaperon, soy flour Bûcheron, the delightfully rustic round loaf of stone-ground wheat flour and the Kamut newly revive the baker's spirit of Alsace. Aficionados of local produce need not worry, though: he also purveys a superb kouglof, streussel, Chinois, pretzel and onion tart all well worth the detour. A word of advice: at peak times, you can expect to join a long line of customers!

▼ Charles Woerlé

10, rue de la Division-Leclerc.
Tel. 03 88 15 19 30.

The kouglof alone is worth a visit and what can we say about the gingerbread, Annecy cake, grès des Vosges, streusel, bredele, apple or fromage blanc tarts and breads (rye, poppyseed, sesame, beer, walnut, raisin, cumin, bacon and onion)?

CHARCUTERIE

▼ Frick-Lutz

16, rue des Orfèvres.
Tel. 03 88 32 60 60.

Here, Jean-Paul Kirn serves quality knacks, cooked ham, ham baked in pastry, torte with Riesling, sausages with beer, presskopf, choucroute and smoked pork filet.

▼ Kirn

19, rue du 22-Novembre.
Tel. 03 88 32 16 10.
www.kirn-traiteur.fr

Torte with white wine, irreprochable galantine, choucroute, housemade foie gras mousse, delicious knacks, bacon and smoked pork shoulder to be enjoyed at home or on the second floor.

▼ Klein

28, bd d'Anvers.
Tel. 03 88 61 16 10.

We savor the pork filet mignon in pastry, feuilleté with munster and chèvre or meat-filled friands.

▼ Porcus

6, pl du Temple-Neuf.
Tel.-Fax 03 88 23 19 38.
www.porcus.fr

Sausages sold by length: smoked, cooked, with liver and herbs, Toulouse-style, merguez and smoked duck breast are Olivier Klein's stock in trade. Light dishes on the second floor.

CHEESE

▼ Fromagerie des Tonneliers

32, rue des Tonneliers.
Tel.-Fax 03 88 52 04 03.

A keen cheesemonger, René Tourette presents fine mountain cheeses, farm-made artisanal roquefort, farm chèvres from the Loire and munsters at the peak of their form.

▼ Au Vieux Gourmet

3, rue des Orfèvres.
Tel. 03 88 32 71 20.

Fine, meticulously matured mountain cheeses made with raw milk (reblochon, tomme de Savoie, cantal, laguiole), farm-made munster and chèvres are the pride of Cyrille and Christelle Lorho.

CHOCOLATE

▼ Epice et Chocolat

5, rue du Temple-Neuf.
Tel. 03 88 32 43 80.
www.mulhaupt.fr

Lime ganache, chocolate bars with Sichuan peppercorns and Guérande sea salt, and other astute blends, along with spices, rosemary, ginger, lemongrass, tea and fruit make up the fresh, light, sparingly sugared pastries prepared by Thierry Mulhaupt.

▼ Gillmann

20, quai des Bateliers.
Tel. 03 88 36 47 05.

Delicious chocolates, nougats, fruit pastes, jams, truffles, muscadines (chocolate truffles coated with powdered sugar), dark chocolate lace cookies, petit fours and ganaches in a variety of flavors are appealing indeed.

In Geispolsheim.

▼ Musée "Les Secrets du Chocolat"

Parc de la Porte Sud, rue du Pont du Péage.
Tel. 03 88 55 04 90.
www.musee-du-chocolat.com

Jean-Paul Burrus, who runs the Marquise de Sévigné, founded this fascinating museum devoted to Montezuma's divine bean. After the tour, visitors can purchase items that are a joy to admire, touch and savor.

GROCERIES

▼ La Cabane des Anges

14, rue du Bain.
Tel. 03 88 35 46 54.
Goritsa and Zoritsa Urosevic bring life to this little gourmet showcase on the edge of Petite France. Organic products, oils, vinegars and selected wines are enshrined in their fragrant emporium.

▼ O & Co

1, rue du Miroir.
Tel.-Fax 03 88 22 33 77.
Hedi Bentsair watches keenly over this store devoted to olive oils of the Mediterranean. From Provence, Lebanon, Israel, Morocco, Italy or Spain, they all bear the seal of quality.

▼ Les Trois Etoiles de Strasbourg

111, Grand-Rue.
Tel. 03 88 22 63 30.
Stéphanie Scharf has turned this bright store into a temple to the fine oils and apéritifs of Provence. Honey vinegars, liqueurs or digestifs are appealing indeed.

▼ Le Panier des Pâtes

7, rue d'Austerlitz.
Tel. 03 88 25 53 59.
Italy (spaghetti, linguine, gnocchi, lasagne) meets Alsace (bidelekäs, knepfles, gaenzeknepfle, buewespaetzle, fleischschnaka) in François Morabito's store.

COFFEE

▼ Café Reck

8, rue de la Mésange.
Tel. 03 88 32 37 22.
www.cafereck.com
Designer coffee machines by major brands, services for espresso, cappuccino, Blue Mountain, Sidamo and a vast range of teas and chocolates form an impressive array indeed in this paneled setting. Tasting in the store.

FOIE GRAS

▼ Edouard Artzner

7, rue de la Mésange.
Tel. 03 88 32 05 00.
www.edouard-artzner.com
Jean and Monique Schwebel have taken over this illustrious establishment founded in 1803. Duck or goose foie gras in glass jars, as well as rilettes, stuffed duck breast and goose presskopf are of the finest quality.

▼ La Boutique du Foie Gras

8, rue Friesé.
Tel. 03 88 32 28 42.
Exuding a timeless charm, this establishment continues to supply spices, foie gras in all its forms, table wines or grand crus. Mail order sales.

▼ La Boutique du Gourmet

26, rue des Orfèvres.
Tel.-Fax 03 88 32 00 04.
Georges Bruck's duck or goose foie gras—sliced, in jars, in a parfait, in a pastry crust—and wines and alcohols draw a gourmet crowd.

▼ Jean Lutz

5, rue du Chaudron.
Tel. 03 88 32 00 64.
Smoked salmon, Petrossian caviar, delicious duck and goose foie gras—fresh, semi-preserved, or in jars, with Port, or four-spice—at reasonable prices.

PREPARED FOODS

▼ La Boutique d'Antoine Westermann

1, rue des Orfèvres.
Tel. 03 88 22 56 45.
www.buerehiesel.com
Spices, wines, teas, eaux de vie, oils, condiments, vacuum-packed food to take away and kitchen utensils fill the first floor and basement here.

In Schiltigheim.

▼ Kieffer

3 km via D46810, rue du Colvert.

Tel. 03 88 83 45 45.

www.kieffer-traiteur.com

Quality baeckeofe, ham baked in pastry, suckling pig. A catering service and organization of receptions.

GINGERBREAD

▼ Mireille Oster

14, rue des Dentelles.

Tel.-Fax 03 88 32 33 34.

In her 1643 establishment on the edge of Petite France, Mireille Oster supplies gingerbread that she produces in her atelier. Gingerbread with fruit, seven spices ("*graines d'ange*"), and the "*cameliesel*" with chocolate are a delight.

ICE CREAM

▼ Le Glacier Franchi

5, rue des Francs-Bourgeois.

Tel. 03 88 23 16 15.

www.leglacierfranchi.fr

This ice cream specialist offers 40 quality flavors. Cookies, spéculos, fleur d'Alsace (vanilla cream with cherries and kirsch) and Carribean rum are superb.

PASTRIES

▼ Jean-Claude Ziegler

23, av de la Forêt Noire.

Tel. 03 88 61 45 95.

www.ziegler-jc.com

Having served at the Buerehiesel for ten years, this industrious confectioner now displays his artistic gifts here, with his classic Opéra cake, his macaron dessert —both delightful—and his "raspberry milk" with pine nuts.

▼ Christian

12, rue de l'Outre.

Tel. 03 88 32 04 41 / 03 88 22 12 70.

www.christian.fr

Christian Meyer creates superb chocolates (truffles with sandalwood, ganache with beer, pure Java chocolate bars) and his pastries, desserts, brioches (the famous pastry ring with frangipane— a creamy pastry filling with powdered almonds), and the ice creams (particularly the fromage blanc) are among the best of their kind.

▼ Falcinella

17, rue du Général-de-Castelnau.

Tel. 03 88 35 27 02.

Jean-Claude Grosskost prepares streusel, kouglof, cheesecake, lemon tart, linzer torte, banana-chocolate or raspberry desserts and nice bittersweet chocolates.

▼ Gerber

28, allée de la Robertsau.

Tel. 03 88 37 13 59.

Valrhona chocolate concentrate, "blancheneige" (fromage blanc, fresh fruit, raspberry coulis), "*séducteur*" (chocolate, praliné, a sprinkle of walnuts) establish the reputation of this fine store.

▼ Gross

24, pl des Halles.

Tel. 03 88 22 22 77 / 03 88 49 98 50.

www.gross.fr

Michel Gross offers iced kouglofs, triple-chocolate festival cake, the grape cluster with Marc de Gewurz and "vergers d'Alsace" (mirabelle plum mousse, quetsche plum marmalade, gingerbread).

▼ Thierry Mulhaupt

18, rue du Vieux-Marché-aux-Poissons.

Tel. 03 88 23 15 02.

www.mulhaupt.fr

The great Thierry subtly prepares millefeuille, "Chicago" (pistachio macaron, apricot chutney, fromage blanc pastry cream), guanaja chocolate tart and iced desserts.

▼ Naegel

9, rue des Orfèvres.

Tel. 03 88 32 82 86.

At the Naegels', tradition has never been healthier, with special breads (fig-hazelnut, fiber), wild strawberry or raspberry tartlets, ice creams and homemade chocolates.

FRESH PRODUCE

▼ Ziegler

2, pl du Marché-Neuf.

Tel. 03 88 32 55 38.

www.ziegler-a.net

Celebrated for his made-to-order cornucopias of fruit, the store also supplies seasonal produce, fruits and vegetables of the world, vinegars, oils, jams and Vosges honey.

IMPORTED PRODUCTS

▼ Spagna

29, rue des Tonneliers.

Tel. 03 88 32 16 09.

Artisanal pastas, balsamic vinegars, olive oils, Parma or San Daniele ham, cheeses from the "Boot" and quality wines make an excellent impression here. There is a second store at 8, rue de Londres.

TABLETOP & KITCHENWARE

▼ Arts et Collections d'Alsace

4, pl du Marché-aux-Poissons.

Tel.-Fax 03 88 14 03 77.

In this store, you will find kelsch and linen tablecloths, engraved carafes, beer mugs, Soufflenheim pottery, and Betschdorf stoneware.

▼ La Cour Renaissance

3, rue de l'Ail

Tel.-Fax 03 88 52 01 21.

With Soufflenheim pottery, molds, antique glasses, earthenware, kelsch fabrics and polychromatic furniture restored by Christine and Bernard Demay, this store is something of a folk art gallery.

▼ Faïencerie de la Petite-France

33, rue du Bain-aux-Plantes.

Tel. 03 88 32 33 69.

faiencerie-petite-France.com

Hand painted reproductions of 18th-century objects, ceramics, old Strasbourg plates and precious (and costly) items fill the Deutschler family's little museum.

▼ Lalique

25, rue du Dôme.

Tel. 03 88 75 55 52.

www.lalique.com

Claudine Mage presents Lalique creations: crystal, jewelry, perfumes, leather goods and china produced in the Wingen-sur-Moder workshops.

▼ Vitrines d'Alsace

18, pl de la Cathédrale.

Tel. 03 88 75 10 90.

Isabelle Siegel recommends Beauvillé tablecloths, Nusbarner eaux de vie, Soufflenheim pottery, Elchinger ceramics, Lunéville earthenware and Spindler marquetry.

TEAS

▼ Le Palais des Thés

124, Grand-Rue.

Tel. 03 88 22 21 23.

www.palaisdesthes.com

This bright, elegant emporium serves all kinds of tea: smoked, green, from China, India, Japan, Ceylon or elsewhere. Attractive teapots too.

WINE

▼ La Cave du Sommelier

28, rue du Maréchal-Foch.

Tel.-Fax 03 88 36 57 71.

Expert "consultant sommelier" Roger Dahlen watches over his grand cru Riesling, Kastelberg, Côtes Rôties from the house of Guérin, Santenay, Banyuls and Margaux of good vintage.

▼ Au Millésime

7, rue du Temple-Neuf.

Tel. 03 88 22 30 20.

This prestige store holds great Bordeaux, rare wines, collectors' cognacs, champagnes, Alsatian eaux de vie, whiskeys and 60 or so Armagnacs dating from 1931 to 1990.

▼ Terres à vin

1, rue du Miroir.

Tel. 03 88 51 37 20.

www.terresavin.com

Cellar, *table d'hôte* and wine bar coexist harmoniously in Eric Demange's establishment, where he presents his personal favorite vintages.

▼ Le Vinophile

10, rue d'Obernai.
Tel.-Fax 03 88 22 14 06.

Wine lover Michel Le Gris lays on tastings of vintages from all over France, commenting shrewdly on each one. Also a splendid range of Italian, Spanish, Hungarian, Romanian, South African and German wines.

 | RENDEZVOUS

BEER BARS

◆ Aux Douze Apôtres

7, rue Mercière.
Tel. 03 88 32 08 24.

A step away from the cathedral, Bernard Rotman has turned this bar, with its wooden banquettes and counter, into an oasis for beer lovers. Patrons enjoy the 15 keg beers and an impressive range of bottled brews with a pretzel or knack.

◆ Le Schluch

3, rue de l'Outre.
Tel. 03 88 32 45 68.

This old *bierstub* has all the atmosphere of a vintage tavern with its oval bar lined with regulars. A second, more unobtrusive room also has paneling and a polychrome entrance.

CAFES

◆ Café Brant

11, pl de l'Université.
Tel. 03 88 36 89 05.
www.cafe-brant.com

Students love this Thirties café with its high ceilings, attractive lighting and terrace near the statue of Goethe.

◆ Café Broglie

1, rue du Dôme.
Tel. 03 88 32 08 08.

Customers can lunch here or enjoy one of the five draft beers or an espresso in the Parisian café setting. A terrace in summer.

◆ L'Epicerie

6, rue du Vieux-Seigle.
Tel.-Fax 03 88 32 52 41.

The Provençal grocery store setting has its charm. A drink and an interesting tartine provide an enjoyable break.

◆ Jeannette et les Cycleux

30, rue des Tonneliers.
Tel. 03 88 23 02 71.

This neo-Fifties café continues to do a roaring trade in tartines (tuna, chicken, roast beef) and selected desserts (chocolate fondant). "VT" Gewurz from Metz and barrel-aged aperitifs practically drink themselves.

◆ Le Montmartre

6, rue du Vieux-Marché-aux-Poissons.
Tel.-Fax 03 88 32 40 58.

With its wooden benches, this café has a touch of yesteryear's subway. Inside or on the terrace, we enjoy a draft beer or an espresso, and can also nibble on quiches, croque-monsieurs or sandwiches.

◆ La Passerelle

38, quai Bateliers.
Tel. 03 88 36 19 95.

From 11 am to 4 pm, this minimalist bar serves refreshing drinks and very honest dishes (duck confit parmentier, oat milk crème brûlée). DJ evenings on the weekend.

◆ La Place

3-5, pl des Tripiers.
Tel.-Fax 03 88 22 22 20.

Bastien Sengel has turned this designer brasserie into a permanent attraction, serving drinks from 10 am to 11:30 pm, and feeding customers with foie gras ravioli with mushrooms, salmon tartare, cod in an herb crust, poultry vol-au-vent and banana dumplings, all impeccably reliable.

◆ Le Roi et son Fou

37, rue du Vieil-Hôpital.
Tel. 03 88 23 22 22.

A Strasbourg style "Flore" where we enjoy "*salade du Roy*", tartare, tomato-mozzarella salad and tartines, along with a cappuccino or a tea.

TEA SALONS

◆ Café Stein

29, rue du Vieux-Marché-aux-Poissons.
Tel. 03 88 22 25 25.

The sandwiches and pain bagnat are as delicious as are the sweeter delights prepared by Jean-Marie Steinmetz. His mille-feuille, éclairs, apple-cinnamon mousse or little pains au chocolat are such a success that he has opened a second tearoom (55, bd G.-Clemenceau).

◆ Christian

10, rue Mercière / 12, rue de l'Outre.
Tel. 03 88 22 12 70 / 03 88 32 04 41.

A quality establishment where Strasbourg society gathers to savor a rhubarb tart, a strawberry cookie and, especially, melon or banana ice cream and rhubarb or fromage blanc sorbet.

◆ Riss

35, rue du 22-Novembre.
Tel. 03 88 32 29 33.

A cozy atmosphere in this *pâtisserie*, where the specialty is the chocolate truffle, although we should not forget the fruit tarts, strawberry mille-feuille, triple-chocolate mousse and other delicacies prepared by Jean-François Hollaender.

◆ Winter

25, rue du 22-Novembre.
Tel. 03 88 32 85 40.

Georges Winter's pastries are delightful. The hot chocolates, desserts and sandwiches made with pretzel dough are as good as they were in the days of his mother Francine.

STUTZHEIM-OFFENHEIM

67370 Bas-Rhin. Paris 478 – Strasbourg 13 – Saverne 23.

A village of Kochersberg, like a signpost to the countryside, reputed for its taverns that serve tartes flambées.

●	RESTAURANTS

● Le Marronnier   🅝 SIM

18, rte de Saverne.
Tel. 03 88 69 84 30. Fax 03 88 69 87 82.
Closed lunch (exc. Sun.).
A la carte: 25€.

A former farm transformed into a charming inn with interminable dining rooms. An entire family, the Friedrichs, serve satisfied customers in the very busy restaurant. Exquisite tartes flambées, plain or with cheese, are what one finds at sensible prices every evening. Pretty multicolored wood fittings and wide culinary range (presskopf, tartiflette, caramelized pork ribs or ham shank).

● Le Tigre   🅝 SIM

Rue Principale.
Tel. 03 88 69 88 44.
Closed Sat. lunch, Mon. dinner, Wed., 1 week Feb. vac., 3 weeks July–mid-Aug.
Prix fixe: 22,50€ (Sun.), 25€ (lunch). A la carte: 28€.

From the road, one can see this establishment with its modern facade and interior, its parasol-covered terrace and its active waitresses. Emmanuel Wolfromm is the talented but modest practitioner of all the culinary arts: a potato and Munster gratin, breaded and fried squid, trout with white summer truffles, spicy pork trotters and tartes flambées in the evening have the best society of the region coming in droves.

THANN

68800 Haut-Rhin. Paris 472 – Mulhouse 22
– Colmar 44 – Guebwiller 25.
office-de-tourisme.thann@wanadoo.fr.
The collegiate church of Saint-Thiébaut, the horizontal donjon known as "the witch's eye" and the glorious Rangen wine-growing region are sufficient to ensure the reputation of Thann. The valley of Saint-Amarin deploys its verdant ribbon.

 HOTELS-RESTAURANTS

■ La Cigogne

35-37, rue du Général-de-Gaulle.
Tel. 03 89 37 47 33. Fax 03 89 37 40 18.
mangelhotels@yahoo.fr
www.hotellacigogne.com
Closed Feb. Rest. closed Sun. dinner, Mon.
27 rooms: 48–76€.
Prix fixe: 13,50€, 26€, 32€ (dinner),
11€ (child). A la carte: 55€.

The Mangels' modern hotel is known for its efficient service, its comfortable rose-toned rooms and its honest family cooking. In the lemon and blue pastel dining room Claude's dishes—Andalouse-style langoustine tart, pike-perch on sauerkraut, venison medallion with lingonberries and a frozen vacherin—go down well with local wines.

■ Moschenross

42, rue du Général-de-Gaulle.
Tel. 03 89 37 00 86. Fax 03 89 37 52 81.
info@le-moschenross.com
www.le-moschenross.com
Closed 2 weeks beg. July
Rest. closed Sun. dinner, Mon. lunch.
23 rooms: 31–46€.
Prix fixe: 11€ (weekday lunch), 16€, 22€,
46€, 7,30€ (child).

This large red house dating from 1880 in the center of the town has bright and lively colored rooms. The Geyer-Pontals extend a hearty welcome and Isabelle's finely prepared dishes reflect the seasons. The pork trotter served over sauerkraut, escargots, pike-perch served over slow-cooked leeks, veal hanger steak with morels and the chocolate desserts are very well made.

■ Le Parc

23, rue Kléber.
Tel. 03 89 37 37 47. Fax 03 89 37 56 23.
reception@alsacehotel.com
www.alsacehotel.com
Rest. closed 3 weeks Jan.
21 rooms: 65–180€.
Prix fixe: 37€, 17€ (child).
A la carte: 49€.

In their country house set in wooded grounds, the Martins offer period-style furniture in opulent rooms, elegant lounges, a fitness center—sauna, Turkish bath and Jacuzzi—and a swimming pool. In the richly colored dining room, extending onto the terrace in summer, Sonia Kassis presents classic cuisine adapted to today's taste. Foie gras terrine with fruit chutney, grilled pike-perch with pepper sauce, duck breast with honey and figs and a chestnut crème brûlée are all well prepared. Paulo Soarès suggests appropriate wines to match these dishes.

▼ SHOPS

BREAD, BAKED GOODS & PASTRIES

▼ Gérard Freyburger

146, rue de la 1re-Armée.
Tel. 03 89 37 06 63.
Organic breads and loaves with spelt, whole grains or wheatberries; baguette; fougasse; house ice creams and fruit tarts abound in this establishment founded in 1933.

CHARCUTERIE

▼ Michel Meyer

82, rue de la 1re-Armée.
Tel. 03 89 37 01 65.
Pâté baked in a pastry crust, beer sausage, country bacon, raw cured ham, choucroute, farm-raised meats and a handful of cooked dishes make a delightful impression here.

PASTRIES

▼ Kaelbel

19, rue de la 1re-Armée.
Tel.-Fax 03 89 37 11 62.
"Vénus", "*délice*" (strawberry mousse
cake with white chocolate mousse frost-
ing), "Engelbourg" (raspberry mousse,
vanilla, ganache) or "*crescendo*" (with
cooked plums) make a visit to Jean-Marc
Kaelbel's store worthwhile indeed.

THANNENKIRCH

68590 Haut-Rhin. Paris 436 – Colmar 21 –
Bergheim 7 – Sélestat 15.
This pretty forest village on a rise across from
the Haut-Koenigsbourg and not far from the
wine route, symbolizes bucolic Alsace.

■ / HOTELS-RESTAURANTS

■ La Meunière

30, rue Sainte-Anne.
Tel. 03 89 73 10 47. Fax 03 89 73 12 31.
info@aubergelameuniere.com
www.aubergelameuniere.com
Closed 20 Dec.–20 Mar.
23 rooms: 63–105€.
Prix fixe: 13€, 17€, 22€, 34€, 36€,
7€ (child).

This picture postcard Alsatian inn overlooking the valley is a haven of peace. The
rooms are mountain style, half-rustic, half-
modern, and the bay windows of the dining
rooms look out on the surrounding countryside. The fitness center, the panoramic
terrace and the garden are all enchanting.
In the kitchen, Jean-Luc Dumoulin serves
up robust and cheerful food using local
market produce. In the rustic dining room
the crunchy Munster cheese bonbon with
lentil salad, perch filet on a bed of cumin-
seasoned sauerkraut, veal hanger steak
with lemon and ginger, the Reinette apple
dessert and crème brûlée left us with delicious memories.

■ Le Touring

Rte du Haut-Koenigsbourg.
Tel. 03 89 73 10 01. Fax 03 89 73 11 79.
touringhotel@free.fr
www.touringhotel.com
Closed beg. Jan.–end Mar.
Rest. closed lunch (exc. weekends).
45 rooms: 50–94€.
Prix fixe: 16€ (weekdays), 21€, 41€.
A la carte: 37–42€.

In the heart of the village and in sight of the
pine crests, Antoine Stoeckel's hearty hotel
has kept up with the times, with its rooms
with wood furniture and its serious cuisine with Jean-Louis Biechler at the helm.
In the old-style light wood dining room,
foie gras ravioli with vegetable bouillon,
rosemary-seasoned and grilled Atlantic
sea bass and a strawberry frozen meringue
go down without any difficulty.

● S'Waldstebel `SIM`

24, rue Sainte-Anne.
Tel.-Fax 03 89 73 11 84.
Closed Mon., mid-Jan.–end Feb.
Prix fixe: 12,50€ (lunch), 16,50€, 20€.
A la carte: 30–35€.

With its pine benches and panoramic terrace, this mountain tavern exudes the
charm of the Vosges. Eric Bechdolff cooks
up timeless dishes and finely wrought
concoctions that go well with the rustic
wooden dining room when escorted by
local wines. House duck foie gras, pike-
perch served on sauerkraut with beurre
blanc, pork cuts and charcuterie served on
sauerkraut and a Kirsch-flavored mousse
have no difficulty convincing us, particularly since the Marcaire menu is devilishly generous.

TOURTOUR

67310 Bas-Rhin. Paris 470 – Strasbourg 25 – Molsheim 8 – Saverne 22.

The northern part of the wine route. The local glory is an Altenberg *grand cru* that gives splendid Rieslings and Muscats.

● | **RESTAURANTS**

● **Zum Loejelgücker**

17, rue Principale.
Tel. 03 88 50 38 19. Fax 03 88 76 02 46.
loejelgucker@traenheim.net
www.Loejelgücker-auberge-traenheim.com
Closed Mon. dinner, Tue., Feb. vac.
Prix fixe: 10,40€ (lunch), 16,50€, 26€, 40€.

The heart of Alsace rings out here in Claude Fuchs' magnificent half-timbered house decked out with wood and frescoes illustrating work in the vineyards. The menu and wine list, with nearly 200 listings, proves without any difficulty that here we concentrate on good eating and drinking. The green- and mint tea-marinated tuna carpaccio with grilled eggplant, the roasted cod filet with fresh sweet peas, the fried veal kidneys napped with a mustard-seasoned herb sauce and the white chocolate and sour cherry jelly verrine swing delicately between regional tradition and modernity. A charming inn that we also appreciate for its moderate prices.

LES TROIS-EPIS

68410 Haut-Rhin. Paris 439 – Colmar 11 – Munster 17 – Gérardmer 50.

The scene of a miracle: it was here that Thierry Schoeré, a resident of Orbey, saw three ears of corn appear in the hand of the Virgin in 1491. Since then, Les Trois-Epis has never ceased to welcome pilgrims who have climbed the 658 meters in search of the benefits of good air.

 | **HOTELS-RESTAURANTS**

■ **Hôtel des Trois Epis**

10, rue Thierry-Schoeré.
Tel. 03 89 49 81 61. Fax 03 89 78 90 48.

hotel3epis.1@wanadoo.fr
40 rooms: 80–85€. 2 suites: 145–160€.
Prix fixe: 29,90€, 39,90€, 45€.
A la carte: 50€.

In the middle of its flowery garden, this sixties vacation resort still continues to work its charm. As witnessed by the welcome provided by Helmut Hautzinger and the carefully laid-out rooms with a view of the Vosges. In the rustic dining room, the regional cooking based on organic produce exudes gentle perfumes. Goose foie gras, cod filet cooked skin-side down, slow-cooked pork cheek medallions and a cold yellow nectarine soup leave no room for criticism.

■ **Turckheim Croix d'Or**

3, rue Thierry-Schoeré.
Tel. 03 89 49 83 55. Fax 03 89 49 87 14.
hostelleriecroixdor@wanadoo.fr
www.hostelleriecroixdor.com
Rest. closed Mon., Jan.
12 rooms: 42–52€.
Prix fixe: 13,10€ (exc. Sun.), 24€, 29€, 7€ (child).
A la carte: 36€.

We appreciate the panoramic view of the Vosges from the terrace or the dining room with its large bay windows. The smiling Fabrice Kolb, who trained at Lucas-Carton, Arpège and Taillevent, delights us with simple yet classic dishes that he executes to perfection. Pan-tossed mixed mushrooms, pansimmered salmon with creamy bacon sauce, veal steak with chanterelles and the berry soup are a pleasure.

TURCKHEIM

68230 Haut-Rhin. Paris 441 – Colmar 7 – Munster 12 – Gérardmer 45.

The night watchman in his greatcoat calling out the hours, the memory of Turenne before the battle, the fortified gates, the *Coteau du Brand*, renowned for its Riesling, its busy winemakers and its gourmet stopovers: a town that is an honor to beautiful Alsace!

HOTELS-RESTAURANTS

■ Berceau du Vigneron

10, pl Turenne.
Tel. 03 89 27 23 55. Fax 03 89 30 01 33.
www.berceau-du-vigneron.com
40 rooms: 43–85€.

Built on the ramparts of the old city, this half-timbered house with its typical Alsatian rooms that are comfortable and equipped—carpet, hair dryer and television—has an agreeable *winstub*, the Caveau du Vigneron. A buffet lunch in the inner courtyard in summertime costs 8€.

● L'Homme Sauvage   COM

19, Grand-Rue.
Tel. 03 89 27 56 15. Fax 03 89 80 82 03.
homme.sauvage.sarl@wandoo.fr
Closed Sun. dinner (exc. off season), Wed. (exc. off season), 1 week Oct., 2 weeks Feb., 1 week at end Aug.
Prix fixe: 13–25€ (weekday lunch), 34€, 9,50€ (child). A la carte: 46€.

There is a satisfying irony in the name of this 1609 inn (The Wild Man), given that John Oed of Strasbourg—who trained in the Cerf de Marlenheim, in the Chambard and in the Fer Rouge—serves up very civilized cuisine. In the pretty dining room with wooden beams that is both rustic and contemporary or in the cobblestone courtyard in summer, foie gras brochettes with jumbo shrimp and mirabelle plum chutney, sea bream with tapenade served with tapenade-seasoned mashed potatoes, jumbo shrimp, stuffed rabbit saddle with chanterelle risotto and a fresh seasonal fruit mille-feuille with mascarpone cream make up seductive dishes that swing between tradition and modernity.

● Caveau du Vigneron   SIM

5, Grand-Rue.
Tel. 03 89 27 06 85.
Closed lunch, Mon.
A la carte: 40€.

Malou and Coco Helschger have brought youth and vibrancy to this 16th-century cellar with its smart and sassy atmosphere. Masterpieces, old wood paneling and a winepress are the hallmarks of this carefully chosen décor. The traditional cuisine wins us over with the onion tart, escargots, boneless frog legs with parsley sauce, potatoes and braised ham shank, berry soup and the frozen kouglof. Local wines wash it all down artfully.

● Auberge du Brand   SIM

8, Grand-Rue.
Tel. 03 89 27 06 10.
www.aubergedubrand.com
Closed lunch, Wed.
9 rooms: 56–110€.
Prix fixe: 23€, 31€, 45€, 9€ (child).
A la carte: 55€.

This goodly inn with its wooden beams and rustic atmosphere has comfortable old-style rooms that are spacious and tastefully furnished. Christian Zimmerlin, who has been through the Ducasse school, serves up very satisfying traditional dishes. Duck foie gras seasoned with eau-de-vie and quince, fish with Riesling cream sauce, beef with Munster sauce and Gewurz-seasoned roast peaches bring a smile to the lips.

● Auberge du Veilleur   SIM

12, pl Turenne.
Tel. 03 89 27 32 22. Fax 03 89 27 55 56.
auberge.veilleur@wanadoo.fr
Closed Sat. lunch, Tue.
Prix fixe: 19,90€, 29,50€, 7,50€ (child).
A la carte: 38€.

Sabrina Chelly and Nicole Dos Santos have taken over and renovated the *winstub* that Christiane Kretz made fashionable without breaking with the spirit of the place. We are welcomed with a smile to the dining room decked out in the colors of Alsace. Jean-Marc Parlato's regional cuisine is authentic: grilled bone marrow with sel de Guérande, pot-au-feu salad with crisp vegetables, fish choucroute, steak tartare and the frozen kouglof go down a treat.

● Le Caveau du Chemin de Ronde

1, rue des Vignerons.
Tel.-Fax 03 89 27 38 27.
lecheminderonde@wanadoo.fr
www.lecheminderonde
Closed Mon. dinner, Jan.–beg. Feb.
A la carte: 36€.

On the ramparts of the old city, this rustic tavern, now in the hands of Franck Heinrich, serves up traditional fare with enthusiasm. The house salad, sirloin steak with béarnaise sauce, beef tartare and pain perdu are authentic.

▼	SHOPS

BUTCHER

▼ Geismar

21, Grand-Rue.
Tel. 03 89 27 14 12.
Heir to this establishment founded in 1784, Jacques Geismar prepares garlic or liver sausages, honey-braised ham, smoked or country bacon, county-style pâté, pickelfleisch (beef breast in brine) and torte vigneronne, along with a wide range of kosher products (Lyonnais sausage made with beef).

TABLETOP & KITCHENWARE

▼ Staub

2, rue Saint-Gilles.
Tel. 03 89 27 77 77.
www.staub.fr
Francis Staub, king of the wrought iron casserole dish, presents a range of high quality winter and summer products. Also, appealing ceramics and Guy Untereiner's renowned tablecloths.

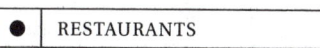

67350 Bas-Rhin. Paris 459 – Haguenau 18 – Saverne 32 – Strasbourg 38 – Pfaffenhoffen 2.
An industrious town in the Hanau region at the entrance to the great forest of Haguenau.

●	RESTAURANTS

● Restaurant de la Forêt

94, Grand-Rue.
Tel. 03 88 07 73 17. Fax 03 88 72 50 33.
Closed Mon. dinner, Tue. dinner, Wed.,
4 days beg. Jan., 3 weeks July–Aug.
Prix fixe: 8€ (lunch),
14,25€ (weekdays), 34€.

This former beer depot has become a fine restaurant in the hands of Caroline and Bernard Ohl. Bernard, who has already worked in the Anthon in Obersteinbach and in the Cygne in Gundershoffen, manages to blend the rustic and refined in masterly fashion. We could come simply for the *plat du jour*, the leek quiche and the braised smoked ham with cream sauce served with a potato gratin, but there are also other things to please us here: the variety meats (kidneys with shallots in Port, oven-crisped tête de veau) or the seafood (scallops and Mediterranean sea bass with olive oil, shrimp salad) or even the classic Alsatian dishes as always (frog legs, a marbled foie gras terrine), not to mention the pretty desserts (frozen praline parfait and cherry soup with vanilla ice cream) or the nicely laid tables and excellent glasses.

▼	SHOPS

EAUX DE VIE

▼ Bertrand

3, rue du Maréchal-Leclerc.
Tel. 03 88 07 70 83.
www.distillerie-bertrand.com
Since 1874, the finest fruits of the Hanau region have gone to make spirits and liqueurs here. kirsch, plum, mirabelle plum, elderflower, sorbier (sorbe-apple),

poire Williams, *alisier* (service berry), quince or fleur de bière reign.

◆   RENDEZVOUS

BRASSERIE

◆ **Brasserie d'Uberach**

30, Grand-Rue.

Tel. 03 88 07 07 77.

www.brasserie-uberach.com

Lager, dark, amber, white and organic beers: superb beverages lovingly concocted in this artisinal brewery.

UNGERSHEIM

68190 Haut-Rhin. Strasbourg 97 – Mulhouse 18 – Ensisheim 5 – Guebwiller 8. All of Alsace summed up in a series of splendidly reconstituted houses: don't miss the ecomuseum!

■   HOTELS

■ **Les Loges de l'Ecomusée**

Chemin du Grosswald.

Tel. 03 89 74 44 95 / 03 89 74 44 49.

Fax 03 89 74 44 68.

28 rooms: 38–45€. Prix fixe: 15€, 29€.

By the entrance to the ecomuseum, a very smart modern hotel in the regional style enables us to visit everything without undue hustle and bustle. Pleasant and functional rooms that are also practical for families in the mezzanine. Regional cuisine in a large ground-floor dining room with a counter where draught beer is served.

◆   RENDEZVOUS

CAFE

◆ **L'Auberge de Gommersdorf**

In the Alsace Ecomuseum, chemin du Grosswald.

Tel. 03 89 74 44 49.

Prix fixe: 17€, 8,20€ (child).

A la carte: 30€.

In the heart of the Ecomusée, two antique residences dated 1564 and 1682. The first is from Hegenheim, with its fine 16th-century yard; the second from Gommersdorf, as its name implies. With fine Fifties lighting, portraits of ancestors and a huge terrace by the water, this scrubbed, waxed village café is "too good to be true".

URMATT

67280 Bas-Rhin. Paris 421 – Molsheim 17 – Saverne 36 – Wasselonne 22. A sentinel between the valley of the Bruche and the forest, on the pathway through the rocks and a true village of the Vosges.

   HOTELS-RESTAURANTS

■ **Le Clos du Hahnenberg**   🏠
   Chez Jacques

65, rue du Général-de-Gaulle.

Tel. 03 88 97 41 35. Fax 03 88 47 36 51.

clos.hahnenberg@wanadoo.fr

www.closhahnenberg.com

Hotel closed Fri. dinner, Feb. vac.

Rest. closed Fri. dinner, Christmas, New Year's, Feb. vac.

33 rooms: 49,50–61€.

Prix fixe: 13€ (weekday lunch), 19€, 26€, 7,50€ (child). A la carte: 37€.

With its renovated bedrooms, games and sports facilities (boules, tennis and swimming pool), this inn is a pleasant stopover. Bruno Baur, whom we know from the Louis XIII in Strasbourg, presents a very pleasant cuisine: goat cheese salad, monkfish slice with Colombo spices, pikeperch with Riesling sauce, a Milan-style piccata and a local steamed bread dessert with mixed spice ice cream make a good impression.

■ **La Poste**   🏠

74, rue du Général-de-Gaulle.

Tel. 03 88 97 40 55. Fax 03 88 47 38 32.

www.multimania.com/hotelrestlaposte

Closed Sun. dinner, Mon., 1 week Christmas–New Year's, Feb. vac., 2 weeks July.

14 rooms: 40–57€.

Prix fixe: 17,50€, 48€, 8,50€ (child).

Doris Gruber and her brother Jacques run this welcoming inn in the center of town.

The rooms are pleasant and the garden is ideal for daydreaming. Installed in the fine dining room, we continue our journey as we enjoy the classic but very well-executed cuisine: quail terrine with foie gras, turbot with beurre blanc sauce and scallops, beef filet medallions with béarnaise sauce and flambéed raspberries served over vanilla ice cream.

LA VANCELLE

67730 Bas-Rhin. Paris 420 – Colmar 31 – Saint Dié – Ribeauvillé 17 – Sélestat 12.
The Vosges, the forest and the call of the great outdoors.

 HOTELS-RESTAURANTS

■ Hôtel Elisabeth

5, rue du Général-de-Gaulle.
Tel. 03 88 57 90 61. Fax 03 88 57 91 51.
info@hotel-elisabeth.fr
www.hotel-elisabeth.fr
Closed 8 Jan.–15 Jan., 26 Feb.–12 Mar., 26 June–3 July
Rest. closed Sat. lunch, Sun. dinner, Mon.
10 rooms: 49€.
Prix fixe: 10€ (weekday lunch), 25€, 32€ (wine inc.), 38€, 12,50€ (child).
A la carte: 45€–50€.

Before wielding kitchen utensils, Gérard Dehaye juggled with figures in an accounting firm. His stays with Bras at Laguiole and Didier Oudill in Paris have enabled him to now present an honorable à la carte menu that is not lacking in flair. The pan-tossed chanterelles with jumbo shrimp in an acidulated reduction, roasted scallops with a creamy saffron-seasoned herb risotto, the thick-cut veal chops accompanied by roasted hazelnut bulgur and Arabica-heightened pan juices and a Gariguette strawberry dessert, a pistachio cream dessert and a house saffron-flavored ice cream are a gourmet's delight. Afterwards we allow ourselves a little nap in one of the hotel's rooms with red and wood tones.

● Auberge Frankenbourg

13, rue du Général-de-Gaulle.
Tel. 03 88 57 93 90. Fax 03 88 57 91 31.
info@frankenbourg.com
www.frankenbourg.com
Closed mid-Feb.–10 Mar., end June–10 July.
Rest. closed Tue. dinner, Wed.
11 rooms: 49€.
Prix fixe: 26€, 43€, 56€, 72€ (wine inc.), 14€ (child). A la carte: 55–65€.

This friendly hotel with a considerable reputation is undergoing a gentle renovation. The rooms have been redecorated and the furniture in the restaurant has changed. In the kitchen, Sébastien Buecher has taken over from his father Aimé in the last few years. After training with the best chefs in Alsace—Mischler in Lembach, Jung at the Crocodile, Albrecht in Rhinau and Brendel in Riquewihr—he is reasserting his desire to bring creativity to the fore. Pan-tossed langoustine served on a pork trotter and headcheese cake, served with warm basil aspic, Atlantic sea bass with Swiss chard ravioli and ricotta poached in a broth made with the fish bones, served with polenta frites and the pigeon breast with vegetables in aspic with the thighs wrapped in crunchy angelhair pastry blend local and more exotic flavors with daring and precision. The house chocolate mint dessert is a sweet and extremely tempting way to finish off a meal. Fabien Steip uses his talent to recommend wines that put the finishing touch to this cocktail of gourmet pleasures.

VILLE

67220 Bas-Rhin. Paris 418 – Sélestat 16 – Strasbourg 58 – Saint-Dié 39.
tourisme@cccanton-de-ville.fr.
This pastoral and forested region where wild berries drop into our hands and where we only have to raise our arms to pick the fruit from the trees, has an abundance of home distilleries.

 HOTELS-RESTAURANTS

■ La Bonne Franquette
6, pl du Marché.
Tel. 03 88 57 14 25. Fax 03 88 57 08 15.
bonne-franquette@wanadoo.fr
www.hotel-bonne-franquette.com
Closed Nov. 1 vac., Feb. vac., 1 week at end June–beg. July. Rest. closed Sun. dinner, Mon.
10 rooms: 33,50–53,50€.
Prix fixe: 19,50€, 27,60€, 38,50€, 10€ (child).

A flowery facade, carefully kept rooms and rustic furniture make this attractive, cen-

trally located inn a choice stopover. Véronique's welcome and Pascal Schreiber's cuisine are equally pleasing. Everything here is "informal". A locally smoked trout carpaccio, pike-perch filet with Riesling cream sauce, thinly sliced duck breast with mountain honey and a frozen kirsch mousse go down easily.

 SHOPS

CHARCUTERIE
▼ Munschina
3, pl du Marché.
Tel.-Fax 03 88 57 17 07.
Philippe Munschina deftly prepares country bacon, ham in pastry, spiced sausages, Ville-style ficelle and torte vigneronne, and chooses the livestock for his milk-fed veal or farm-raised beef.

EAUX DE VIE
▼ Massenez
In Dieffenbach-au-Val.
Tel. 03 88 85 62 86.
www.eaux-des-vies.com
Manou Heitzmann-Massenez runs this celebrated establishment with tact and a smile. Pear, plum, kirsch, mirabelle plum or wild raspberry are at the peak of their genre. Note the Los Boldos, produced on the family property in Chile with chardonnay, merlot and cabernet sauvignon grapes.

In Hohwarth.
▼ Meyer
19, rue Principale.
Tel. 03 88 85 61 44.
www.distillerie-meyer.fr
Jean-Claude Meyer's renowned eaux de vie come in fine blown glass bottles. Raspberry, kirsch, poire Williams, quetsche plum and fruit liqueurs are in excellent form.

In Maisonsgoutte.
▼ Marie-Françoise Hubrecht
6, rue Kuhnenbach.
Tel. 03 88 57 17 79
Marie-Françoise Hubrecht keeps a close watch on her outstanding mirabelle. The Marc de Gewurz, pear, quince, wild sloe,

rose-hips, sorbe-apple and pine bud are also of the highest quality.

In Steige.

▼ Nussbaumer
23, Grand-Rue.
Tel. 03 88 57 16 53.
www.joss-nussbaumer.com
This half-timbered house on the Steige pass road is now a museum of quality eaux de vie. Mariane Willm, who took over from King Jos, watches over the matchless kirsch, pear, raspberry, quetsche plum, quince or sloe here.

SEAFOOD

▼ Le Nautilus
5, pl du Général-de-Gaulle.
Tel. 03 88 57 26 36.
Rémy Wendling chooses the best of the catch from small fishing boats. Fine platters of oysters and crustaceans.

 RENDEZVOUS

TEA SALON

◆ Pfister
9, pl du Gal.-de-Gaulle.
Tel. 03 88 57 17 56.
This food lovers' haunt offers tarts, bredele (small Alsatian cakes, baked in a variety of flavors), gingerbreads, mille-feuille and florentins, as well as light dishes at lunchtime. A pretty doll's house décor.

WANGENBOURG

67710 Bas-Rhin. Paris 469 – Strasbourg 42 – Saverne 20 – Molsheim 40.
At the heart of Alsace's Little Switzerland, a village made for convalescence, relaxation and quiet strolls in the pure air. In the ruins of its medieval forest château, you can feel time standing still.

 HOTELS-RESTAURANTS

■ Parc Hôtel ❀⌂
39, rue du Général-de-Gaulle.
Tel. 03 88 87 31 72. Fax 03 88 87 38 00.
parchotel@wanadoo.fr
www.parchotel-alsace.com
Closed beg. Nov.–end Mar.
31 rooms: 51–84€. 3 suites: 93–109€.
Prix fixe: 16€, 19€, 24€, 33€, 10€ (child).

Set in its grounds overlooking the valley, the Gihrs' establishment is just the place to enjoy a little fresh air. Elisabeth's welcome and the tennis court, indoor swimming pool and sauna induce an immediate sense of well-being. On the food side, son Olivier prepares dishes of true character, such as the foie gras and sauerkraut terrine, oven-crisped langoustine with vegetable tartare, Riesling-poached chicken with buttered pasta and the pear served two ways, in warm wine and in a spice-infused aspic.

In Engenthal-le-Bas (67710). Junction D218 and D224.

■ Hôtel des Vosges ⌂
5, rue de Winsbourg.
Locale known as Steigenbach.
Tel.-Fax 03 88 87 30 35.
Closed Wed.
8 rooms: 43€.
Prix fixe: 14,50€, 27€.

This inn standing on a crossroads in a forest clearing is an address to remember. The rustic rooms are full of character, as is the dining room, a hunters' haven. The theme continues with Cunibert Klerlein's dishes, which include some very sound traditional cuisine. Game terrine, pike fish quenelles, veal cutlets with mushrooms and a caramel flan slip down smoothly.

In 67710 Freudeneck. 3 km e via D224.

■ **Freudeneck**

3, rte de Wangenbourg.
Tel. 03 88 87 32 91. Fax 03 88 87 36 78.
hotel-freudeneck@wanadoo.fr
www.hotelfreudeneck.com
9 rooms: 53,50–56,50€.
Prix fixe: 8,50€ (weekday lunch), 15€ (weekday lunch), 18€ (weekday lunch), 20€ (dinner), 7,50€ (child).

This forest inn offers bright, comfortable rooms and a tasteful traditional restaurant. Jean-Claude Wagner stoutly prepares escargots prepared in the style of Alsace (stuffed with spiced butter and herbs and cooked in local wine), mixed pepper-seasoned cod filet, venison steak and a simple fruit sabayon.

LA WANTZENAU

67610 Bas-Rhin. Paris 476 – Strasbourg 12 – Brumath 17.
This town was famous for its "chick". Now, only the bird's name remains. Another tradition has survived, though: the Strasbourg Sunday meal, when local families like to linger at the table.

 HOTELS-RESTAURANTS

● **Le Relais de la Poste**

21, rue du Général-de-Gaulle.
Tel. 03 88 59 24 80. Fax 03 88 59 24 89.
info@relais-poste.com
www.relais-poste.com
Closed 3 weeks Jan.
Rest. closed Sat. lunch, Sun. dinner, Mon.
12 rooms: 80–130€. 2 suites: 130€.
Prix fixe: 37€ (weekdays lunch, wine inc.), 45€, 68€, 150€, 23€ (child).
A la carte: 92€.

This old post house converted into a "Romantik Hotel" has been completely renovated, but still has the woodwork, frescoes and coffered ceilings that form

its Old World charm. The functional rooms are refined but welcoming. Jérôme Daull has turned the restaurant into a gourmet haunt acclaimed for its reliable cuisine. We pay proper tribute to the delicate fresh foie gras served with Muscat aspic on country bread, grilled cod filet with tomatoes served in tartare and also sundried, the home-style roasted young chicken with vegetables and a dark chocolate puff pastry dessert with mandarin orange sorbet. The lush, green terrace is a joy in summer. Highly attentive service.

■ **Hôtel du Moulin**

3, impasse du Moulin.
Tel. 03 88 59 22 22. Fax 03 88 59 22 00.
moulin-wantzenau@wanadoo.fr
www.moulin-wantzenau.com
Closed Christmas–New Year's.
19 rooms: 67–88€. 1 suite: 101€.
Half board: 71€.

On the Strasbourg road, this former mill is an excellent place to stay. Béatrice Wolf and Andrée Dametti provide a cheerful welcome and the rooms furnished with selected fabrics have plenty of character. (See Restaurants: Au Moulin de Wantzenau.)

● **Zimmer** `V.COM`

23, rue des Héros.
Tel. 03 88 96 62 08. Fax 03 88 96 37 40.
zimmer-nadeau@club-internet.fr
www.zimmer-nadeau.fr
Closed Sun. dinner, Mon., Nov. 1 vac., Feb. vac.
Prix fixe: 19,70€, 30€, 37€, 59€ (wine inc.), 15€ (child).
A la carte: 64€.

Dominique Nadeau, who trained at the Robuchon school, has refurbished this traditional establishment in white. At the stove, he applies his talents to preparing a solid cuisine that still leaves room for innovation. A layered scallop and potato dish with ceps, sole meunière with Mont Saint-Michel mussels, oven-crisped veal sweetbreads with morels in a sherry sauce and the mirabelle plum crème brûlée served next to a hot soufflé with a quenelle

of ice cream are attractive propositions.
An excellent cellar.

● Les Jardins Secrets N 🍴 COM

At Hôtel La Roseraie. 32, rue de la Gare.
Tel. 03 88 96 63 44. Fax 03 88 96 64 95.
www.hotelroseraie.fr
Rest. closed lunch (exc. Sun., Mon., Tue.).
15 rooms: 48–56€.
Prix fixe: 28€, 34€.

The décor is Zen, the welcome serene,
the cuisine deft and the set menus well-
chosen: here is the restaurant you should
try in this gourmet village. Foie gras with
Berawecke chutney, black mullet filet with
white beans and guinea hen with pumpkin
purée make a fine impression. The appealing, classical desserts are finely crafted
(crème brûlée with vanilla ice cream and
coffee and whiskey served over shaved ice,
"Irish coffee" style). You will rise from the
table a happier person.

● Les Semailles 🍴 COM

10, rue du Petit-Magmod.
Tel. 03 88 96 38 38. Fax 03 88 68 09 06.
info@semailles.fr
www.semailles.fr
Closed Sun. dinner, Wed., Thu., 3 weeks Feb.,
3 weeks Aug.
Prix fixe: 26 (lunch, weekdays), 39€.

Jean-Michel Loessel is a chef with a prom-
ising future. The Rosenmeer at Rosheim,
the Julien in Strasbourg and the Cheval
Blanc in Lembach already feature among
his trophies. His crisp foie gras mille-feuille,
scallops and shrimp with citrus flavorings,
thyme-seasoned roasted lamb, the house
strawberry dessert and a light mascarpone mousse are the expression of a skilled,
inventive culinary approach. In the dining room, Laurence looks after each of her
guests with talent and charm. She will also
unearth the right wine to flatter the dish you
choose. The prices keep a cool head.

● Au Moulin de Wantzenau COM

2, impasse du Moulin.
Tel. 03 88 96 20 01. Fax 03 88 68 07 97.
philippe.clauss@wanadoo.fr
www.moulin-wantzenau.com

Closed Sun. dinner, bank holiday evenings,
1 week beg. Jan., 1 May, 3 weeks July.
Prix fixe: 25€ (weekdays), 28€, 34€, 48€,
60€, 14€ (child), 60€. A la carte: 65€.

The comfortable dining room and shady
terrace here are delightfully cozy. Philippe
Clauss, the prudent heir who trained at
the Beau Site in Ottrott and Gavroche in
London, presents dishes that are a touch
more imaginative than in the past. Crab,
avocado and grapefruit tartare, orange-
seasoned Atlantic sea bass served with
chanterelles and artichokes, venison cannelloni with ceps and foie gras and an
exotic fruit cappuccino incite us to come
again. The huge cellar was put together
by Clauss the elder.

● Le Grillon 🍴 SIM

18, rte de Strasbourg.
Tel. 03 88 96 27 84. Fax 03 88 96 65 40.
Closed Sat. dinner, Sun., Wed. dinner,
mid-Dec.–beg. Jan., 1 week at end July,
1 week beg. Aug.
Prix fixe: 20€, 25€.
A la carte: 35–40€.

Yves Matter, Jérôme Daull's disciple at
the Poste, wins us over with moderate
prices and a pleasant ambiance. The terrace is crowded in summer. Guests feast
on smoked salmon with house potato
chips, pike-perch poached in wine and
the duck breast with pan-tossed chanterelles. If you find it impossible to choose
between the frozen chocolate truffle
and a house berry gratin with vanilla ice
cream, remember you can afford both at
these prices. The service deserves extra
credit. Exquisite flambéed tarts in the
evening.

● Il Forchettone SIM

25a, quai des Bateliers.
Tel. 03 88 96 37 30. Fax 03 90 29 25 18.
restaurantilforchettone@wanadoo.fr
Closed Mon., Tue. lunch, Aug.
Prix fixe: 25€, 36,50€.
A la carte: 45–50€.

The spacious terrace in front of this modern establishment in the heart of a residen-

tial neighborhood by the canal is instantly overflowing whenever the sun shines. The service is a ballet of proficiency and the menu focuses on the regions of Italy. Pizza as in Naples, fritto misto as in Campania, mushroom tortelloni as in Emilia-Romagna, fish tagliolini as in the Veneto and orechiette as in Puglia (the native country of the owners, Tina and Franco Albanese): all this and more awaits you here, prepared with no frills but a great deal of precision. A fine Italian wine list and a tiramisu ice cream to melt the most hardened soul.

● **Le Pont de l'Ill**   `SIM`

2, rue du Général-Leclerc.
Tel. 03 88 96 29 44. Fax 03 88 96 21 18.
aupontdelill@wanadoo.fr
www.aupontdelill.com
Closed Sat. lunch, Aug.
Prix fixe: 22€, 25€, 28€, 30€,
10€ (child). A la carte: 45€.

Pierre Daull, brother of Jérôme at the Poste, manages this neo-1900 brasserie nonchalantly but efficiently. Chef Fabrice Bienvenot tends to the seafood platters and prepares duck foie gras, a fisherman's stew, pike-perch in red wine sauce, goose breast seasoned with pepper and a soft-centered chocolate cake at prices that fail to torpedo our budget.

▼	SHOPS

LOCAL PRODUCTS

▼ **Paul Hirsch**

1, rue de l'Ecole.
Tel. 03 88 96 20 14.
This champion of goose or duck foie gras at low prices also prepares faultless rillettes, confits and quail with foie gras.

◆	RENDEZVOUS

TEA SALON

▼ **La Cour de Honau**

Allée de Honau.
Tel. 03 88 96 33 44.
A stone's throw from a fitness center (sauna, steam bath, solarium), Patrick and Caroline Tonussi serve salads and

fruit or chocolate desserts, as well as ice creams to be enjoyed on the terrace in summer.

WASSELONNE

67310 Bas-Rhin. Paris 461 – Haguenau 39 – Saverne 14 – Strasbourg 25.
A welcoming crossroads town, boasting the antique ruins of a castle bombarded by Turenne, timber-framed houses, the wine route just a step away and Alsace's Little Switzerland next door.

■/	HOTELS-RESTAURANTS

■ **Hostellerie de l'Etoile**   △

Pl du Maréchal-Leclerc.
Tel. 03 88 87 03 02. Fax 03 88 87 16 06.
luxetoile@aol.com
www.hostellerie-etoile.com
Rest. closed Sun. dinner, Christmas, New Year's.
33 rooms: 38–48€.
Prix fixe: 11€ (weekdays), 17€, 27€.

On the main square, this traditional hotel offers modern rooms and simple, blameless dishes served in a porch dining room. The oyster mushrooms in puff pastry, pike-perch and salmon filets, lamb medallion in a pastry crust and rich chocolate cake are unpretentious.

● **Au Saumon**   `COM`

69, rue du Général-de-Gaulle.
Tel. 03 88 87 01 83. Fax 03 88 87 46 69.
thierry.welty@neuf.fr
Closed Feb. vac., 2 weeks beg. July.
Rest. closed Sun. dinner, Tue. dinner, Wed.
6 rooms: 40€.
Prix fixe: 11,50€ (lunch, weekdays),
17,50€, 45€, 9€ (child). A la carte: 50€.

Thierry Welty has taken over the family establishment and renovated the place, but refrained from making any radical changes. The bucolic rooms, warm welcome, pleasant dining room and faultless service reflect the quality of the food. The cuisine is regional and first-rate: pan-tossed liver with mushroom ravioli, pike-perch served on a bed of sauerkraut, braised veal sweetbreads served with potato purée and a cinnamon parfait with prunes soaked in Armagnac are appetizing classics that never stale. In the summer, the terrace on the edge of the main square is delightful.

● Dolce Vita SIM

17, pl du Marché.
Tel. 03 88 87 27 17. Fax 03 88 87 02 06.
Closed Sun. lunch, Tue. dinner, Wed. dinner.
Prix fixe: 24€, 32€, 8,50€ (child).
A la carte: 40–45€.

Hervé Giagnorio-Schall has turned this very cheerful trattoria into a restaurant worthy of interest. The décor, featuring photos of stars and trompe-l'oeil, is highly imaginative. We cheerfully sit down to our soft melting pizzas, succulent pasta and also the rouget alla Calabraisi, the saltimbocca alla Romana and the panna cotta. The cellar is run by "Bill" Siebenschuh, ex-sommelier at the Kochersberg in Landersheim, who even plays the pizzaiolo, teasing dough into discs (dare we say "whenever kneaded'?).

● La Petite Suisse SIM

69, rte de Cosswiller.
Tel. 03 88 87 05 38.
Closed Tue. dinner, Wed., 2 weeks beg. July.
Prix fixe: 15€, 30€, 6,50€ (child).
A la carte: 33€.

This "Little Switzerland", with its mountain refuge air, is run by Hervé Feldis, who trained at the Etoile and then with his stepfather at the Salmon. Sandrine, née Welty, is charmingly attentive as we feast on the simple, plain, local cuisine. The escargots, headcheese and aspic terrine, salmon with sorrel sauce, pork shank with sauerkraut and the profiteroles are delightful. A terrace when the weather is fine.

In Romanswiller (67310). 3,5 km e via D224.

● Les Douceurs Marines ♙🛏SIM

2, rte de Wangenbourg.
Tel.-Fax 03 88 87 13 97.
Closed Mon.–Thu. (dinner), Wed. lunch,
Nov. 1 vac., 1 week in summer.
Prix fixe: 11€ (lunch, weekdays), 15€,

17,50€, 23€, 30€, 40€ 7,50€ (child).
A la carte: 36€.

On the border of Little Switzerland, this blue and white house offers a change of air. The shady terrace is a joy when the sun shines. Emmanuelle greets us with all the charm of a hostess welcoming us to her home. Cooking comes as naturally to Claude, who trained at the Métropole Palace in Monaco and the Sporting in Roquebrune-Cap Martin, as song to a thrush. Certain specialties recur throughout the year: bouillabaisse, a simpler local fish soup and fish poached in red wine. The prices are angelically restrained and the set menu at 23€, which, the other day, included the surf and turf salad, then the delicate fish couscous and finally a berry Melba, is quite simply a steal. Add the fish soup, bursting with flavor, Atlantic sea bass in an orange infusion and a frozen marbled coconut and exotic fruit dessert and you will soon come to the conclusion that this affable establishment is a treasure trove, well-worth another visit.

▼ SHOPS

BREAD AND BAKED GOODS

▼ René Neyman

46, rue du 23-Novembre.
Tel. 03 88 87 03 57.
Jean-Claude Neyman bakes modern-style flatbreads. His sanita with bran, crackers (with onion, sesame or cumin) and crispy matzah with rye or whole grains are splendid.

WESTHALTEN

68250 Haut-Rhin. Paris 460 – Colmar 21 – Mulhouse 29 – Thann 26.
In this pretty, unspoiled, rustic village to the south of the wine route, modesty reigns unchallenged, from the shrewd wines to room at the inn.

 | HOTELS-RESTAURANTS

● **Au Cheval Blanc**
20, rue de Rouffach.
Tel. 03 89 47 01 16. Fax 03 89 47 64 40.
www.auberge-chevalblc.com
Closed 10 days end June–beg. July,
15 Jan.–8 Feb.
Rest. closed Sun. dinner, Mon., Tue. lunch.
10 rooms: 85–100€. 2 suites: 120€.
Prix fixe: 36€, 65€, 76€, 87€,
13€ (child). A la carte: 72€.

The Koehler family have been winegrowers from father to son since 1785. Today, in this luxurious, typically Alsatian establishment, Gilbert Koehler regales guests with his presentation of goose foie gras served three ways, jumbo shrimp served two ways (simply roasted and in a spicy bouillon), the local-style venison medallion served with house spätzle and the berry mille-feuille. Vintages from the family property naturally head the wine list, which focuses on the region's production, but still has room for other libations. The hotel rooms have been fully renovated in bright, warm colors.

WETTOLSHEIM

68920 Haut-Rhin. Paris 453 – Colmar 8 – Eguisheim 4 – Ribeauvillé 17.
Travelers pass through this slightly suburban wine-growing village to bypass the city of Colmar to the west. It is the starting point for hikers heading for southern Alsace, where mountain meets vine.

 | HOTELS-RESTAURANTS

● **La Palette**
9, rue Herzog.
Tel. 03 89 80 79 14. Fax 03 89 79 77 00.
lapalette@lapalette.fr

www.lapalette.fr
Hotel closed 3 weeks Jan.
Rest. closed Sun. dinner, Mon., Tue. lunch,
10 days Jan.
15 rooms: 64–74€. 1 suite: 110€.
Prix fixe: 14€ (lunch), 22€, 25€, 35€,
59€, 10€ (child).
A la carte: 52€.

Henri Gagneux, a native of Bonneville in Savoy, who trained with Jacob in Courchevel and at the Bourget-du-Lac, paints from a palette of endless shades, reflected in both the colors of his rooms and the dishes that make up the delicious, demanding menu here. The rooms have been modernized, but the jigsaw-cut wooden ceiling remains intact, gracing a dining room whose walls are now brightened by works from contemporary artists. Assisted by a young reception and waitstaff, Henri puts his skills into practice in the kitchen, teasing the finest produce to perfection. The whole grain cake with lobster, the monkfish medallion with sun-dried tomatoes and a lentil risotto with olives, the duck breast in a cocotte of sweet-and-sour radishes, the rich chocolate or hazelnut cake and the amaretto parfait with hot wine-poached cherries are simply splendid.

WEYERSHEIM

67720 Bas-Rhin. Paris 474 – Brumath 8 – Hoerdt 3 – Strasbourg 15.
Surrounded by bucolic scenery to the north of Strasbourg, a step away from the asparagus fields, the Zorn nods its melancholy way through the countryside.

● | RESTAURANTS

● **Auberge du Pont de la Zorn**
2, rue de la République.
Tel.-Fax 03 88 51 36 87.
Closed Sat. lunch, Wed., Thu., 3 weeks Sept.,
2 weeks Feb.
Prix fixe: 32,50€ (Sat., Sun., lunch).
A la carte: 34–42€.

On the bank of the Zorn, Myriam and Hervé Debeer have made a good-natured, resolutely Alsatian tavern of this country inn. The ambiance is friendly in the dining room and in the garden when summer comes. We happily set to work on the local flat garnished pies cooked in a wood oven, foie gras nougat, rabbit presskopf, pike-perch in a horseradish crust, caramelized pork ribs and the regional flat apple tart.

WILLGOTTHEIM

67370 Bas-Rhin. Paris 462 – Saverne 16 – Strasbourg 22 – Wasselonne 13.
In the heart of Kochersberg and its lush countryside, an old-style village with timber-framed homes.

●	RESTAURANTS

● L'Oie Gourmande

51, rue Principale.
Tel. 03 88 69 90 65.
Closed Sat. lunch, Wed., 2 weeks end Aug.
A la carte: 28€.

Pleasant, inexpensive and fun with its blue facade and picturesque dining rooms adorned with antique furniture and Alsatian engravings, the Schmitt establishment is something of a convivial museum. Sandrine offers a lively welcome and Olivier provides reliable cooking. Sometimes he overdoes it a little, but such are the perils of generosity. The exquisite local flat garnished savory pies, house headcheese and aspic terrine, pork cheeks with Melfor vinegar and the frozen Kouglof are gratifying.

WINTZENHEIM

68920 Haut-Rhin. Paris 445 – Colmar 6 – Turckheim 5.
A crossroads town in the suburbs of Colmar, on the wine and Vosges mountain routes.

●	RESTAURANTS

● Le Bon Coin

4, rue de Logelbach.
Tel. 03 89 27 48 04. Fax 03 89 27 51 14.

au-bon-coin2@wanadoo.fr
Closed Tue. dinner, Wed., 3 weeks Feb., 3 weeks mid-Aug.–beg. Sept.
Prix fixe: 12,50€, 21€, 36€, 6,50€ (child).
A la carte: 30€.

The flowered half-timbered facade invites visitors to step inside and taste the dishes prepared by Rémy Haeffelin, who enthusiastically concocts Alsatian classics. We enjoy hot pâté with spring sprouts in salad, the pike-perch poached in Riesling with noodles, the local Wickerschwihr choucroute and the frozen kouglof.

WISSEMBOURG

67160 Bas-Rhin. Paris 483 – Haguenau 33 – Strasbourg 66 – Karlsruhe 41.
tourisme.wissembourg@wanadoo.fr.
The banks of the Lauter, the houses on the quai Anselman and memories of L'Ami Fritz: this is the most regionalist of Alsace towns. It was here that an adaptation of the Erckmann-Chatrian novel was shot in the thirties. The décor has remained intact, like a Hansi drawing.

	HOTELS-RESTAURANTS

■ Au Moulin de la Walk

2, chemin de la Walk.
Tel. 03 88 94 06 44. Fax 03 88 54 38 03.
info@moulin-walk.com
www.moulin-walk.com
Closed 3 weeks Jan.
Rest. closed Sun. dinner, Mon., Fri. lunch, 3 weeks Jan., mid-June–beg. July.
25 rooms: 50–65€.
Prix fixe: 32€, 38€, 50€, 10€ (child).
A la carte: 42–50€.

Peace and greenery in this former mill, and relaxation in its comfortable rooms, five of them attic conversions. We appreciate the Schmidts' thoughtfulness and Eric's polished recipes: his foie gras or game terrine, the roasted lamb tenderloin and the frozen mirabelle plum soufflé.

■ Hostellerie au Cygne

3, rue du Sel.
Tel. 03 88 94 00 16. Fax 03 88 54 38 28.
www.hostellerie-cygne.com
Closed 2 weeks Nov., 2 weeks Feb.–beg.
Mar., 2 weeks beg. July, Wed.
Rest. closed Sun. dinner, Wed., Thu. lunch.
16 rooms: 50–75€.
Prix fixe: 20€ (lunch), 30€, 45€, 60€,
13€ (child).

In the dining room and kitchen respectively, Cathie and Georges Eberhardt go out of their way to make sure the customers and friends who frequent this smartened up old post house enjoy their visit. The facade is charming and the paneled rooms refined. The cuisine consists of a succession of reliable, updated traditional recipes: a salted pork cheek and aspic terrine with baby vegetables in sauce, salmon trout pot-au-feu with horseradish-seasoned heirloom vegetables and sel de Guérande, beef filet medallions with Pinot Noir sauce and slow-cooked mushrooms and the chocolate and salted-butter caramel truffle. On the accommodation side, the rooms are snug in a cozy, romantic way.

■ Hôtel d'Alsace

16, rue Vauban.
Tel. 03 88 94 98 43. Fax 03 88 94 19 60.
hotel.d.alsace@wanadoo.fr
www.hotel-alsace.fr
Rest. closed Fri., Sat., Sun.
41 rooms: 41–54€.
Prix fixe: 13€.

The small rooms in this modern hotel slightly outside the center of town, some of them attic accommodations, are all well-equipped. The prices are reasonable and the breakfast generous. Simple catering during the week.

● Le Carrousel Bleu

17, rue Nationale.
Tel. 03 88 54 33 10.
Closed Mon., Wed., 2 weeks beg. Aug.
Prix fixe: 26€, 36€, 46€.

This recent little main street restaurant is not much to look at; the modern setting is a tad neutral in gray tones with brown seats. At the helm, Annabelle and Michael Heid offer flawless, reliable set menus that lure us away to the South. The "cecina" cannelloni (cured beef) with peppers and melon, a tartare of tomatoes and shrimp seasoned with vanilla, pike-perch with chanterelles, a goat cheese–stuffed pork cutlet, raspberry tiramisu and the rosemary-seasoned pan-simmered apricots with lavender ice cream offer a pleasant conclusion.

● L'Ange

2, rue de la République.
Tel.-Fax 03 88 94 12 11.
info@restaurant-ange.com
www.restaurant-ange.com
Closed Mon., Tue., Christmas vac.,
2 weeks June.
Prix fixe: 28,50€, 38€.
A la carte: 43€.

In his 16th-century post house, Pierre Ludwig seems to have set aside any former excess of ambition. This former lieutenant of Antoine Westermann prepares a multifaceted regional cuisine that sometimes looks to the shores of the Mediterranean for inspiration. In summer, guests are served on a charming courtyard terrace. Although he has done little to renovate his two adjoining dining rooms, pleasant but simple, we are still happy to gorge ourselves on rabbit terrine with foie gras, trout with onion confiture, pork cheeks with crunchy vegetables and pan-seared liver with balsamic vinegar and apples, which do little damage to our pocket. To conclude, the individual wild blueberry tart served with fresh fromage blanc ice cream makes an excellent impression.

In Cleebourg (67160). 3 km via D77.

■ Le Tilleul

94, rue Principale.
Tel. 03 88 94 52 15. Fax 03 88 94 52 63.
Closed Mon., Tue., Christmas–New Year's
vac., 2 weeks beg. Mar.
8 rooms: 40–45€.
Prix fixe: 19€, 29€, 8,50€ (child).

This hotel-restaurant deep in the heart of a winegrowing village is a pleasant place to stay. Martine and Gérard Franck provide attractive, peaceful rooms and respectable dishes. The house foie gras, sole meunière, scallops with endives, veal steak with morels and the frozen meringue dessert are unpretentious.

In Hohwiller (67250). 10 km s via D263.

● **La Grange Fleurie** `SIM`

38, rue Principale.
Tel. 03 88 80 55 71.
Closed Sat., Sun.
Prix fixe: 19,50€, 26€, 7,50€ (child).
A la carte: 30–40€.

A delightful inn where we stop to try the cuisine prepared by André Goaziou, who makes deft use of his market produce. We enjoy a fine gourmet salad with foie gras, a mixed fish dish, beef filet medallion Rossini and the rich chocolate cake.

In Seebach (67160). 5 km e via D245.

● **La Vieille Grange** `SIM`

77, rue des Eglises.
Tel. 03 88 53 18 40. Fax 03 88 53 18 39.
Closed lunch, Mon.–Thu.
A la carte: 25€.

Local flat garnished savory pies, mixed local salad, chilled beef muzzle with vinaigrette and sautéed potatoes, smoked beef tongue served on a bed of sauerkraut, potato cakes and bibelaskäs (local fromage blanc specialty) favorably impress in Joanna and Jean-Marc Bayer's establishment. They have turned this old village barn into a tasteful inn.

▼	SHOPS

BREAD & BAKED GOODS

In Soultz-sous-Forêts. 13 km s via D263.

▼ Paul Heumann

42a, rue de Lobsann.
Tel. 03 88 80 40 61.
Loyal to Soultz-sous-Forêts since 1907, Guy Heumann's establishment produces flatbreads, organic galettes, crackers (onion, sesame or whole grain), buckwheat croustia and other special organic bread products.

CHARCUTERIE

▼ Schimpf

9, rue Nationale.
Tel. 03 88 94 00 34.
Black or white boudin sausage, liver sausages, ham, smoked bacon and duck liver all look delicious at Christophe Schimpf's store.

PASTRIES

▼ Matern-Criqui

6, rue de la République.
Tel.-Fax 03 88 94 02 62.
Ice creams (wild raspberry, white peach), raspberry tart, ganaches, kouglof and éclairs are the star acts in Edith and Laurent Criqui's *pâtisserie* and tearoom.

▼ Rebert

7, pl du Marché-aux-Choux.
Tel. 03 88 94 01 66.
www.rebert.fr
This tearoom and store with its trompe l'oeil façade by Edgar Mahler is attractive indeed. We relish the Venezuelan araguani chocolate, milk-chocolate ganache infused with cinnamon or "prince" (soft almond cake, sheets of crispy praline).

WINE

▼ Les Vignes de la Couronne

6, quai Anselmann.
Tel. 03 88 54 24 19.
Laurent Habouzit, former sommelier at the Cheval Blanc in Lembach, has opened a select cellar on the waterfront here, where he presents delicatessen products and his favorite wines from Bordeaux, Portugal and Languedoc, not to mention Alsace (with bottles from Muré and Stoeffler). Pay him a visit and taste the tartes flambées, charcuterie, cheeses and savory tart of the day.

◆ RENDEZVOUS

TEA SALON

◆ **Au P'tit Kougelhopf**

Rue Nationale.

Tel. 03 88 94 00 56.

Exquisite pastries (Black Forest cake, fruit tarts, delicious little individual kouglofs) to be enjoyed inside or on the terrace, or taken away.

ZELLENBERG

68340 Haut-Rhin. Paris 430 – Colmar 14 – Saint-Dié 45.

Its silhouette is easy to make out on the wine route: a village stretching along the crest of a hillside, just a step away from its big brothers, Hunawihr, Riquewihr and company.

 HOTELS-RESTAURANTS

■ **Au Riesling**

5, rte des Vins.

Tel. 03 89 47 85 85. Fax 03 89 47 92 08.

auriesling@wanadoo.fr

www.au-riesling.com

Closed end Dec.–1 Mar.

Rest. closed Sun. dinner, Mon., Tue. lunch.

36 rooms: 61–75€.

Prix fixe: 17€, 24€, 29€, 8€ (child).

Surrounded by vineyards, this quiet hotel offers rooms with all modern comforts, some of them just refurbished, and an affable, classical restaurant. Beef carpaccio, pan-seared scallops, pork tenderloin medallions and cherries in Kirsch can hardly be faulted. We naturally drink wines produced by the Rentz family, our hosts.

■ **Caveau du Schlossberg**

59a, rue de la Fontaine.

Tel. 03 89 47 93 85 / 03 89 49 00 89.

Fax 03 89 47 82 40.

hotel-le-schlossberg@wanadoo.fr

www.eschlossberg.com

Open daily. Winter: by reserv.

7 rooms: 56–115€. 4 suites: 135–198€.

Prix fixe: 29€, 17€ (child).

Charles Maierboerck has turned this welcoming hostelry into a fine stopover on the wine route. Its renovated rooms and suites provide a panoramic view of the surrounding villages and vineyards. The cuisine, which is gratifying but not overdone, includes foie gras, pike-perch in filo pastry, a rabbit haunch in Riesling sauce and Marc de Gewurz sorbet.

● **Maximilien**   ⓥ V.COM

19a, rte d'Ostheim.
Tel. 03 89 47 99 69. Fax 03 89 47 99 85.
www.le-maximilien.com
Closed Sun. dinner, Mon., Fri. lunch,
Feb. vac.
Prix fixe: 31€ (lunch), 43€, 63€, 79€.
A la carte: 77€.

This neo-Alsatian establishment, standing on the hillside among the vines, belongs to Jean-Michel Eblin, who set up in business near to his parents' property after a conspicuous stay at the Valet de Coeur. His resume also includes Taillevent and the Auberge de l'Ill, a testament to his tried-and-true technique and skills. He knows how to prepare precisely cooked, refined dishes with finely calculated flavors, and offers proof in the form of the shrimp tail tartlette seasoned with basil-infused oil, pan-tossed pike-perch filet with a mixed herb sauce, roasted Mediterranean sea bass filet, pigeon breast, roasted lobster with an orange reduction sauce and the venison medallion with red beet sauce. The elegant dining room looking out onto the vineyards, with the village in the background, is the perfect setting for our feast.

● **Auberge du Froehn**   SIM

5, rte d'Ostheim.
Tel. 03 89 47 81 57. Fax 03 89 47 80 28.
Closed Tue., Wed., 2 weeks end Nov.,
end Feb.–mid-Mar., end June–beg. July.
Prix fixe: 11€ (weekday lunch), 19€, 23€,
26€, 35€, 10€ (child), 35€.
A la carte: 34–39€.

Dedicated to the great local vintage, Jean-Marc and Brigitte Hatterman's cellar offers wine from close at hand and further afield, especially the libations produced by their friends and neighbors, the Beckers. Duck foie gras with fruit compote, pan-seared scallops with herb sauce, herb-encrusted lamb with rosemary sauce and a raspberry sorbet with eau-de-vie are a delightful experience.

INDEX

INDEX

W

Z